The New Science of the Mind

The New Science of the Mind

From Extended Mind to Embodied Phenomenology

Mark Rowlands

A Bradford Book
The MIT Press
Cambridge, Massachusetts
London, England

MIT Press books may be purchased at special quantity discounts for business or sales promotional use. For information, please email special_sales@mitpress.mit.edu or write to Special Sales Department, The MIT Press, 55 Hayward Street, Cambridge, MA 02142.

This book was set in Stone Sans and Stone Serif by Toppan Best-set Premedia Limited. Printed and bound in the United States of America.

Library of Congress Cataloging-in-Publication Data

Rowlands, Mark.
The new science of the mind : from extended mind to embodied phenomenology / Mark Rowlands.
  p. cm.
"A Bradford book."
Includes bibliographical references and index.
ISBN 978-0-262-01455-7 (hardcover : alk. paper)
1. Cognitive science. I. Title.
[DNLM: 1. Mental Processes. 2. Philosophy, Medical. BF 441 R883n 2010]
BF311.R685   2010
153—dc22

                                                          2010003182

10 9 8 7 6 5 4 3 2 1

For Emma

Contents

Preface and Acknowledgments

I suppose that for a book entitled *The New Science of the Mind* there isn't, in fact, a lot of science in it; and some of the science that does find its way in isn't particularly new. The underlying reason is that the expression "new science" is as much aspirational as descriptive. There is, as yet, no new science, not understood as something comparable to mature cognitive science in its classical guise. Rather, "new science" picks out a cluster of related views that are emerging, or have emerged, from a variety of disciplines, including cognitive and developmental psychology, situated robotics and artificial intelligence, perceptual psychology, cognitive neuroscience, and philosophy. The role of philosophy is not so much to detail these developments as to provide a logical or conceptual foundation for them. That is the task of this book. It might have been called "Foundations of the New Science of the Mind," but that is a bit of a mouthful.

The book is written for philosophers, cognitive scientists, and any interested lay persons who want to understand what is being talked about when people throw around phrases like "situated cognition," "embodied cognition," "the extended mind," and their perhaps more arcane variants ("enactivism," "vehicle externalism," "locational externalism," "architecturalism," and the like). When writing for a disparate constituency, the danger is, of course, that at least some of this constituency, at least some of the time, might be tempted to think that I am in the business of teaching their grandmothers to suck eggs. I have tried to avoid this as much as possible, and in cases where I can clearly envisage it happening, I have inserted the offending passages into boxes.

Over the past decade or so, conversations with Fred Adams, Ken Aizawa, Andy Clark, Shaun Gallagher, Richard Menary, Robert Rupert, John Sutton, and Mike Wheeler have helped shape my thinking about matters embodied, embedded, enacted, and extended. Their influence has no doubt found its way into this book in a variety of ways. My thanks to all.

Tony Chemero and Mike Wheeler were kind enough to read an earlier draft of this book, and made a number of very helpful suggestions which significantly improved the final version. The mistakes that remain are entirely my fault.

At MIT Press, my thanks to Tom Stone for getting this project off the ground in the first place, and to Marc Lowenthal and Philip Laughlin for seeing it through to completion. Finally, my thanks to Judy Feldmann, for faultless copyediting (as usual).

1 Expanding the Mind

1 The Expanding Mind?

There is a new way of thinking about the mind and things mental that has started to seep out of the ivory tower and set up residence in popular consciousness.[1] Actually, to call it a *new* way of thinking about the mind is not entirely accurate. It is an old way of thinking about the mind that has taken on new form. Previously the preserve of a few scattered, and distinctly renegade, philosophers and psychologists spread out over the centuries, this way of thinking about the mind has started to acquire what many would regard as more persuasive credentials. This is because it is now emerging, in a reasonably consistent and recognizable way, from the confluence of various disciplines in cognitive science, including situated robotics and artificial intelligence (Webb 1994; Brooks 1994; Beer 1995), perceptual psychology (O'Regan and Noë 2001; Noë 2004), dynamical approaches to developmental and cognitive psychology (Thelen and Smith 1994), and cognitive neuroscience (Damasio 1994).

Some people think—and, for what it's worth, I am one of them—that upon this new way of thinking about the mind will be built a new *science* of the mind. The new science in question will employ different methods for studying the mind, and will supply explanations of mental processes that are, at least in some ways, quite different from traditional accounts. But these transformations in methods and forms of explanation are just symptoms of something far deeper and more important. Fundamentally, the new science would be *new* because it is underwritten by a novel conception of what sort of thing the mind is. The subject matter of this book is not the mooted new science of the mind but the conception of the mind that underlies it—a conception that can, I think, be evaluated independently of whether anyone actually gets around to making a science of it.

Traditional attempts to study the mind are based on the idea that whatever else is true of mental processes—perceiving, remembering, thinking, reasoning, and so on—they exist in brains. Mental processes are either *identical* with brain processes or *exclusively realized* by brain processes (see box 1.1). The word "traditional," here, is slightly idiosyncratic. The scientific study of the mind is not much more than a hundred years old, and in that time it has undergone several significant transformations: introspectionism, gestalt psychology, behaviorism, and finally, from the early 1960s onwards, cognitive science. Cognitive science, in its traditional form, is based on the idea that mental processes—specifically cognitive processes, for these are the purview of cognitive science—are abstract "programs" realized in the "hardware" of the brain (an analogy with computers guided much of the early work in cognitive science). The principal tasks of cognitive science are, accordingly, to identify the programs (cognitive psychology) and work out how these programs are implemented in the brain (cognitive neuroscience). For reasons that will be fully explained shortly, I am going to refer to cognitive science, in its traditional form, as *Cartesian cognitive science.*

Cartesian cognitive science is, in many respects, a broad church. There are many important differences in the way cognitive science has developed over the years. For example, in early cognitive science, the emphasis was very much on the "programs" or cognitive "software"; early cognitive science understood itself as engaged in the task of providing abstract formal descriptions of cognitive processes. However, from the mid-1980s on, this emphasis gradually gave way to a renewed emphasis on "hardware" in the form of *connectionist* or *neural network* approaches: approaches to understanding cognition based on neurally realistic models of its underlying architecture.[2] Neural network models base their accounts of cognition on a hardware that is explicitly (if roughly) modeled on the brain (Rumelhart, McClelland, and the PDP Research Group 1986). It is not clear that these two approaches are incompatible. It may be that neural network models are merely accounts of how the more abstract formal descriptions of cognitive processes come to be implemented in the brain. However, nor it is clear that these two approaches are compatible: it may be that neural network models have properties that preclude their being described at a more abstract level by formal descriptions of the sort typically employed.[3]

We do not need to worry about the details of this dispute. What unites these differing faces of Cartesian cognitive science is an unquestioned—indeed seemingly banal—assumption: whatever else is true of mental processes, whether they are abstract formal processes or patterns of activity in a neural network (or both)—they are processes that occur inside the head of the thinking organism. Cognitive processes—the category of mental processes with which cognitive science is concerned—occur inside cognizing organisms, and they do so because cognitive processes are, ultimately, brain processes (or more abstract functional roles realized exclusively by brain processes). It is this unquestioned assumption that makes Cartesian cognitive science Cartesian. And it is this assumption that I shall try to undermine.

The new way of thinking about the mind is inspired by, and organized around, not the brain but some combination of the ideas that mental processes are (1) *embodied*, (2) *embedded*, (3) *enacted*, and (4) *extended*. Shaun Gallagher has referred to this, in conversation, as the *4e* conception of the mind.[4] The idea that mental processes are *embodied* is, very roughly, the idea that they are partly constituted by, partly made up of, wider (i.e., extraneural) bodily structures and processes. The idea that mental processes are *embedded* is, again roughly, the idea that mental processes have been designed to function only in tandem with a certain environment that lies outside the brain of the subject. In the absence of the right environmental *scaffolding*, mental processes cannot do what they are supposed to do, or can only do what they are supposed to so less than optimally. The idea that mental processes are *enacted* is the idea that they are made up not just of neural processes but also of things that the organism *does* more generally—that they are constituted in part by the ways in which an organism acts on the world and the ways in which world, as a result, acts back on that organism. The idea that mental processes are *extended* is the idea that they are not located exclusively inside an organism's head but extend out, in various ways, into the organism's environment. We shall examine each of these ideas in much more detail in the following chapters. These characterizations are very rough, and in several ways inadequate; but they will probably give us enough to work with for present purposes.

Each of these ideas—embodiment, embeddedness, enactedness, and extendedness—has been understood as denying, or at least questioning, the central assumption of Cartesian cognitive science: mental processes are identical with, or exclusively realized by, brain processes. It is not clear, however, whether it is *correct* to understand all of the ideas in this way. I shall argue, later in this chapter and in more depth in chapter 3, that not all strands of 4e are equally anti-Cartesian. Moreover, even if it were true that all of these ideas deny the central assumption of Cartesian cognitive science, this denial would take a quite different form in each case. And

Box 1.1
Identity and Exclusive Realization

For the purposes of this book, the difference between identity and exclusive realization is of no real importance—that is why I have hitherto used them in the same breath. But it is probably time to explain why the difference is of no real importance. First of all, identity itself can actually be understood in two ways. Broadly speaking, to say that mental processes are identical with brain processes is to say that they are one and the same thing as brain processes. It is not that there are two things there—mental processes and brain processes—that are correlated; there is only one thing there. However, there are two different ways of thinking about this. According to one, this is a claim about mental and neural processes understood as *kinds*—or as philosophers like to call it, *types*—of process (Smart 1959). So, the claim is that kinds or types of mental process are identical with kinds or types of brain process. This is known as a *type identity theory*. According to this, mental processes are one and the same thing as brain processes in much the same way that water is H_2O, and as lightning is an electrical discharge to Earth from a cloud of ionized water particles.

There is another—currently more popular—way of understanding the identity theory. According to this, the identity between mental and physical holds between individual *instances*—or, as philosophers like to call them, *tokens*—of each kind (Davidson 1970). It is the individual episode of pain that I, a particular person, feel at a particular time (e.g., 4:19 PM on March 21, 2008) that is identical with a particular firing of a brain process (that takes place in me at this time). This is an identity between individual episodes, instances, or tokens, rather than an identity of general kinds or types. This view is known as the *token identity theory*.

The token identity theory has proved more popular for reasons that connect up with the notion of *realization* mentioned above. The idea of realization is drawn from the computer metaphor that dominated early cognitive science (Putnam 1960). One and the same program can be run on different sorts of computer—and these computers can, within limits, be built in different ways. Therefore, we can not identify the program with any particular configuration of hardware. But, nonetheless, the program cannot be run without some hardware or other. Therefore, the idea is that though the program cannot be regarded as the same thing as configurations in the underlying hardware—because it can be run on different hardware—the program is, in any particular case, realized by given type of hardware. To say that A realizes B, therefore, is to say, very roughly, that A makes B possible by providing a physical basis for it.

Box 1.1
(continued)

The token identity theory became popular because it is compatible with the idea that mental kinds are *functional* (see box 2.1) kinds that are, in any given instance, realized by some or other physical hardware—but not necessarily the same hardware in all cases. The idea that mental kinds are functional kinds is the claim that they are best understood in terms of what they *do*. To see what this means, consider another example of something defined by what it does. A carburetor is a physical object located somewhere in the innards of a car's engine (or older cars anyway—fuel injection systems have replaced them in more recent models). What is a carburetor? Roughly, it is (or was) something that takes in fuel from the fuel inlet manifold, takes in air from the air inlet manifold, mixes the two in an appropriate ratio, and sends the resulting mixture on to the combustion chamber. It is fulfilling this role that makes something a carburetor, and anything that fulfils this role in a car thereby counts as a carburetor. Most carburetors tend to look pretty similar. But this is at best a contingent fact, because it doesn't matter what a carburetor looks like as long as it fills this role. The details of its physical structure and implementation are of secondary importance compared to the role it fills, for it is filling this role that makes something a carburetor, and not the details of its physical structure or implementation. Of course, not everything physical thing is *capable* of playing the role of a carburetor. A lump of Jell-O inserted into your car engine would have a hard time mixing fuel and air—or doing anything except melting, for that matter. A lump of Jell-O is simply not the right sort of thing for fulfilling the functional role of a carburetor. So, the details of the how the functional role is physically implemented are not irrelevant. But as long as you have a suitable physical structure—one that is capable of fulfilling the role of a carburetor, then it doesn't matter what it is as long as it, in fact, fulfills this role. If it does, then it is a carburetor.

At the level of tokens, each individual carburetor is a physical object. There is a token identity between a carburetor and a physical thing. However, since carburetors can, in principle, be realized by different kinds of object, there is no type identity between carburetors and specific types of physical object. That is, it is not plausible to say that a carburetor as a kind is the same thing as this kind of physical object, because other kinds of physical objects are capable of playing the role of carburetors—and thus of being carburetors. The kind or type carburetor is *realized* by physical kinds or types, but it is not the same thing as them.

By far the most popular version of materialism over the past few decades has combined an identity of mental and physical tokens with a functionalist

Box 1.1
(continued)

> account of mental kinds or types. So, the general idea is that mental process-tokens are *identical* with brain process-tokens, but mental process-types are *realized* by brain process-types. Since, it has almost universally been assumed, there is nothing outside the brain that realizes mental types, this realization is *exclusive* to the brain. Together these claims—token identity combined with exclusive neural realization—form the default view of the nature of mental phenomena that 4e attacks.

once we venture beyond the simple denial, we shall see that the ideas of embodiment, embeddedness, enactedness, and extendedness are far from equivalent. Indeed, not only are these ideas different, some of them may actually be incompatible with the others. Indeed, at least one of the strands of 4e can, and indeed has, been employed as a sort of Cartesian fifth column—one designed to acknowledge the force of anti-Cartesian arguments but also strictly limit their scope. In chapter 3, we shall begin the process of tidying these ideas up: working out exactly what each one claims, the ways in which it denies (if it does) the central assumption of Cartesian cognitive science, and thereby working out which ideas are and which are not mutually compatible.

To avoid these difficulties, and to avoid anticipating the results of arguments yet to be given, I shall, for now, simply talk of *non-Cartesian* cognitive science (or, depending on context, of the non-Cartesian conception of the mind that underlies this science), and understand this as made up of at least some, but not necessarily all, of the strands that make up 4e: embodiment, embeddedness, enactedness, extendedness. The diversity and potential incompatibility of the ideas of embodiment, embeddedness, enactedness, and extendedness do present us with a problem. If a new, non-Cartesian, cognitive science were to be built on these ideas, and if some of these ideas didn't really cohere with the others, then the prospects for our new science would be at best uncertain and at worst bleak. What we need, it seems, is a way of identifying with precision the content of each of these ideas, and, on this basis, putting them together in the best way we can and discarding the ones that cannot be thus assimilated. This, in effect, is where philosophy comes in. It would not be entirely true to say that philosophy has *driven* the development of the ideas of embodiment, embeddedness, enactedness, and extendedness. It is true that the history of philosophy has contained figures that have developed views of the mind that are entirely amenable to, and may even be (philosophical) versions of these ideas. We shall encounter several of these figures later in the book. However, most of the recent impetus for 4e comes from developments in fields of cognitive science such as situated robotics, developmental cognitive psychology, and theories of visual perception. The primary role of philosophy is not to provide new empirical evidence for non-Cartesian cognitive science, but to place this science on a solid conceptual footing.

To this end, this book aims to identify, clarify, render consistent, and, where appropriate, defend the central concepts on which a non-Cartesian cognitive science is to be based. This process begins in chapter 3. There, we shall examine the ideas of embodiment, embeddedness, enactedness, and extendedness with a view to identifying the content of each idea—what it actually says or claims. Then we shall examine the ways in which each idea fits together with the others and the ways in which it does not. That is, we are going to look at the extent to which each idea either entails the others, or is compatible with the others, or is incompatible with the others. In the process, choices will have to be made. Perhaps one idea will simply turn out to be a version of another. In this case, our non-Cartesian cognitive science may turn out to be 3e (or even less), rather than 4e. More worryingly, perhaps one idea will prove incompatible with one or more of the others. Then, it seems, one of the ideas will have to go, and our task is to work out which one, and how to do justice to the overall framework of the non-Cartesian conception of the mind given these constraints.[5]

Once the process of identification, clarification, and rendering consistent has been completed, we get to the most important part of the project: *defending* the new, non-Cartesian, conception of the mind.[6] In a work of philosophy, this means defending the concepts out of which this new conception is going to be built—the concepts we have succeeded in identifying, clarifying, and rendering consistent. This is the principal task of the book, and most of the book will be devoted to it. None of these tasks is particularly easy. Even if we are witnessing the birth of a new science of the mind, some births are protracted and painful. Nonetheless, this book contends that all these tasks can be successfully completed.

Before we get to them, however, there are a few more preliminary matters that need our attention. The idea that the mind is not "in the head"—that the mind can extend out into the body and even into the world—will strike many as a truly crazy idea that no one who is even remotely sane could ever accept. In the rest of this chapter, I want to sketch, in a preliminary way, the general motivation for thinking that this idea is not as crazy as it seems.

2   Minds and Mental Phenomena

The new way of thinking about the mind is sometimes characterized as the claim that the mind, or even the self, is *outside the head*. Now that, at least on one way of thinking about the mind or self, *would* be a truly crazy claim. Happily, no version of non-Cartesian cognitive science commits us to this. That is, none of the various strands that make up 4e—the theses of embodiment, embeddedness, enactedness, and extendedness—should be interpreted as saying anything at all about the mind (and a fortiori, the self)—unless you want to think of this as a construction out of mental states and processes. What a non-Cartesian cognitive science is actually concerned with is mental states and processes, and not whatever it is that has them.[7]

Where does your mind begin, and where does it end? This is an unusual question. The usual question, at least if the history of philosophy and psychology is anything to go by, is: what is the mind? And the usual answer is: the brain. If this is right, then your mind begins and ends where your brain begins and ends—for your mind is simply your brain and nothing else. But where does your brain begin and end? People who think that the mind is the brain typically draw a firm distinction between the central and peripheral nervous systems. The brain is the lump of gray, gooey matter located in your head, made up of brain stem, hippocampus, and cerebral cortex. And if that is what the brain is, then that is what the mind is. Or more accurately, your mind is part of this triune structure, the part that is responsible for your being able to think and feel, and so on: your mind is (parts of) your cerebral cortex and hippocampus.

This idea is probably still unacceptably vague. But the most serious problem is with it is this: between you and me, I'm not sure I even have a mind—if this is understood as something different from my mental states and processes. This point, or at least something recognizably similar to it, was made a long ago by the philosopher David Hume:

Whenever I enter most intimately into what I call *myself*, I always stumble on some particular perception or other, of heat or cold, light or shade, love or hatred, pain or pleasure. I never catch *myself* at any time without a perception and never can observe anything but the perception. . . . If anyone upon serious and unprejudiced reflection thinks he has a different notion of himself, I must confess I can reason no longer with him. All I can allow him is that he may well be in the right as well as I, and that we are essentially different in this particular. He may, perhaps, perceive something simple and continued, which he calls *himself*, though I am certain there is no such principle in me. (1739/1975: 252)

Hume's remarks, here, are addressed to the existence of what he calls the *self*. It is not clear that the self and the mind are the same thing for Hume.[8] For our purposes, however, this does not matter. We can make a precisely parallel point about the mind. When I enter, as Hume put it, "most intimately into what I call myself"—that is, when I turn my attention inward or introspect—I never encounter my mind: all I ever come across are mental states and processes. That is, when I introspect, I might become aware of what it is I am thinking, what it is I am feeling, and so on. I might become aware of my beliefs, my desires, my sensations, my emotions; my hopes, fears, aspirations, and anticipations. But what I never come across is the *subject* of these states and processes, at least if this is understood as something different from these states and processes. I never come across my *mind* thought of as something lying behind these states and processes.

We must be careful here, because we can easily transform this Humean-inspired observation into a very bad argument. Suppose I am looking at something—say, the can of diet Coke that invariably sits next to my laptop when I work, bearer of the psychotropic substance that I need to give my aged and rather reticent brain the morning kick start it needs. I can see the shape of the can, and its shiny silver surface. I can see the writing on that surface in black and red. But do I ever see the can itself? Well, what I don't see is the can as something separate from, or over and above, these properties. I don't see the shape, the surface, the adornment, and then, in addition, see the can. But does this mean I don't see the can? That would be the bad argument advertised at the beginning of this paragraph. I see the can in virtue of seeing the shape, surface, and adornment. In general, we see objects by way of, or in virtue of, seeing their properties.

That is the best way of understanding this Humean-inspired observation. I am not claiming that when you introspect you don't ever encounter your mind. Rather, I am making a point about what it is to introspectively encounter your own mind: to encounter your mind is to encounter your mental states and processes. You are aware of your mind in virtue of being aware of your mental states and processes, just as you are aware of the can of diet Coke in virtue of being aware of the shape, surface, and adornment of the can.

Nevertheless, lack of subtlety often has a habit of creeping back into our thinking. Often, when we think of the mind we have an idea of something that underlies all our mental states and processes: something to which those states and processes attach—something that holds them all together. Similarly, when we think of the can, we typically think of it as something that underlies its various properties—as something to which those properties attach. To avoid this questionable way of thinking about the mind—the mind as a *bare substratum*—I am, in the rest of the book, going to do my best not to talk about the mind at all (unless I am talking about someone else who is talking about the mind in this sense). I am only going to be concerned with mental states and processes: mental *phenomena* broadly construed. The non-Cartesian conception of the mind defended in this book is not, in fact, a conception of the mind at all—not if we understand this as something underlying mental states and processes. It is a conception of mental phenomena: it claims that at least some mental phenomena are either embodied, embedded, enacted, or extended. In this, it rejects the conception of mental phenomena embodied in Cartesian cognitive science: mental states and processes begin and end with the brain, because mental states and processes are *identical* with, or *exclusively realized by*, brain states and processes.

The view that mental states and processes are identical with, or exclusively realized by, brain states and processes is not a peculiar eruption of contemporary thought. On the contrary, it derives from a view of the mind that emerged in seventeenth-century France.

3   Descartes's Ghosts

It is easy to understand why the ideas of identity of mental and neural tokens combined with exclusive realization of mental types by neural types assumed such position of dominance in scientific thinking about the mind. To deny it seemed, at least at first glance, to commit you to an untenable position: to a form of *dualism* about the mind. Dualism received its most famous development at the hands of the philosopher, mathematician, and sometime mercenary René Descartes.

According to Descartes, the mind is a nonphysical *substance*. Today, we tend to use the word "substance" to mean something like "the stuff from which a thing is made." However, Descartes inherited his use of this term from medieval philosophers, and, for them, "substance" meant "thing" or "object." So the mind, according to Descartes, is a nonphysical object. In some respects, Descartes thought of the mind as similar to other bodily organs. The heart, liver, kidneys, and so on, are all objects found in the body and, more importantly, they are objects of a certain sort: ones defined by their *function* or *what they are supposed to do*. The function of the heart is to pump blood around the body; the function of the liver is to regulate metabolism; the function of the kidneys is to process waste products; and so on.

According to Descartes, the mind, like other things found inside the body, is defined by its function: and its function is to *think*. However, he argued that there is a crucial difference between the mind and all other organs found inside the body: the mind is a *nonphysical* substance. By this, he meant, fundamentally, that the mind is *nonspatial*. Physical things, Descartes claimed, have a single defining feature: *extension*. By this he meant that physical things *occupy space* or *take up room*. This, he thought, is precisely what makes them physical things. Therefore, the mind, being nonphysical, must also be nonspatial.

However, there are actually two different aspects of the idea of space, and Descartes never clearly distinguished between them. On the one hand, there is spatial *extension*—taking up room. On the other hand, there is spatial *location*—existing *at* a particular place. If an object has spatial extension then it must also have spatial location. It is not possible for an object to occupy space without the space that it occupies being somewhere or other (even if this "somewhere or other" is rather vague). But just because an object has spatial location, it does not necessarily follow that it has spatial extension. For example, scientists are willing to countenance (and some even insist on) the existence of *point particles*: particles that exist at some particular place but do not take up any room. Even if they ultimately turn out to be wrong, their willingness to countenance the possibility shows, at least prima facie, that the *ideas* or *concepts* of spatial extension and spatial location are not the same. The idea of spatial extension seems to entail the idea of spatial location. But the idea of spatial location does not entail the idea of spatial extension.

Although Descartes never clearly distinguished between the ideas of spatial extension and spatial location, this distinction can be used to make sense of Descartes's position.[9] In effect, Descartes's view was that minds do not have spatial extension—this is what makes them nonphysical—but they do have spatial location. Every mind is located inside a (functioning) brain, and every (functioning) brain is located inside a body. Descartes was never exactly clear on the precise location of the mind; but somewhere in the vicinity of the brain's pineal gland seemed to be his favored hypothesis.[10]

Descartes's view is known as *dualism*—since it asserts that each one of us is composed of two different kinds of thing: physical bodies and nonphysical minds. Despite making something of a recent, limited comeback (e.g., Chalmers 1996), dualism is still almost certainly one of the most reviled philosophical views ever invented. Generations of professional philosophers have spent much time and energy (a) showing that Descartes's arguments for dualism don't work, (b) arguing that dualism itself has empirical and conceptual difficulties so serious as to render it an effectively untenable position, and (c) inventing catchy slurs with which to disparage his view—most famous of which is, perhaps, Gilbert Ryle's (1949) dismissal of the view as the dogma of the *ghost in the machine*. Today, even the word "Cartesian" is often used as a term of abuse.

The popularity of the mind–brain identity/exclusive neural realization combination stemmed, in large part, from the belief that to deny it was to be committed to dualism of a broadly Cartesian sort. This, we are now beginning to understand, is not true. Indeed, what has been overlooked until very recently is just how much the mind–brain identity theory/ exclusive neural realization combination has inherited from Descartes: they are, in effect, fashioned in the image of the Cartesian conception of the mind.

The Cartesian conception of the mind in fact has two distinguishable aspects. First, there is the claim that the mind is a nonphysical thing. Second, however, there is the idea that the mind is something that exists inside the head. So, when Ryle dismissed Descartes's view as the myth of the ghost in the machine, this dismissal actually has two distinguishable aspects. First, Ryle was rejecting the idea that the mind is a *ghost*—that is, a nonphysical thing. But second, and for our purposes more significantly, he was rejecting the idea that the mind is the sort of thing that can be found *inside* the bodily machine. If you reject only the first idea, then you have not fully rejected the Cartesian conception of the mind, but only part of it. And that, in effect, is precisely what the mind–brain identity/exclusive neural realization combination did. It rejected Descartes's idea that the mind is ghostly or nonphysical, but it left intact the second defining idea of the Cartesian conception: the idea that the mind is something that exists *inside* the head. In other words, the mind–brain identity/exclusive neural realization model is a view fashioned partly, but as things turned out, decisively in the image of the Cartesian view of the mind.

Non-Cartesian cognitive science is based on a more complete rejection of the Cartesian view of the mind. This science is, of course, materialistic: there will be no reversion to nonphysical substances—that particular

Cartesian ghost remains well and truly exorcised. However, non-Cartesian cognitive science also rejects, or is at least thought of as rejecting, Descartes's second idea, the idea inherited by the mind–brain identity/ exclusive neural realization model. That is, it rejects the claim that mental states and processes occur purely inside the brains. Some of them do; but not all of them do. Mental states and processes are not just things that happen inside our brains; they are also things that happen, *partly*, in our bodies and even, *partly*, in the world outside of our bodies. The qualification "partly" is (i) obvious, (ii) crucial, and (iii) ignored with surprising frequency. With (iii) in mind, let me risk being tediously overemphatic. No one is going to claim that there can be free-floating mental processes hovering around in the world outside the head. That *would* be an example of a truly crazy idea that no remotely sane person would want to hold. Almost as insane would be the idea that there can be mental processes that are entirely made up of processes occurring inside the body but outside the brain. No one wants to maintain that either. The idea, rather, is that in the case of some mental processes but not all, *part* of that mental process—but *never* all—is made up of factors that occur outside the brain of the subject.

Our next obvious question is: why think this?

4 Best Friends and Barking Dogs

The starting point for non-Cartesian cognitive science is the extent to which we make use of things around us in order to solve problems and get things done. Our tendency to do so has become more and more obvious in recent years. Consider, for example, a relatively new acquaintance of mine: my car's GPS (global positioning system). Actually remembering how to get to a destination: that was *so* 2007 (or, for more those of a less technophobic persuasion than I, so 2005). In 2009, my GPS will tell me how to get anywhere I want to go. "Make a safe and legal U-turn," the reassuring, and apparently vaguely stoned, voice tells me. OK, will do.[11]

The knowledge afforded me by my GPS is essentially *situated*. That is, it provides me with practical and easily digestible instructions because it uses my physical location to encode at least some of the information I require to follow those instructions. The information with which my GPS provides me is, in this sense, *indexical*: it has a meaning that is partly made up of is made up of the meaning of words such as "here," "there," "this," "that," and associated locutions. Because of this the instructions, we might put it, *show* more than they *say*. If the instruction is "make a safe and legal

U-turn": then that is precisely what the instruction *says*. But what it shows is that you should make the U-turn at the next intersection—which is "there," in front of you.[12] The instructions show more than they say because part of their informational content—part of their *meaning*, broadly construed—is encoded in my physical location at the time the instructions are given.

Think about the difference between my GPS and its precursor: Map-Quest. For our purposes, both the similarities and differences between the GPS and MapQuest are important. Consider, first, the similarities. Both the GPS and MapQuest are external forms of information storage—external to *my body*. I don't need to remember how to get somewhere, because the information about how to get there is contained in both the GPS and in MapQuest. These external forms of information storage, therefore, reduce the burden on my biological memory. Memory tasks that I would find difficult are offloaded onto the environment.

The differences between the GPS and MapQuest concern how this external information is stored. MapQuest works by providing you with an *algorithm*: a set of instructions such that if you follow them faithfully you will arrive at your destination—at least in theory. Leaving your residence, you turn west on 156th. Then at 77th you turn north. At the second light, you turn east on 144th, and so on. When MapQuest wants you to turn left, it needs to provide you with information that specifies precisely where you are to do this (e.g., at the intersection of 77th and 144th). There is no need for your GPS to do this. With your GPS, the time and place of the utterance is inextricably linked to the meaning of the utterance. The information contained in the GPS instructions is situated in a way that the information contained in the MapQuest algorithm (typically) is not. The GPS information is both external and situated. The MapQuest information is external but not situated (or, at least, not *as* situated).

We all know the problem with MapQuest directions. The chances are there are too many instructions for you to remember, and so you have to take them with you in printed form. And then, consulting your sheet to find out what you should do next, you slam into the back of the Camry that's stopped in front of you. Your GPS, on the other hand, gives you easily digestible snippets of information as and when you need them— which it can do precisely because the information it provides is situated. Nevertheless, although they accomplish it in different ways, both the GPS and MapQuest have essentially the same function. You need to accomplish a task—getting from A to B. If you couldn't avail yourself of MapQuest or a GPS or some other form of external information storage system, then you would have to remember how to get from A to B "all by yourself." That is, the task would have to be entrusted to your naked biological—that is, neural—memory. However, to the extent that you are able to avail yourself of an external information source, the complexity, and therefore difficulty, of the task you have to accomplish in your head is correspondingly reduced. The task that you would have had to accomplish in your head is, in part, *off-loaded* onto the environment. Equivalently, we might say that the task is *distributed* onto the environment.

It is the possibility of this sort of off-loading that provides the starting point for the new science of the mind. However, recent technological developments of the sort that result in MapQuest or GPS systems are only the most recent manifestations of a process that began almost as soon as humans became humans. Human cultural development is, in part, a process of creating external information-bearing structures: structures that could be used to enhance our ability to accomplish important tasks. One of the most significant of these structures is the development of written language. In a classic early study, the Soviet psychologists Alexander Luria and Lev Vygotsky (1930/1992) identified the implications of this development for human biological memory.

Consider an early form of written language—a simple system of visuographic representation. Imagine two people (the example is Luria and Vygotsky's). One is an African envoy, entrusted with the task of remembering word for word the message of his tribal chief. The other is a Peruvian *kvinu* officer—an "officer of knots"—who uses a conventional system of knots tied in string to achieve the same purpose. As Luria and Vygotsky point out, for each new message, the African envoy must employ anew his (biological) memory. The *kvinu* officer, on the other hand, need employ his memory resources only once—in learning the "code" that allows him to access the information contained in the knots. Once he has done this, a potentially unlimited amount of information becomes available to him since a potentially unlimited number of knots can be presented to him. The African envoy faces a comparatively difficult task. But, for the *kvinu* officer, part of the difficulty of this task has been off-loaded onto the environment. By making use of an appropriate environmental structure, the *kvinu* officer significantly reduces the complexity and difficulty of the task that he must accomplish in his head (see also Rowlands 1999, 134–137).

Suppose you have to do something; it doesn't matter what. And suppose successfully doing this thing requires you to put in a certain amount of work. Then, this is a truism: if you can get something (or someone) else to do some of this work for you, you will have correspondingly less work to do yourself—as long, and here is a crucial caveat, as the work you put into to getting that something or someone to do the work for you is less than the work they thereby do. There is an old adage that captures this idea quite nicely. It says: why keep a dog if you are going to bark yourself? If there is some barking to be done, and you have a dog that will do at least some of it for you, then you have correspondingly less barking to do yourself (Rowlands 1999, 79–80). At the conceptual heart of non-Cartesian cognitive science is this *barking dog principle*.[13]

Any cognitive science, whether Cartesian or non-Cartesian, will be concerned with, at the very least, the following sorts of tasks: (1) *perceiving* (visually, aurally, etc.) the world, (2) *remembering* perceived information, (3) reasoning on the basis of information perceived or remembered, and (4) expressing this information, or listening to information expressed by others, in the form of *language*. Perceiving, remembering, reasoning, and the processes involved in the production and comprehension of language may not exhaust the legitimate business of cognitive science; but they certainly lie at the core of this science.

The central idea of non-Cartesian cognitive science is that cognitive tasks are not, in general, the sort of thing that need be accomplished only in the head or by a brain. If we had to accomplish a cognitive task using only our brains, then complex and difficult neural maneuvers might be required. However, if we are able to use relevant structures in our environment, then some of the complexity and difficulty of this task might be reduced: we off-load at least some of the task onto the environment around us. Roughly: we get the environment to do some of the work for us; and this reduces the work that we need do. What makes an environmental structure relevant? Again roughly: it carries information relevant to the task that we need to accomplish, and by using this structure, or acting on it in the right sort of way, we are thereby able to appropriate—make available—and employ this information in the accomplishing of the cognitive task in question.

If this sounds a little abstract, just think of our MapQuest instructions that we have printed out prior to our journey. This printout contains information relevant to the task we need to accomplish—getting from A to B. I am able to make this information available and use it by manipulating the page in the right way—for example, by picking it up, turning it the right way up, and holding it in front of my eyes. In the absence of this sort of manipulation, the information I require is present on the page but unavailable to me. Because I am able to act on the external structure—the page—in such a way as to make the information it contains available to me, the number and complexity of neural operations that I must perform to accomplish the task of getting from A to B is accordingly reduced (given that we are encultured in linguistic communities, we generally find reading novel information easier than remembering it). Acting on external structures in such a way that the information they contain is transformed from the merely *present* to the *available* lies at the heart of non-Cartesian cognitive science. This sort of action is, according to the non-Cartesian conception of cognition, *part* of what cognition is. That is, action of this sort—action that transforms information that is merely present in external structures to information that is available—forms a properly cognitive part of an overall cognitive process.

Consider another example that makes much the same point. Imagine how fiendishly difficult it would be to do jigsaw puzzles if we weren't allowed to pick up and manipulate the pieces (Kirsh and Maglio 1994). If we couldn't do this, then we would have to form detailed mental images of each individual piece, and by a process of mental rotation try to work out with which other pieces it fits. In such circumstances, jigsaws would be even less fun than they already are. But this, of course, is not how we do jigsaws. We don't do them this way because the pieces themselves contain information about which of the other pieces they are going to mesh with and which they are not. By picking up individual pieces and "trying them out"—bringing them into close proximity with other pieces and adjudicating the likelihood of their fitting together—we make this information available to us. Therefore, we don't need to construct this information in the form of mental images and processes of mental rotation. We get the world to do some of the work for us, and we do this by acting on the world—manipulating and exploiting structures that contain useful information and thereby making this information available to us. Each piece of the jigsaw contains information that uniquely specifies the pieces with which it will fit. By manipulating the pieces, we transform this from information that is merely present to information that is available. And this, according to non-Cartesian cognitive science, is, in part, what cognition is.

5 Non-Cartesian Cognitive Science: Framework

We are beginning to glimpse at least the general contours of the non-Cartesian conception of mental phenomena that underlies the prospective new science:

1. External structures carry information relevant to the accomplishing of a given cognitive task (or task that has a cognitive component). This information is *present* in these structures.

2. By using such structures in appropriate ways, I can transform the information they contain from information that is merely present to information that is *available*—available for detection by my sensory apparatus, and for deployment by my subsequent cognitive operations.

3. The information thus made available is, therefore, information that I need only *detect* rather than information I need *construct* or *store*.

4. Detection of information is *cheaper* than construction or storage.

And, finally, the *money ball*:

5. Action on external structures that transforms the information they contain from the merely present to the available (and so amenable to detection rather than requiring construction or storage) is part of what cognition is.

To see these principles in action, let us once more revisit MapQuest. The external structure in question is the printout of the directions. This printout contains information relevant to the accomplishing of a given task: getting from A to B. This information is *present* in the printout. Moreover, this is a task that is part locomotive, but also part cognitive (that is, it has a clear cognitive component). Therefore, condition 1 is satisfied. By using the structure in appropriate ways—for example, by picking it up, turning it the right way up, and holding it up in front of my eyes—I transform the information contained on this page from information that is merely present to information that is *available* for detection by me and deployment in my subsequent cognitive operations. This is condition 2. The information that is made available is information that I need only detect, for example, through perception. I do not need to store this information in the form of memory. Nor do I need to construct this information by way of a process of reasoning. This is condition 3. We find perceiving of information easier to accomplish than storing or constructing it. Typically—not always, not necessarily, but typically—perceiving makes fewer demands on our neural apparatus than either reasoning or storage. This is condition 4, and we shall look at reasons for thinking it is true later on. It is condition 5 that is the controversial one. We will look at this principle, and why it is controversial, in the next section.

The first condition of this general framework appeals to external information-bearing structures. In this context, to call something "external" is to say that it is outside the brain (or central nervous system). The structure in question is not a neural state or process. The structures I have looked at so far are also ones that are outside the body as a whole—GPS devices, printed pages, knots, and so on. However, like its Cartesian counterpart, non-Cartesian cognitive science is a broad church—as we shall see later, perhaps too broad. In some cases, the external structures in question might be bodily ones: things located inside the body of the organism but not part of the brain or central nervous system. This means that the notion of "use" referred to in the second condition must also be understood in a very broad sense. The way in which we use bodily structures in accomplishing our cognitive tasks is typically very different from the way in which we use structures outside our body. We shall return to this point in a later chapter.

At present, however, we need to look at a more fundamental question, one that pertains to condition 5.

6   The Big Question (Or, How Many Es Are Enough?)

It is easy to understand the attraction of utilizing external forms of information storage in the ways we have encountered above. The attraction, bluntly put is: *thinking is hard.* The perils and pitfalls of irresponsible brain-use were, as far as I am aware, first pointed out by the philosopher Alfred North Whitehead, early in the twentieth century:

It is a profoundly erroneous truism, repeated by all copy-books and by eminent people making speeches, that we should cultivate the habit of thinking of what we are doing. The precise opposite is the case. Civilization advances by extending the number of operations we can perform without thinking about them. Operations of thought are like cavalry charges in a battle—they are strictly limited in number, they require fresh horses, and they must only be made at decisive moments. (Whitehead 1911, 55)

As if we needed reminding, this idea has been the subject of extensive empirical confirmation in recent years (e.g., Baumeister et al. 1998). Cognizing is hard, especially when we use only the naked brain, and is something one should do only at decisive moments. The rest of the time, it is a good idea to *cognitively delegate*. As Andy Clark (1997) once put it, we make the world around us smart so we don't have to be. Underlying this delegation, of course, is the barking dog principle. Delegating works, as long as the work you put into the delegation is less than the work your delegates then actually do for you.

However, this idea begs one crucial question: what reason, if any, do we have for thinking that the sorts of extraneural processes invoked by non-Cartesian cognitive science are cognitive processes?[14] Take, for example, manipulating the MapQuest printout—picking it up, turning it the right way around, holding it up in front of my eyes, and so on. This is an action that transforms the information merely present in the printout into information that is available. But what reason, if any, do we have for regarding this as a part of my cognitive processing? Intuitively, this seems far-fetched. It seems far more natural to divide up what is going on in the following way. First of all, there are the processes of perceiving, recognizing, and understanding the words contained on the page. These are genuinely cognitive processes, and they occur in the brain. That is, they are processes occurring somewhere in the brain's visual and language modules. The processes are *facilitated* by actions that I perform. It is, of course, much easier to read the page if I turn it the right way up. Everyone knows that. But that doesn't mean that this manipulation forms part of my processes of cognition. The right way to think about things, surely, is that my genuinely cognitive processes—ones occurring in my brain's visual and language modules—are supplemented and supported by actions that I perform on the world. To be supported by actions that I perform on the world is not the same thing as to be partially constituted by those actions (Rupert 2004; Adams and Aizawa 2001, 2010).

We can make the same point about the jigsaw puzzle. The real cognitive processes involved here are ones of visual perception and mental image formation and rotation. Of course, it is true that if I were not able to pick up the pieces and manipulate them, then I would have to engage in far more complex processes of image formation and rotation. The need to do this is considerably reduced by the fact that I can pick up pieces and manipulate them—bring them into close proximity and see if they fit together. Nonetheless, the need for image formation and rotation is not eliminated. At any given time, I select which piece to pick up on the basis of an antecedent sense of whether it is a likely candidate for fit. And I get this sense through prior processes of at least partial image formation and rotation. So, it is natural to think that the process of completing a jigsaw puzzle can be divided into two sorts. First, there are the *real* cognitive processes: perception of the pieces, and subsequent image formation and rotation. These occur exclusively in the brain. Second, there are bodily actions I can perform on the individual pieces: picking them up and "trying them out." These are not real cognitive processes at all; but they do provide a useful supplement to those processes—a supplement that reduces the extent, and perhaps alters the nature, of the real cognitive processes that we must perform.

These questions are obvious ones. The inference from the claim that external operations I perform on the world *supplement* or *complement* my cognitive processing to the claim that these operations therefore form *part of* that processing is unsound. We cannot afford to run together the question of whether things going on in the environment *drive* (i.e., causally contribute to) a cognitive process with the question of whether things going on the environment partially *constitute* a cognitive process. The answer to the former question is, of course, yes. Things going on in the environment do causally drive cognitive processes. Even René Descartes could have agreed to that—assuming he could work out his problems with understanding how mental–physical interaction took place. The idea that things going on in the environment causally drive cognitive processes is an utterly mundane claim that anyone should accept. Cartesian cognitive science would not only accept this idea, it would insist on it.

Indeed, not only is this question an obvious one that must be answered in any development of a non-Cartesian alternative, it also makes it clear why we shouldn't be in any rush to blithely identify non-Cartesian cognitive science with 4e. In effect, the question begins the process of whittling down 4e into something that is leaner and, I hope to show, meaner. To see this, consider a way of rephrasing the objection developed above. In the case of MapQuest and the jigsaw puzzle, we might say that the external operations I perform provide a useful *scaffolding* or *framework* within which the real cognitive processes can operate. That is, the actions I perform on the world provide a scaffolding or framework within which my cognition can be usefully *embedded*. And this is the thesis of the embedded mind. This scaffolding in which my cognition is embedded considerably reduces the amount of (real) cognitive processes that I must perform in working out how to get from A to B, or in completing the jigsaw puzzle. But this doesn't mean that the framework is literally part of the cognitive processes in which I engage when I am navigating or jigsaw-completing.

The traditional—Cartesian—way of thinking about cognitive processes draws a firm distinction between cognitive processes proper and the framework or scaffolding within which these processes occur. This scaffolding can causally affect, and so facilitate, the cognitive processes proper. But, according to Cartesian cognitive science, we must be careful not to confuse real cognition with extraneous causal accompaniments (Adams and Aizawa 2001). Notice that this point has, in effect, been developed in terms of the language of embedding. Thus, endorsing the thesis of the embedded mind can actually provide a way of attacking non-Cartesian cognitive science—at least in the way I have developed this idea.

The correct response to this is not to deny the distinction between cognition and scaffolding. Such a move might be tempting, but only, I suspect, because it has, as Bertrand Russell once put, all the advantages of theft over honest toil. We need to reiterate the distinction between causation and constitution and cannot fall into the trap of supposing that whatever causally contributes to a cognitive process is part of that cognitive process (cf. Wheeler 2008). To say that the distinction between cognition and scaffolding has been drawn in the wrong place (or has, in general, not been drawn in the right place) is not to deny that there is a distinction between cognition and scaffolding. Without this distinction, non-Cartesian cognitive science becomes true by stipulation.

If non-Cartesian cognitive science is to provide a genuine (i.e., interesting and informative) alternative to its Cartesian counterpart, then it must be based on a stronger claim than the mere environmental embedding of cognitive processes. The required claim, I am going to argue, is that processes occurring in the environment—that is, outside the brain—can, in part, literally *constitute* cognitive processes. That is, things existing or occurring outside of the brain can be partial constituents of cognitive processes. So, the question that should be used to demarcate non-Cartesian cognitive science from the Cartesian alternative is this: can states, processes, and structures that exist outside the brain form part—a genuinely cognitive part—of cognitive processes? Cartesian cognitive science answers *no*: cognitive processes are exclusively realized by brain processes. To the extent that cognitive processes rely on processes occurring outside the brain, these form part of the scaffolding or framework within which these processes are situated, but do not literally form part of cognition.

Non-Cartesian cognitive science, at least as I shall develop this idea, answers *yes*: some cognitive processes—not all by any means, but some—can have, as literal constituents, processes occurring outside the brain. "Outside the brain," of course, does not necessarily mean "outside the body." Here, the new science bifurcates. The *embodied* strand of the science emphasizes the way on which cognitive processes can, in part, be constituted by processes and structures occurring outside the brain but inside the body of the cognitive organism. The *extended* strand, however, argues that cognitive processes can, in part, be made up of processes and structures that occur outside the body in the wider environment of the cognitive organism.

At stake, of course, is the Cartesian vision of mental phenomena as ones located inside the heads of thinking subjects. This vision has under-

written both our commonsense conception of the mind, and the scientific attempts to study the mind that have been erected on the foundation
of common sense. The Cartesian vision stands or falls on this question:
can processes occurring outside of the brain form genuinely cognitive
parts of cognitive processes? If they can, and if cognitive processes are
mental processes, then the Cartesian vision of the mental must be abandoned. The aim of this book is to show that the Cartesian vision must in
fact be abandoned.

2 Non-Cartesian Cognitive Science

1 Cartesian Cognitive Science at Work: Marr's Theory of Vision

The primary aim of this chapter is to show that non-Cartesian cognitive science is not a peculiar eruption of philosophy or philosophers of idiosyncratic bent. Rather, at least in its most recent incarnation, it is motivated by empirical work in a variety of cognate disciplines. This chapter is, therefore, aimed at the uninitiated. It comprises a survey—necessarily brief and for that reason unsatisfactory—of this empirical work. Those already familiar with this work can safely skip to chapter 3.

In the previous chapter I used the expression "non-Cartesian science of the mind"—a science built on a non-Cartesian vision of mental phenomena. At present this expression is largely aspirational rather than descriptive. It applies to something that does not yet exist. However, the expression is not entirely empty. It has meaning to the extent that it picks out, or denotes, a collection of theories of, or approaches to, the mental phenomena that, though often quite different, cluster around a recognizable and recurring theme: mental operations are not confined to processes occurring in the brains of cognizing organisms. Instead, they can be made up, in part, of processes that extend into the organism's body and even into the organism's world.

It would be both inaccurate and premature to describe this cluster of theories as a *new science*. It would be inaccurate because some of the theories that make this up are not new; shortly, we shall look at some work conducted within this general framework that is nearly a century old. It would be premature because, despite their antipathy toward the central tenet of traditional cognitive science, the theories involved are often disparate; some might even prove to be incompatible. Traditional cognitive science is a systematic and comprehensive framework for understanding cognitive processes, a framework whose foundational principles are explicit and well understood. The aspiring new science is, as yet, not even on nodding terms with this sort of systematic self-awareness that constitutes a mature science. The new science, as yet, has no clear conceptual foundation. This chapter is going to focus on identifying some of the accounts of mental processes that make up the cluster of theories that are candidates for the new science. The rest of the book will be concerned with supplying the relevant foundation for this science. It would, however, be useful to begin with an examination of a classic—indeed paradigmatic—exemplar of Cartesian cognitive science. This will allow us to identify more precisely exactly what it is that the aspiring new science brings to the table. And, as far as Cartesian cognitive science goes, you just do not get more paradigmatic than David Marr's (1982) theory of vision.[1] Indeed, so canonical is Marr's account, it not only provides an example of traditional cognitive science at work, it also played an important role in shaping how cognitive scientists came to understand their enterprise. The example is, therefore, both illustrative and partly constitutive of traditional cognitive science at its best. That is why I am going to use it to provide a foil to much of the discussion to follow—both in this and subsequent chapters.

From the perspective of common sense, visual perception seems to be an obvious example of a process that takes place both in the world and in the brain. For visual perception to occur, light has to first strike the retina, and this is a worldly occurrence rather than an intracranial one. Admittedly, for visual perception to occur, the brain must then process the information it receives. But, one might think, visual perception straddles both worldly and intracranial processes. However, traditional cognitive science relegates the first half of the process to *sensation* as opposed to *perception*. The study of perception is, therefore, the study of the processes occurring in the brain whereby it transforms visual input or sensation into visual perception.

According to David Marr's (1982) theory of vision, visual perception begins with stimulation of the retina (sensation) and culminates with the construction of a visual representation of the world (visual perception proper). To understand vision is to understand the processes in between— the processes whereby stimulation of the retina is progressively transformed into genuine visual representation. If we think of retinal stimulation as input, and the production of a visual representation of the world as output, then to understand vision is to understand the intervening steps whereby input is transformed into output.

Stimulation of the retina takes the form of electromagnetic energy distributed over an array of retinal locations. This pattern of stimulation is often called the *retinal image*. The retinal image, however, falls far short of a visual representation. Images are flat, static, and notoriously ambiguous. Vision, on the other hand, yields perception of a three-dimensional, mobile, and interpreted world. It seems, therefore, that visual perception must involve processes that embellish and augment the information contained in the retinal image: the image must be *processed* in some way. To understand vision, according to Marr, is to understand this processing.

The retinal image consists in varying intensities of light distributed over an array of locations on the retina. The variation in light intensity is a result of the way in which light is reflected by structures in the observer's environment. The goal of what Marr calls *early* visual processing is to create from the retinal image a representation of the *visible* structures of observed objects, where visible structures are ones that can be observed directly without, as Marr sees it, any need for postperceptual cognitive processes. The shapes of surfaces, and their orientations to and distances from the observer are examples of visible structures in this sense. In contrast, recognition of an object as being of a certain type—table, dog, car, and so on—would involve inferential processes that fall outside the scope of early visual processing.

The first stage in early visual processing consists in the construction of what Marr calls the *primal sketch*. The primal sketch represents the intensity changes present in the retinal image and makes some of the more global image structures present. Construction of the primal sketch consists of two stages. First, there is the construction of the *raw primal sketch*. The raw primal sketch is a representational structure instantiated in the brain: a representation of the pattern of light distributed over the retina in which information about the edges and textures of objects is made explicit. To make this information explicit, the brain registers the information contained in the retinal image, and then applies certain *transformational rules* to it.

These transformational rules are, in essence, something like a process of *inference*—although this does, of course, undermine Marr's distinction between direct perception and perception based on inference. Alternatively, we can think of them as something like *guesses* that the brain makes. The brain registers the information contained in the retinal image, and then attempts to work out from this the sorts of edges and textures and object would have to possess in order to produce a retinal image like that. Consider, for example, the transformational rule known as *good continuation*. The brain detects in the retinal image the presence of a line, which it takes to be indicative of an object's edge. The line stops at a certain point, but shortly after this, another line is found that continues the course of the original line. The rule of good continuation allows the brain to infer that the two lines belong to the same edge. In other words, the brain interprets the gap in the line to indicate the occlusion of a single object rather than the presence of two distinct objects. This "guess" is, of course, fallible. But it is based on a rule of good continuation that is hardwired in the brain. And it became hardwired in the brain only because, all things being equal, it was correct more often than the alternative inference to two distinct objects. So, by way of transformational rules of this sort, the brain essentially *embellishes* the information contained in the retinal image.

This process of inference continues in the construction of the *full primal sketch*. Here the brain applies various grouping principles—proximity, similarity, common fate, closure, and so on. Again, the underlying idea is the same. Suppose you have a mishmash of regions, edges, and textures—and this, according to Marr, is essentially what the raw primal sketch is. The next task you will have to accomplish is working out which regions, edges, and textures go together. That is, does this edge belong with this region or that one? Does this texture go together with this edge or that one? The function of the grouping principles is to answer these sorts of questions. Again, these principles are akin to a form of inference whereby the brain embellishes the information contained in the raw primal sketch with its best guess as to what this must mean for the full primal sketch. The result of the application of the various grouping principles is the identification of defined larger structures, boundaries, regions, and so on. This new representational structure is the full primal sketch.

The brain then further embellishes the information contained in this new representational structure with further forms of inference. Here principles concerning depth, motion, shading, and so on are brought into play. The result is the construction of a new representational structure: the *2½D sketch*. This is the culmination of early visual processing and describes the layout of structures in the world from the perspective of the perceiver.

A further, and equally essential, aspect of vision is recognition of objects. Marr argued that in order to recognize the object to which a particular shape corresponds, a third representational layer of processing is required, a layer that centers on the object rather than the observer. This level of processing yields what Marr calls *3D object representations*. Again, construction of this new representational structure is akin to a process of inference. Here, the brain utilizes a stored set of object descriptions, and works out which description is most likely to be satisfied by the information contained in the 2½D sketch.

The language of "inference" and "guessing" is, of course, metaphorical. The brain does not *infer* in the way we do when we solve a logical puzzle. And it does not *guess* in anything like the way we do when we guess who it was that just knocked on our door. Nevertheless, Marr's account of what the brain does when we visually perceive the world employs ideas that are similar enough to these familiar concepts to make this language illuminating. Abstracting from the details, Marr's account is built around two related concepts: *representations* and *rules*. And these are inseparable.

The retinal image is *not* a representation (although there has been much confusion on this score). The retinal image can be neither true nor false; neither correct nor incorrect. And it is simply caused by whatever in fact caused it. The key to any representation is that it makes a *normative* claim on the world. What this means is that a representation makes a claim about the way the world is, and if the representation is instantiated or activated then the world *should* be that way. If the world is not that way, then the representation is false or incorrect. The retinal image is not the sort of thing that can be false or incorrect: it simply is what it is. Even the raw primal sketch, however, is different. For example, in applying its good continuation guess, and constructing the primal sketch in one way rather than another, the brain is, in effect, making a claim about the way the world is. If the brain applies the good continuation rule, then the observer's world *should* contain a single occluded object rather than two distinct objects. If this world in fact turns out to contain two distinct objects, the representation is incorrect; and it is incorrect because the brain's "guess," although generally reliable, was in this case erroneous.

So, the primal sketch (in either form) is a representation, whereas the retinal image is not. But what makes the primal sketch into a representation is precisely the fact that it has been constructed via the application of transformational rules (such as good continuation). It is because these rules have been applied that the primal sketch makes a claim about the way the world is—as opposed to the retinal image that is simply what it is. And, therefore, it is because these rules have been applied that, if the world should turn out otherwise, we can legitimately talk of the primal sketch being incorrect or inaccurate. It is the application of these rules that makes the primal sketch the sort of thing that can make a claim on the world, and therefore be either true or false. It is the application of transformational rules that makes the primal sketch a normative item. But being normative is a necessary condition of an item's being a representation.

Therefore, ultimately, it is the application of transformational rules to a structure that, at least in part, makes that structure into a representation. In Marr's theory of vision, and in Cartesian cognitive science in general, the concepts of a representation and (transformational) rule are indissolubly entwined.

The Cartesian idea that the mind is located somewhere inside the head was, therefore, underwritten in Cartesian cognitive science by way of two claims:

1. Mental representations are structures instantiated in the brains of cognizing animals—structures that make claims on the world.
2. Cognitive processes consist in the application of transformational rules to mental representations.

The internality of cognitive processes, therefore, follows from the internality of mental representations. Cognitive processes are rule-governed operations performed by the brain on mental representations. Both the representations and the operations by which they are transformed are internal to the brain.

2 Check This Out!

A perfect place to begin exploration of the cluster of theories that are candidates for the new, non-Cartesian, science of the mind is Kevin O'Regan's Web site (http://nivea.psycho.univ-paris5.fr/). O'Regan is a perceptual psychologist, working at the CNRS in Paris, who made his name studying a phenomenon known as *change blindness*; and his Web site provides some very good examples of this phenomenon. There you will find photographs of various scenes: Notre Dame Cathedral is in one of them; a fighter plane landing on an aircraft carrier is another; people canoeing on a lake against a backdrop of mountains; and so on. The pictures are going to change— significantly. I won't tell you precisely how, as that would spoil things. But the changes are significant enough that you would easily notice them under normal circumstances. However, in a change blindness experiment, circumstances are very far from normal.

A change in a visually presented scene, like a photograph, would normally cause a transient signal in your visual apparatus. This transient signal is detected by low-level (i.e., unconscious) visual mechanisms in this apparatus, and the result is that your attention is automatically attracted to the location of the change. This is why you notice the change. In a change-blindness experiment, however, a way is found of nullifying the role of the visual transient. This can be done in several ways (and if you visit O'Regan's Web site, you will see all of these). One method involves superimposing a very brief global flicker over the whole visual field at the moment of the change. In other words, the scene is momentarily replaced by a simple gray frame. During the period of *gray-out*, a change is made in the photograph. Another method involves creating a number of simultaneous local disturbances—which appear something like mud splashes on the scene—that act as decoys and so minimize the effect of the local transient. The same sort of effect can also be achieved by making the change in the photograph coincide with an eye saccade, an eye blink, or a cut in a film sequence. In all these cases, a brief global disturbance swamps the local transient and thus prevents it from playing its normal role of grabbing your attention.

Experiments conducted by O'Regan (1992) and others (e.g., Blackmore et al. 1995; Rensink, O'Regan, and Clark 1997) showed that under these sorts of conditions, observers have great difficulty seeing changes, even though they are large and occur in full view. If you are at all typical, you will find some of the changes easier to spot than others. But some of them will be very difficult to spot, and all of them will be harder to spot than if you were just looking at a changing scene where the change was not masked. In one version of the experiment, O'Regan even showed that an observer could be looking directly at the change at the moment it occurs and still not notice it (O'Regan et al. 2000).

Simons and Levin (1997) have show that the same sorts of results can be obtained when one switches from computer screens to real-world situations. One striking experiment turned on a slapstick scenario—of which Simons and Levin are the undisputed world heavyweight champions—in which an experimenter, pretending to be lost on the Cornell Campus, would approach an unsuspecting passerby to ask for directions. Once the passerby started to reply, two people carrying a large door would walk between the inquirer and the passerby. During the walk through, however, the original inquirer is replaced by a different person. Only 50 percent of the direction-givers noticed the change. Yet the two experimenters were of different heights, wore different clothes, had different voices, and so on. Moreover, those who did notice the change were students of roughly the same age and demographics as the two experimenters. In a follow-up study, the students failed to spot the change when the experimenters appeared as construction workers, placing them in a different social group. The conclusion that Simons and Levin (1997, 266) draw is that our failures to detect change arise because "we lack a precise representation of our visual world from one view to the next." We encode only a "rough gist" of the current scene—just enough to support a broad sense of what's going on insofar as it matters to us, and to guide further intelligent information retrieval as and when it is needed.

In a related experiment, one that gave rise to a paper with almost certainly the best title ever to grace the pages of an professional academic journal—the paper was called "Gorillas in Our Midst"—Simons and Chabris (2000) had their experimental subjects watch a video of two teams (one in white, one in black) passing basketballs (one per team). Each subject was asked to count the number of successful passes made by the white team. Afterward, subjects are asked whether they saw anything else, anything unusual. A short time into the film (about 45 seconds) an intruder will make an appearance—walking through the middle of the players. The intruder may be the semitransparent figure of a woman holding an umbrella or a semitransparent man in a gorilla suit. On some trials, the woman or man in gorilla suit were presented in fully opaque form. In the semitransparent condition, 73 percent of subjects failed to see the gorilla, and even in the opaque condition 35 percent of subjects failed to see it (Simons 2000, 152). Simons concludes, "We do not realize the degree to which we are blind to unattended and unexpected stimuli, and we mistakenly believe that important events will automatically draw our attention away from our current task or goals" (2000, 154). This is an example of *inattentional blindness*, a phenomenon closely related to change blindness.

In the next chapter, we shall examine attempts to explain these phenomena in more depth. For present purposes, however, two points are worthy of note. First, the phenomena of change and inattentional blindness seem to indicate—at least arguably—that the role traditionally assigned to visual representations has been somewhat overplayed. Instead of providing us with complex and detailed simulacra of the visual world, the role of internal visual representations is to provide us with the "rough gist" of the situation. That is, in general, visual representations provide us with a map of the perceived world that is partial, incomplete, and lacking in the sort of detail we take as unproblematically given in our visual experience. We do not, after all, visually experience the rough gist of the world around us: we experience it in all its concrete, rich, and detailed glory. Therefore, visual representations, by themselves, cannot explain the phenomenological character of our visual experience.

Second, the slack left by this downgrading of the role of visual representations, and the resulting gap between visual representations and visual phenomenology, is taken up by the ability of an organism to act on the world around it. We do not need to reproduce internally the complexity, detail, and richness that we take, correctly, to be part of the phenomenology of visual experience. Instead, we make use of the complexity, detail, and richness that make up the visually detectable world around us. By constantly directing and redirecting our attention to this world, we avail ourselves of the complexity, detail, and richness it contains, and thereby obviate the need to reproduce these internally.

We shall look at these ideas in much more detail in the next chapter. For now, we can simply note that the general explanatory profile— *attenuation of the role of representation* coupled with *augmentation of the role of action* is one that is replicated throughout the cluster of theories that make up our prospective new science.

3   The Ecological Theory of Visual Perception

Some of the most important features of this sort of *enactive* account of perception discussed in the previous section were anticipated by a Cornell University psychologist—James J. Gibson. Gibson's account, which he developed from the late 1950s until his death in 1979, became known as the *ecological theory* of visual perception. During the first two decades of its life, this theory was widely reviled, by psychologists and philosophers alike, as a hopelessly confused, "magical" account of vision. Now, however, it is slowly beginning to be appreciated that the rise of non-Cartesian cognitive science is, in effect, a vindication of the work of James Gibson.

As we have seen, traditional approaches to visual perception, of the sort exemplified by Marr, adhere closely to the following sort of explanatory framework:

1. Perception begins with stimulation of the retina by light energy impinging on it.
2. This results in a retinal image, characterized in terms of intensity values distributed over an array of different locations.
3. Retinal images carry relatively little information, certainly not enough to add up to genuine perception.
4. In order for perception to occur, the information contained in the retinal image has to be supplemented and embellished (i.e., processed) by various information-processing operations.
5. These information-processing operations occur inside the skin of the perceiving organism.

This framework assumes that visual perception begins with the retinal image. Gibson's first insight—and perhaps his most important one—was to see that this is not so: visual perception begins not with the retinal image but with what Gibson (1966, 1979) called the *optic array*.

Light from the sun fills the air—the *terrestrial medium*—so that it is in a "steady state" of reverberation. In this steady state, the environment is filled with rays of light traveling between the surfaces of objects. At any point in space, light will converge from all directions. Therefore, at each point there is what can be regarded as a densely nested set of solid visual angles, which are composed of inhomogeneities in the intensity of light. Thus, we can imagine an observer, at least for now, as a point surrounded by a sphere, which is divided into tiny solid angles. The intensity of light and the mixture of wavelengths vary from one solid angle to another. This spatial pattern of light is the optic array. Light carries information because the structure of the optic array is determined by the nature and position of the surfaces from which it has been reflected.

The optic array is divided into many segments or angles. Each of these contains light reflected from different surfaces, and the light contained in each segment will differ from that in other segments in terms of its average intensity and distribution of wavelength. The boundaries between these segments of the optic array, since they mark a change in intensity and distribution of wavelength, provide information about the three-dimensional structure of objects in the world. At a finer level of detail, each segment will, in turn, be subdivided in a way determined by the texture of the surface from which the light is reflected. Therefore, at this level also, the optic array can carry information about further properties of objects and terrain.

The realization of the importance of the optic array is, in many ways, Gibson's essential insight. In effect, the rest of his ecological approach stems from placing the optic array in its proper position of conceptual priority. The optic array is an *external information-bearing structure*. It is external in the quite obvious sense that it exists outside the skins of perceiving organisms and is in no way dependent on such organisms for its existence. It also carries information about the environment. Indeed, according to Gibson, there is enough information contained in the optic array to specify the nature of the environment that shapes it. Information, for Gibson, is essentially *nomic dependence*. The structure of the environment depends, in a lawlike (i.e., nomic) way on the structure of the physical environment that surrounds it. In virtue of this dependence, the optic array carries information about this wider environment. The optic array is, as Gibson puts it, *specific* to the environment. Because of this, an organism whose perceptual system detects optical structure in the array can thereby be aware of what this structure specifies. Thus, the perceiving organism is aware of the structure and not the array and, more importantly, is in a position to utilize the information about the environment embodied in the array.

Once we allow that the optic array is an external structure that embodies information about the environment, we are, of course, forced to admit that some of the information relevant to perception exists in the environment of the perceiver. This may seem like a mundane observation. However, an important conclusion follows from it. Suppose we are faced with a particular perceptual task. If we accept the idea of the optic array, we must allow that at least some of the information relevant to this task will be located in the array. Perhaps, as Gibson seems to suggest, this information will be sufficient for us to accomplish the task. Perhaps not—in which case we might find it necessary to postulate internal processing operations that supplement or embellish the information contained in the array. Even if this is so, however, one thing is clear: we cannot begin to estimate what internal processing an organism needs to accomplish unless we understand how much information is already available to that organism in its optic array. The more information available to the organism in its optic array, the less internal processing the organism needs to perform. Understanding the internal processes involved in visual perception is logically and methodologically secondary to understanding the information that is available to the perceiving organism in its environment.

The next stage in understanding visual perception would be to provide an account of how a perceiving organism is able to make the information contained in the optic array available to it. Here we find another distinctively Gibsonian element: the emphasis on *action*. As Gibson points out, and the enactive approach would echo this point nearly half a century later, perception is inextricably bound up with action. Perceiving organisms are not, typically, static creatures but, rather, actively explore their environment. The optic array is a source of information for any organism equipped to take advantage of it. But the optic array does not impinge on passive observers. Rather, the living organism will actively *sample* the optic array. When an observer moves, the entire optic array is transformed, and such transformations contain information about the layout, shapes, and orientations of objects in the world.

By moving, and so effecting transformations in the optic array, perceiving organisms can identify and appropriate what Gibson calls the *invariant* information contained in the array. This is information that can be made available to an observer not by any one static optic array as such but only in the transformation of one optic array into another. Consider, for example, what is known as the *horizon ratio relation* (Sedgwick 1973). The horizon intersects an object at a particular height. All objects of the same height, whatever their distance from the observer, are cut by the horizon in the same ratio. This is one example of invariant information. An organism can detect such information only by moving and, hence, bringing about transformations in the optic array. Information, in this sense, is not something inside the organism. It exists as a function of changes in the organism–environment relation.

Therefore, crucial to Gibson's account are two claims: (i) the optic array, a structure external to the perceiving organism, is a locus of information for suitably equipped creatures; and (ii) a creature can appropriate or make this information available to itself through acting on the array, and thus effecting transformations in it. What the perceiving creature does, in effect, is *manipulate* a structure external to it—the optic array—in order to make available to itself information that it can then use to navigate its way around the environment. And the claim that the organism *makes information available* to itself simply means that the organism makes information susceptible, or amenable, to detection by itself. Thus, information about the relative heights of objects is contained in the organism's environment. However, this information is not directly available to the organism. It becomes available—that is, amenable to detection by the organism—only when the organism moves, and thus brings about transformations in the structure of ambient light.

Gibson has usually been understood as hostile to the idea of mental representations, and it's common to find his account presented as obviating the need for them. However, I think the real value of Gibson's account is safeguarded by another, less sanguine interpretation. Whether or not Gibson would have endorsed it—and I have been made aware that at least some contemporary Gibsonians do not[2]—the interpretation is compatible with his overall theory.

Recall the general contours of the old science, as represented by Marr's theory of vision. Perception consists in the manipulation and transformation of internal information-bearing structures—representational items ranging from the raw primal sketch all the way through to 3D object representations. Gibson's account replaces at least some of the need for manipulation and transformation of internal information-bearing structures with the manipulation and transformation of external information-bearing structures—the optic array. There is nothing in Gibson's theory itself—as opposed, perhaps, to his statements about his theory—that entails or even suggests that *all* of the role traditionally assigned to manipulation and transformation of internal information-bearing structures can be taken over by the manipulation and transformation of external information-bearing structures (Rowlands 1995). Precisely how *much* of the role traditionally assigned to the manipulation and transformation of internal information-bearing structures can be taken over by the manipulation and transformation of external information-bearing structures is, of course, an empirical question. And there is no reason at all for thinking that Gibson's theory entails that all of the role of the former can be taken over by the latter. However, crucially, we will not know what sorts and how many kinds of internal information-processing operations we need to posit in order to explain an organism's perceptual ability unless we understand the ways in which, and the extent to which, the organism is able to manipulate and transform relevant structures in its environment and so make available to itself information required for the prosecution of its perceptual tasks.

Therefore, we find in Gibson's work the twin themes characteristic of the nascent new science: attenuation of representation combined with augmentation of action. There is the questioning of, and limited (at least on my interpretation) hostility to, the role played in Cartesian cognitive science by the notion of mental representation. And there is the idea that at least some of the role traditionally played by mental representations can be taken over by the perceiving organism acting on the world in appropriate ways.

4   From Russia with Love

That the work of Gibson should turn out to be a version of what I am calling the new science shows that this science is not, in fact, *that* new. An even more striking example of just how old the new science is can be found in work I briefly mentioned in the previous chapter. This is the work of two Soviet psychologists, Anton Luria and Lev Vygotsky (1930/1992).

A natural expression of the Cartesian conception is what we might, following Hurley (1998), call the *vertical sandwich* model of the relation between sensation, cognition, and action. This model was clearly implicated in Marr's account of vision. This is, in essence, an input–output model of the mind. Sensation provides the input to the system; action is the system's output. And cognition consists in information-processing operations—the manipulation and transformation of information-bearing structures in the brain. One noticeable feature of Cartesian cognitive science is that it locates perception in the middle of the sandwich—as a part of cognition, and therefore, quite different from sensation. Nonetheless, one would also have to acknowledge that, intuitively, perception is far more closely connected to the world than other types of cognitive process, such as thinking, reasoning, and remembering. The starting point for perception is provided by sensation; but, one might argue, this is not true of any other type of cognitive process. Therefore, if perception is to be found in the sandwich's filling, it is in the outer part of that filling. Perception is not so much the burger as the lettuce, gherkins, and mayonnaise.

These intuitive claims suggest what we might call a *deflationary* response to the ecological and enactive arguments we have encountered. The deflationary response accepts the arguments, but tries to severely restrict their influence. Basically, the response goes like this: OK, we'll give you perception. Perception, we'll accept, involves manipulation and transformation of external information bearing structures, and so is a process that extends into a perceiving organism's environment, and is not restricted to processes occurring inside that organism's head. We'll accept all that—but that's as far as it goes. Real cognition—cognition central, if you like—is restricted to processes occurring inside the cognizing organism's brain. In other words, perception is a peculiarly peripheral and decidedly idiosyncratic form of cognition; and we cannot use it as a template for understanding cognition in general.

This response holds on to the sandwich model itself, but merely rearranges our understanding of its ingredients. Perception breaks down into two components, one of which is to be found in the sandwich's filling, and the other to be found in the bread. The conclusion is clear. If the new science is to deal the Cartesian conception anything more than a glancing blow, it cannot restrict its arguments to perception: it must go after *cognition central*. Here the general strategy of the nascent new science has been to try and show that cognition central is not, in fact, as central as we might think. Or, to put the same point another way: cognition is a lot more like perception than we have hitherto realized or been willing to accept.

An early, but nonetheless important, development of this general theme is to be found in the work of the Soviet psychologists Anton Luria and Lev Vygotsky. In a classic series of studies originally published in 1930, but not reproduced in English until 1992, Luria and Vygotsky consider the difference in memory tasks facing two types of people. On the one hand, there is the African envoy who has to remember word for word the message of his tribal chief. On the other, there is the Peruvian *kvinu* officer. *Kvinus* are a system of knots, and were used in ancient Peru, China, Japan, and several other parts of the world. They are conventional external representations—in essence, a forerunner of written language—used to record various sorts of information (e.g., about the state of the army, census statistics, taxes) or to provide instructions (e.g., to remote provinces). The *Chudi* tribe of Peru had a special officer assigned to the task of tying and interpreting *kvinus*. In the early stages of development of the *kvinu* system, such officers were rarely able to read other people's *kvinus*, unless they were accompanied by verbal comment. However, over time, the system was refined and standardized to such an extent that they could be used to record all the major matters of state, and depict laws and events.

Luria and Vygotsky argue that the development of *kvinus* will have had a profound effect on the strategies of remembering employed by those who could use them. The African envoy, who has no similar external system of representation, must remember verbatim the perhaps lengthy message of his tribal chief. He has to remember not simply the general gist of the message, but also, and much more difficult, the precise sequence of words uttered by his chief. The Peruvian *kvinu* officer, on the other hand, does not have to remember the information contained in the knot he has tied. He has to remember only the "code" that will allow him to access the information contained in the knot. The African envoy relies on outstanding biological memory to remember the information he is to transmit. The Peruvian officer's reliance on this sort of memory is much less, amounting to, at most, the remembering of the code. Once he knows this, he is able to tap into a potentially unlimited amount of information contained in the *kvinu* system.

Once an external information store of this sort becomes available, Luria and Vygotsky argue, it is easy to see how memory is going to develop. As external forms of information storage increase in number and sophistication, naked biological memory is going to become progressively less and less important. Therefore, Luria and Vygotksy predict, types of memory that are clearly biological will have a tendency to wither away. The most obvious implication will be for *episodic* memory (see box 2.1): the outstanding episodic memory of both primitive cultures and children will diminish significantly with the process of enculturation. The cultural evolution of memory is, therefore, also *involution*—the withering away of vestigial forms.

The Peruvian *kvinu* officer, having learned the appropriate code, has access to potentially more information than the African envoy could absorb in a lifetime. And this is not brought about by way of internal development of the brain. The internal demands on the Peruvian officer—

Box 2.1
Varieties of Remembering

Today psychologists generally distinguish three distinct types of memory. This tripartite distinction hadn't been made explicit at the time of Luria and Vygotsky's studies. I have translated their claims into this contemporary terminology.

1. *Procedural memory* is the mnemonic component of learned—as opposed to fixed—actions patterns: to have procedural memory is to remember *how* to do something that you have previously learned. For this reason, it is sometimes referred to as *knowing how* (Ryle 1949) or *habit memory* (Bergson 1908/1991; Russell 1921). The most obvious examples of procedural memory are embodied skills such as riding a bicycle, playing the piano, or skiing. Procedural memory has nothing essentially to do with conscious recall of prior events: one can, in principle, know how to do something while having completely forgotten learning to do it.

2. *Semantic memory* is memory of facts (Tulving 1983). You might remember that, for example, Ouagadougou is the capital of Burkina Faso. It is not immediately clear the extent to which this category is distinguishable from the category of *belief*. What is the difference between, for example, believing that Ouagadougou is the capital of Burkina Faso and remembering this fact? Neither beliefs nor memories need be consciously recalled or apprehended by a subject in order to be possessed by that subject. (That is, beliefs are dispositional, rather than occurrent, items [see box 3.1]). Therefore, it seems likely that semantic memories are simply a subset of beliefs. Not all beliefs qualify as semantic memories. If I perceive that the cat is on the mat, and form the belief that the cat is on the mat on this basis, it would be very odd to claim that I remember that the cat is on the mat. However, any semantic memory does seem to be token-identical with a belief: the claim that I remember that p without believing that p seems to be contradictory.

3. *Episodic memory*, sometimes called "recollective memory" (Russell 1921), is a systematically ambiguous expression. Often it is used to denote memory of prior *episodes* in a subject's life (Tulving 1983, 1993, 1999; Campbell 1994, 1997). However, it is also sometimes taken to denote memory of prior *experiences* possessed by that subject. For example, Locke understood (episodic) memory as a power of the mind "to revive perceptions which it has once had, with this additional perception annexed to them, that it has had them before" (1690/1975, 150). In a similar vein, Brewer defines episodic memory as a reliving of one's phenomenal experience from a specific moment in his or her past, accompanied by a belief that the remembered episode was personally experienced by the individual in the past (Brewer 1996, 60). The ambiguity embodied in the concept of episodic memory, then, is that between the episode experienced and the experience of the episode. This ambiguity is significant, but it can be accommodated in a sufficiently sophisticated account of episodic memory.

the amount of information he must process internally—are, if anything, far fewer than those placed on the African envoy. The Peruvian is in a position to appropriate more information at less internal cost. Moreover, *kvinus* form a fairly basic external representational system: the amount and kinds of information they can embody are strictly limited. But with the development of more sophisticated forms of external representation—in particular, language—capable of carrying greater quantities and varieties of information, the benefits of learning the code that allows you to tap into this information increase accordingly.

According to Luria and Vygotsky, remembering in literate cultures follows the sort of dynamic interplay between internal and external processes that we find in the Peruvian *kvinu* officer. It is characteristic of modern memory to *offload* part of the task of remembering into external information-bearing structures—written language being the most obvious and important one. In the case of semantic memory at least, remembering for us consists largely in retaining the "code" that will allow us to plug into the rich and varied stores of information around us.

Luria and Vygotsky's account of remembering parallels, in many essential respects, the ecological and enactive models of perception we examined earlier. Crucial to their account is the idea of structures that (i) are external to the remembering subject, and (ii) carry information relevant to the memory task in question. If in possession of the requisite "code," the remembering subject can use or deploy these structures to reduce the amount of internal information processing that he or she needs to perform in the accomplishing of a given memory task. In Luria and Vygotsky's account, external representational structures can go proxy, at least in part, for internal representational structures. Therefore, at least some of the role played in Cartesian cognitive science by mental representations can be taken over by the remembering subject acting on the world in appropriate ways. Merlin Donald (1991) has supplied an impressive development of this general theme in his account of the origin of the modern mind.

5 Neural Networks and Situated Robotics

The development of robotics in the past two decades has been decisively shaped by two factors. First, there was the development of *connectionist* or *neural network models* of cognition. Second, there was the role assigned to environmental interaction—manipulation and exploitation of environmental factors or circumstances—in the modeling of cognitive processes. These two factors are not unrelated.

Box 2.2
Neural Networks

Neural networks are, in essence, *pattern-mapping* devices. Pattern mapping, in this sense, is made up four different types of process. Pattern *recognition* is the mapping of a given pattern onto a more general pattern. Pattern *completion* is the mapping of an incomplete pattern onto a complete version of the same pattern. Pattern *transformation* is the mapping of one pattern onto a different but related pattern. And pattern *association* is the arbitrary mapping of one pattern onto another, unrelated pattern (Bechtel and Abrahamsen 1991, 106).

A neural network is made up of a collection of *nodes* or *units*—the rough equivalent of neurons. Each node can be connected to various other ones. The underlying idea is that activation in one unit can affect, or have an impact on, activation in the other units to which it is connected. However, the nature of this impact can vary along at least three dimensions. First, the connections can be of varying *strengths*. The strength of a connection between two units A and B is a function of how much of the activation of A is transferred to B. Even if A and B are connected in such a way that activation in A is transmitted to B, it might be that half of the activation of A is transmitted, or a quarter. It might be that the activation of A is augmented when it is passed on to B: for example, A fires at level q, but the quantity of activation passed on to B is $2q$.

The second type of variability derives from the fact that connections can be both *excitatory* and *inhibitory*. The connection between A and B is excitatory if the activation in A tends, all things being equal, to produce activation in B or increase the activity in B if B is already firing (in ways determined by the strengths of the connection between them). The connection between A and B is inhibitory if activation in A tends to stop or dampen down activity in B.

The third source of variability derives from the fact that any unit may (but need not) have a *threshold* level of activation below which it will not fire. Thus, for example, even if the activation q from A is passed on to B, B does not fire because its threshold level is greater than q.

The units of a neural network are arranged into *layers*: an *input* layer, an *output* layer, and one or more *hidden* layers. Connections between units occur both between layers and within layers.

For our purposes, the details of neural networks are less important than their characteristic strengths and weaknesses. Specifically, neural networks are very good at certain tasks, and very bad at others. Much of the allure of these networks is that that the tasks they are good at are the sorts of tasks that can easily, or relatively easily, be performed by human beings. Conversely, the sorts of tasks that neural networks are not very good at are ones that humans also find difficult. With traditional symbolic systems, in contrast, the relation is reversed. Traditional "rules and representations" systems are very good at the tasks that humans find difficult, and very bad at tasks that humans find easy. This suggests that neural networks will provide far more realistic models of human cognition than traditional systems.

The tasks that human beings and connectionist systems seem to be very good at correspond to, broadly speaking, the tasks that can be easily reduced to pattern-mapping—recognizing, completing, transforming, and associating—operations. These include visual perception/recognition tasks, categorization, recalling information from memory, and finding adequate solutions to problems with multiple, partial, and inconsistent constraints. The tasks that humans and neural networks are relatively bad at include, most notably, logical and mathematical calculations and formal reasoning in general.

From a neural network perspective, the problem with a process such as formal reasoning is that it does not seem reducible to pattern-mapping operations: such reasoning conforms to a structure that does not seem to be replicable by way of pattern-mapping. However, the problem cuts both ways. According to the rules and representations approach, the ability of humans to engage in formal reasoning processes is to be explained in terms of there existing inside human brains both mental representations and rules governing the transformation of those representations. These rules and representations mirror those of a formal system—like logic or mathematics. One of the problems with this sort of approach is that it makes it difficult to understand why humans are so *bad* at formal reasoning processes such as those involved in mathematics or deductive logic. More precisely, on the traditional approach, it is difficult to see why humans should be subject to *characteristic patterns of errors* exhibited by humans engaged in formal reasoning processes. If formal reasoning is a matter of manipulating structures according to rules, and if the relevant structures and rules are contained in the brain, then it seems that we should be, if not infallible, at least a lot better than we are at formal reasoning.

Neural network approaches face the opposite problem: explaining how humans can be so *good* at formal reasoning. Neural networks specialize in pattern-mapping operations, and processes of formal reasoning don't reduce to these. Therefore, it seems that neural network approaches are going to have difficulty explaining how humans have achieved the level of competence in formal reasoning that they have in fact achieved. In short, with respect to formal reasoning of the sort of exhibited in mathematics and formal logic, humans are not as good as traditional approaches predict they should be, and they're not a bad as neural network approaches predict they should be.

For our purposes, what is important is the strategy that connectionist theorists adopted to explain the human facility in formal reasoning. Rumelhart, McClelland, and the PDP Research Group's (1986) neural network account of our ability to engage in mathematical reasoning was based on the idea of *embedding* the network in a larger environment, one that the network was able to utilize in appropriate ways. Consider mathematical reasoning. In a fairly simple case of multiplication, say, $2 \times 2 = 4$, most of us can learn to just *see* the answer. This, Rumelhart et al. suggest, is evidence of a pattern-completing mechanism of the sort that can be easily modeled by a neural network. But, for most of us, the answer to more complex multiplications will not be so easily discernible. For example, 343×822 is not easy to do in the head. Instead, we avail ourselves of an external formalism that reduces the larger task to an iterated series of smaller tasks (see also Clark 1989). Thus, we write the numbers down on paper, and go through a series of simple pattern-completing operations (2×3, 2×4, etc.), storing the intermediate results on paper according to a well-defined algorithm. Rumelhart et al.'s point is that if we have a neural network that is *embedded*, in the sense that it is incorporated into a further system that is capable of manipulating mathematical structures external to it, then a process such as long multiplication, which ostensibly requires postulation of internally instantiated mathematical symbols, can be reduced to other processes that require no such thing. The main features of this embedded network are:

1. A pattern-*recognition* device necessary for recognizing external structures such as "2," "×," "3," and so on.

2. A pattern-*completion* device necessary for completing already recognized patterns such as "$2 \times 3 =$."

Both sorts of device are easily implemented in a neural network.

3. A capacity to manipulate mathematical structures in the environment.

Thus, for example, upon recognition of the pattern "2 × 3 =," the embedded system is able to complete that pattern and then, crucially, write or record the numeral "6." This then forms a new pattern for the system to recognize, and its completion and recording of this will, in turn, direct it to a further pattern to be recognized and completed, and so on.

In this way, a process—long multiplication—that seems to require the postulation of internally instantiated mathematical symbols can be reduced to an *internal* process of pattern recognition and completion coupled with a process of manipulation of *external* mathematical structures. The entire process whereby this mathematical task is achieved is, therefore, a *hybrid* that straddles elements both internal and external to the neural network. Neither of these elements involves the postulation of internally instantiated mathematical symbols, and neither requires postulation of internally instantiated rules governing the transformation of such symbols. The role that is thought to be played by *internal* symbols and rules has largely been usurped by *external* symbols and rules, plus the ability to manipulate these symbols as required. The internal residue consists of nonsymbolic pattern recognition and completion operations.

This strategy, in common with the accounts of perception and memory we have so far examined, works by *off-loading* some of the cognitive burden of a task onto the world. Pattern-mapping operations seem to place *relatively* low demands on the human cognitive system in the sense that they seem to be operations that can be implemented fairly easily in such a system. Thus, once again, we find the replacement of a certain type of internal representation—mathematical and other sorts of formal symbol—with an inner process that the human brain finds far easier to implement. And any explanatory slack engendered by this replacement is taken up by the organism's ability to act on the world around it. This attenuation of the role of internal representation coupled with an augmentation of the role of action is a hallmark of the prospective new science.

One way of thinking of the development of situated robotics is as a more general development of this basic idea. This development is organized around a distinction between what Clark (1989) calls *horizontal* and *vertical microworlds*. A microworld is a restricted domain of study. Given that we cannot understand intelligence all at once, we need an approach that breaks it down into easily digestible slices. However, this can be done in two ways. A vertical microworld takes a small piece of human-level cognitive competence as an object of study. Thus, famous research programs in Cartesian cognitive science have focused on things like the production of the past-tense forms of English verbs, playing chess, and planning a picnic. There are several worries engendered by this approach. Perhaps most significantly, in solving problems of this sort—in modeling vertical microworlds—we might find ourselves (unwittingly) employing neat, design-oriented solutions—ones quite unlike biological solutions driven by the need to make use of extant structures. As Clark (1997, 13) puts it: we may be chess masters courtesy of pattern-recognition skills selected to recognize mates, food, and predators. But if we were looking for a neat, design-oriented solution to modeling chess-playing competence, pattern-mapping operations are far from the first place we would look.

A horizontal microworld, on the other hand, consists in the *complete* behavioral competence of a relatively simple creature (whether real or imaginary). The idea is that by focusing on these horizontal microworlds we can simplify the problems posed for human-level intelligence but without forgetting biological imperatives (e.g., making use of extant structures and solutions, coping with damage, real-time response, the integration of sensory and motor functions, and so on). The most influential work in robotics and artificial intelligence of the past two decades has focused on the understanding of horizontal microworlds.

This is where something very like neural networks enters the picture. Many horizontal microworlds are susceptible to modeling by a type of architecture that is similar, in crucial ways, to a neural network: a *subsumption architecture*. Care must be taken here, because one of the most influential advocates of the use of subsumption architectures is careful to distinguish them from neural networks. Rodney Brooks (1991, 147) writes:

Neural networks is the parent discipline of which connectionism is a recent incarnation. Workers in neural networks claim that there is some biological significance to their network nodes, as models of neurons. Most of the, models seem wildly implausible given the paucity of modeled connections relative to the thousands found in real neurons. We claim no biological significance in our choice of finite state machines as network nodes.[3]

Given their simplicity, the claim of biological significance for neural networks was, of course, always a tenuous one. But this acknowledgment should not blind us to the important similarities between subsumption architectures and neural networks. A subsumption architecture is, like a neural network, composed of "layers" of circuitry, and to the extent these layers communicate it is not through the transmission of complex messages but, rather, by way of simple signals that turn one layer off or on when another layer has entered a certain state. Whether we regard subsumption architectures as a species of neural network is largely a matter of stipulation. But even if, like Brooks, we are not inclined to do so, we should be aware of the deep similarities between the two.

Brooks has developed an array of simple "creatures," composed of a number of distinct activity-producing subsystems or "layers." Each of these layers—and this is characteristic of subsumption architectures—is a complete route from input to action. Layers communicate with each other by way of simple signals that either augment (i.e., excite) activity in another connected layer, interrupt that activity, or override it. (The expression "subsumption" architecture derives from the fact that a layer can, in these ways, subsume another layer's activity but cannot communicate in more complex ways.)

Designed along these lines, a creature might be composed of layers of the following sorts (Brooks 1991, 156):

Layer 1   Object avoidance via a ring of ultrasonic sonar sensors. These cause the creature (a mobot—*mo*bile ro*bot*) to *halt* if an object is dead ahead and allow reorientation in an unblocked direction.

Layer 2   If the object-avoidance layer is currently inactive, an onboard device can generate random course headings so the creature wanders.

Layer 3   This layer can override the wander layer, and instead set up a distant goal to take the creature into a new locale.

Layers can be added incrementally, and each new layer yields a new complete functional competence. These creatures do not require a central planner, processing unit, or reservoir of data. Instead, they are driven by a collection of competing behaviors; and these competing behaviors are themselves driven by environmental inputs. In such a creature, there is no precise dividing line between perception and cognition. Nor is there any point at which perceptual codes are translated into a central code to be shared by onboard reasoning devices. Rather, the environment itself guides the creature, courtesy of some basic behavioral responses, to success.

Subsumption architectures decompose systems in a way quite different from that employed by traditional Cartesian cognitive science. The latter decomposition is based on the identification of vertical microworlds. A subsumption architecture, on the other hand, decomposes systems not by local (i.e., vertical) functions or faculties, but rather by global (i.e., horizontal) activities or tasks. Thus Brooks writes:

[This] alternative decomposition makes no distinction between peripheral systems, such as vision, and central systems. Rather, the fundamental slicing up of an intelligent system is in the orthogonal direction dividing it into *activity* producing subsystems. Each activity or behavior producing system individually connects sensing to action. We refer to an activity producing system as a *layer*. An activity is a pattern of interactions with the world. Another name for our activities might well be skill. (Brooks 1991, 146)

The crucial idea is that the activity performed by layers presupposes, and makes no sense without, the system's environment. The activity of each layer consists in close interaction with the environment and can only be understood in terms thereof. So the structures of the respective aspects of the environment are at least as important as the structures of the internal portions of the corresponding layers in rendering the different activities intelligible.

Again, we find the pattern of explanation characteristic of the cluster of theories that vie to make up the new science: the attenuation of representation combined with the augmentation of action. Traditional approaches would attempt to build into the creature or mobot a set of representations and series of rules that governed what to do with those representations. The approach employed by Brooks and others eschews this. Instead, mobots are supplied with subsumption architectures, each layer of which is a functionally complete neural network. And any explanatory slack with respect to the capabilities of the mobot is explained in terms of the mobot's ability to utilize structures in its environment in the right sort of way. With this strategy, no role is assigned to representations in anything like the traditional sense. There is no need for such an assignment. As Brooks famously put it: *the world is its own best representation.*

6   Conclusion

This survey of the cluster of theories that make up the new science is neither comprehensive nor complete. I have, for example, left out any discussion of dynamicist approaches to cognition (van Gelder 1994), and the important accounts of situated child development based on these approaches (Thelen and Smith 1994). However, the survey has been comprehensive enough to serve its purposes. These purposes are twofold. First, enough has been said to show that there is a significant body of scientific research being conducted into the nature of mental processes that diverges in crucial respects from traditional, Cartesian approaches based on rules and representations. Second, enough has been said to identify, at least in broad strokes, the principal points of divergence between the traditional rules and representations approach and this cluster of alternative theories. The cluster of theories—the new and the not so new—is characterized,

relative to the traditional approach, by attenuation of the role of representation combined with augmentation of the role of action. The two are
connected in that the attenuation of the role of representation is made
possible only by the augmentation of the role of action: any explanatory
gap engendered by the attenuation of representation is filled by the augmentation of action.

It is the augmentation of action that makes this cluster of theories anti-
Cartesian—at least ostensibly. Underlying this augmentation is a vision of
cognition, and perhaps other mental processes, not as something occurring
exclusively inside the brains of organisms but as something that organisms
achieve, in part, because of what they do in and to the world that is outside
their brains—whether their bodies or the wider environment.

None of this is, as yet, particularly clear. The function of the next
chapter is to inject at least some of the required clarity.

3 The Mind Embodied, Embedded, Enacted, and Extended

1 Cartesian Cognitive Science (A Recapitulation)

Traditional cognitive science has been a continuation of the Cartesian vision of mental states and processes as located exclusively inside the head of any given subject, person, or organism. Cartesian cognitive science developed this vision by way of a theoretical apparatus of mental *representations* and *operations* performed on those representations. That is:

1. Cognitive processes consist in the manipulation and transformation of structures that carry information about the world.
2. These information-bearing structures are known as *mental representations*.
3. Mental representations are structures located in the brains of cognizing organisms.

Mental representations are typically regarded either as brain states or higher-order functional properties realized by brain states. Since, on either interpretation, mental representations are things that are to be found in the brain, and only in the brain, their manipulation and transformation are also processes that occur in the brain. Since cognitive processes simply are these manipulative and transformative operations, cognitive processes are, therefore, ones that occur in the brain: cognitive processes are brain processes or are processes exclusively realized by brain processes. The manipulation and transformation of mental representations is, of course, not random, but takes place according to certain principles or rules. Therefore, this view is sometimes called the *rules and representations* approach toward understanding cognition. Both the representations and the rules by which they are manipulated and transformed have an implementation that is exclusively neural: they occur inside the brains of cognizing organisms.

Different ways of developing cognitive science can, in varying ways and to varying extents, abandon this rules and representations conception of cognition. Neural network, or connectionist, approaches, for example, are commonly thought of as abandoning the *rules* component of this picture, at least as this had hitherto been understood. Some—both advocates and detractors—even take them as abandoning the *representations* component also; but I think a more plausible way of understanding neural networks is as modifying, rather than abandoning, the guiding concept of representations.

For our purposes, however, these differences between classical and connectionist approaches to cognition are unimportant. For they share a common assumption; and it is this assumption that is going to provide the target for the central arguments of this book. Even if we abandon rules and representations for spreading patterns of activation over neural assemblies, we are still dealing with structures and processes that are internal to the brain. Whatever else is true of cognitive processes, they are processes occurring inside the brains of cognizing organisms. That is something on which both classical approaches to cognition and the connectionist alternative can agree. Non-Cartesian cognitive science is defined by its rejection of this common assumption.

However, as we saw in the opening chapter, the new science is made up of different strands. And even if they all do reject the assumption that cognitive processes always occur inside brains—and at the end of chapter 1, we started to unearth some reasons for doubting this—they do so in quite different ways and for quite different reasons. It is to an examination of the ideas of embodiment, embeddedness, enactedness, and extendedness that we now turn.

2   The Mind Embodied

To begin with, recall my admonition in the opening chapter concerning talk of the mind. There is a persistent tendency in most of us to think of the mind as something that lies behind and holds together our various mental states and processes; to think of it as something to which all those states and processes belong. If we think of the mind in this way, then cognitive science—in both Cartesian and non-Cartesian forms—is not a science of the mind but of mental processes. Of course, if we think of the mind as nothing more than a network of mental states and processes, things are different. On this, what is often known as the *Humean* view of the mind—for Hume might have held a view similar to it—cognitive science would indeed be a science of the mind.[1] However, in the absence of any consensus on whether or not the mind is in this sense Humean, I shall continue to regard the new science of the mind as, fundamentally, a science of mental states and processes. Therefore, what I am going to call the thesis of the *embodied mind* is more accurately rendered the thesis of *embodied mental processes*. This is a bit of a mouthful, so I shall continue talking of the thesis of the embodied mind; but it should be understood that it is a thesis concerning mental processes and not the mind as this is perhaps commonly understood.

According to this thesis, at least some—not all by any means, but some—mental processes are constituted not just by brain processes but by a combination of these and wider bodily structures and processes. This thesis has been defended by Shapiro (2004) and Damasio (1994), among others. Here, I shall focus on the contribution of Shapiro since I think this is more germane to the concerns of this section—that is, providing a conceptual foundation for understanding the claims of the thesis of the embodied mind.

Shapiro (2004) provides a sustained attack on what he calls the *separability thesis* (ST). According to ST, minds make no essential demands on bodies. A humanlike mind could very well exist in a nonhumanlike body. Against this, Shapiro defends what he calls *the embodied mind thesis* (EMT). According to EMT, "minds profoundly reflect the bodies in which they are contained," and, therefore, "it is often possible to predict properties of the body based on knowledge of properties of the mind" (Shapiro 2004, 174). In essence, Shapiro's arguments for EMT are based on the idea that

psychological processes are *incomplete* without the body's contributions. Vision for human beings is a process that includes features of the human body. . . . Perceptual processes include and depend on bodily structures. This means that a description of various perceptual capacities cannot maintain body-neutrality and it also means that an organism with a non-human body will have non-human visual and auditory psychologies. (Ibid., 190)

For example, in processing visual-depth information, the brain deploys disparity information from two eyes. Were there more than two eyes or fewer, or if the distance between the eyes differed, the processes in the brain that compute depth from disparity would require significant revision: "Human vision requires a human body" (ibid., 191). The same is true of other perceptual abilities. The human auditory system is calibrated to the distance between human ears. Because of this distance, sound will reach

each ear at slightly different times, and the difference carries important information about the direction from which the sound is emanating. So, the brain uses the distance between the ears as a way of determining the direction of the sound source. The brain is thus calibrated to this distance: if you change the distance, you would also have to change the calibration of the brain. Moreover, the fact that sound passes through a head of a particular size and density provides further important information about the direction of the sound source, and so on.

Here is an analogy employed by Shapiro in developing the EMT thesis (ibid., 185ff.). Imagine an instruction manual for piloting a submarine. This manual is, of course, specific to submarines. Although there might be some overlap, it would be largely useless for teaching you how to pilot an airplane. There is no general-purpose manual—or program—that affords skill-transferability from piloting a submarine to an airplane to a bus, and so on. The submarine manual, Shapiro argues, is analogous to the computational algorithms underwriting mental activity. That is, in order to work properly, the rules on which the brain runs—the rules by way of which it manipulates and transforms mental representations—depend on the nature of the underlying architecture that implements or realizes them. And this architecture, Shapiro argues, includes not just the brain but wider bodily structures. The rules by way of which the brain manipulates and transforms mental representations depend, partly but crucially, on the body in which that brain is embodied. Indeed, Shapiro argues that, in one crucial respect, the analogy is not deep enough: "the presence of the sub does not change the information that the instructions contain. Destroy the submarine and the instructions in the manual remain unchanged" (ibid., 186). However, the instruction manual for human cognition would make no sense in the absence of the bodily structures in which, in part, they are implemented. Shapiro characterizes his argument as an attack on the idea of *body neutrality*. This is the idea that "characteristics of bodies make no difference to the kind of mind one possesses," and this is in turn associated with the idea that the "mind is a program that can be characterized in abstraction from the kind of body/brain that realizes it" (ibid., 175).

Shapiro's invocation of wider bodily structures in explaining and understanding the nature of cognitive processes is fairly typical of the embodied genre. However, there are at least three different ways of interpreting Shapiro's claims, one significantly stronger than the others. The first interpretation is what philosophers would call an *epistemic* one. "Epistemic," here, means roughly "pertaining to our knowledge or what we can know." Understood in this way—*epistemically*—Shapiro's claim is that it is *impossible to understand* the nature of cognitive processes without understanding the wider bodily structures in which these processes are situated.[2] For example, we cannot understand how the brain computes the direction of a sound without taking into account the facts that (a) the brain is attached to ears, (b) these ears are located at a certain distance from each other, (c) there will typically be a slight difference in the times at which sound arrives at each ear, and (d) this discrepancy in arrival time carries information about the direction of the sound source. We cannot understand how the brain accomplishes the task of identifying the direction of a sound source without knowing these facts, because if the facts were different, the brain would have to do things differently. For example, if we had just one ear, then there would be no disparity information available to us, and the brain would have to do correspondingly more work in order to successfully identify the direction of the sound source.

This epistemic interpretation of the embodied mind thesis is not insignificant, but it does leave much of the traditional conception of cognitive processes intact. It is compatible, for example, with the idea that real cognition occurs in the brain—that it consists in transformations of neural representations—and adds only the qualification that in order to understand the character of these transformational processes in specific cases, we need to understand the wider bodily structures in which these transformations are embedded. The wider bodily structures provide a sort of bodily *context* in which these cognitive processes are situated, and to properly understand how the processes do what they do we have to understand this context. But this does not mean that there is no distinction between cognition and its bodily context. Real cognition, one, might argue, still occurs in the brain; and this claim is compatible with the epistemic reading of the embodied mind thesis.

The second possible interpretation of the embodied mind thesis is what philosophers might call *ontic* rather than epistemic. Here, "ontic" means roughly "pertaining to how things are" (rather than to our knowledge of how things are). According to the second interpretation, the embodied mind thesis is a thesis of the *dependence* of cognitive processes on wider bodily structures. The idea is that cognitive processes are *dependent* on wider bodily structures in the sense that these processes have been designed to function only in conjunction, or in tandem, with these structures. In the absence of the appropriate bodily structures, an organism may be unable to accomplish its usual repertoire of cognitive tasks because the processes it typically uses to perform such tasks work only in conjunction with the missing structures. One can understand this thesis of dependence in various ways. One way might be to understand it as a *contingent* claim about the nature of cognitive processes: as a matter of fact, some cognitive processes have developed in such a way that they are dependent for their proper functioning on wider bodily structures. Things did not have to be that way—cognitive processes might have developed to function independently of wider bodily structures—but that is the way things, in fact, turned out. If one were feeling more sanguine, one might try and convert this into a *necessary* truth. The difference between a contingent and a necessary truth in this context is the difference between *does not* and *could not* (see box 3.1). As a claim of necessary dependency, the embodied mind thesis is the claim that some cognitive processes are such that they *could* not, even in principle, function independently of wider bodily structures. That is, some cognitive processes are such that they could not have been developed to function independently of the bodily context in which they did, in fact, develop. I suspect—strongly—that elevating this claim of dependency to the status of necessary truth is a little too sanguine, but this is not a matter on which we need to adjudicate at the present time.

Again, the dependence interpretation of the thesis of the embodied mind is not insignificant. But there is a clear sense in which it leaves the traditional vision of cognition untouched. Embracing the dependence interpretation still allows one to maintain that real cognition occurs exclusively in the brain. This real cognition may be dependent for its correct functioning on wider bodily structures and processes, but there is no reason for thinking that these wider bodily structures and processes form part of cognition. *Dependence*, even *essential* dependence, does not add up to *constitution*—not without a lot more argument.[3] Sunburn is (essentially) dependent on solar radiation in the sense that any skin discoloration not produced by solar radiation is not sunburn. But this does not mean that solar radiation is literally part of—a component of—sunburn (Davidson 1987).

In the opening chapter, I argued that the Cartesian conception of the mind cannot be challenged simply by pointing out the rather obvious fact that that in many cases the environment *drives*—in the sense of causally contributing to—cognitive processes. Cognitive processes are, thus, dependent on environmental factors. This is an utterly anodyne claim of the sort to which any Cartesian might assent. Even if we try to tighten the connection—perhaps by claiming that some cognitive processes have been designed to function only in tandem with certain environmental circumstances—this does not undermine the Cartesian picture of cognitive processes as occurring in the brain. We can modify Davidson's suntan example to make this point. The transformation of skin color commonly called a suntan has been designed to function only in conjunction with certain environmental circumstances—the presence of UV light—as a mode of protection from those circumstances. But the suntan occurs in the skin and only in the skin (Davidson 1987). To say that cognitive processes are dependent, even essentially dependent, on environmental circumstances does not undermine the claim that they are located in, and only in, the brain of the cognizing subject. We can make precisely the same point with regard to the interpretation of the thesis of the embodied mind as a claim of bodily dependence. The claim that cognitive processes are dependent, even essentially independent, on wider bodily structures and circumstances does not, in any way, force us to reject the claim that cognitive processes occur exclusively inside the brain.

The third—the strongest and therefore most interesting—interpretation of the embodied mind thesis is also *ontic*, but is based on the idea of *constitution* or *composition* rather than dependence.[4] According to this third interpretation, cognitive processes are not restricted to structures and operations instantiated in the brain, but incorporate wider bodily structures and processes. These wider bodily structures and processes in part *constitute*—are *constituents* of—cognitive processes. This final interpretation of the embodied mind thesis is the most interesting because only it directly and fundamentally challenges the Cartesian vision of cognitive processes: the idea that cognitive processes occur exclusively in the brain of cognizing organisms. If the third interpretation of the embodied mind thesis is correct, then, to return to Shapiro's example, the distance between the ears, and the resulting disparity between the arrival times of sound at each ear, can be a literal part, or constituent, of the process of computing the direction of a sound source. This distance, and the resulting disparity, is not something extraneous to cognition, on which cognition merely depends: it is a genuine part of the cognitive process.

This is by far the most radical and interesting interpretation of the embodied mind thesis. For this reason, it is also the most difficult to defend. To endorse this interpretation is to run straight back into what I called, in the final section of the first chapter, the *big question*. Given that we can understand the embodied mind thesis as a thesis of *dependence*, what reason—if any—is there for endorsing the thesis of *constitution*? We might be willing to grant that cognitive processes depend on wider bodily structures and processes in order to do what they are supposed to do. But, why move from this to the more radical—and for that reason also more intuitively implausible—claim that these wider bodily structures and processes constitute, or are constituents of, cognitive processes? Given that the dependence thesis allows us to hold on to both our Cartesian intuitions and, to a considerable extent, the traditional cognitive science built upon them, endorsing the constitution interpretation seems both unnecessary and unmotivated. More than that, it seems positively capricious.[5]

Nevertheless, this book is going to defend the constitution interpretation. I shall argue that some—not all by any means, but some—cognitive processes are composed of, constituted by, wider bodily structures and processes.

3   The Extended Mind

The view that I am going to call the thesis of the *extended mind* goes by a variety of names: *vehicle externalism* (Hurley 1998; Rowlands 2006), *active externalism* (Clark and Chalmers 1998), *locational externalism* (Wilson 2004), and *environmentalism* (Rowlands 1999). "Extended mind" is a label invented by Andy Clark and Dave Chalmers in their 1998 article of the same name. I think all the labels have their problems, and "extended mind" is no exception. However, it is the name that has come closest to sticking, and I propose to use it in this book. However, though I adopt their terminology, what I call the thesis of the extended mind differs from Clark and Chalmers's position in at least one crucial respect.

First of all, let me say what I am going to mean by the thesis of the extended mind. The general idea is that at least some mental processes— not all, but some—extend into the cognizing organism's environment in that they are *composed*, partly (and, on the version I am going to defend, *contingently*), of actions, broadly construed, performed by that organism on the world around it.

The mental processes in question are primarily *cognitive* ones; and my focus, at least for the time being, is going to be on these. The actions that the organism performs on the world around it are ones of manipulating, exploiting, and/or transforming external structures. What is distinctive of these structures is that they carry information relevant to accomplishing a given cognitive task. And by acting on these structures in suitable ways, the cognizing organism is able to make that information available to itself and to its subsequent cognitive operations. That is, the function of the action performed by a cognizing organism on these structures is to trans- form information that is merely *present* in the structures into information that is *available* to the organism and/or to its subsequent processing opera- tions. This, according to the thesis of the extended mind, can form part—

a properly cognitive part—of a process of cognition. Thus, as I shall understand it and defend it, the thesis of the extended mind is the thesis that some cognitive processes are made up, in part, of the manipulation, exploitation, and/or transformation of information-bearing structures in the cognizing organism's environment. That is, the thesis of the extended mind is defined by the following claims:

The Extended Mind

1. The world is an external store of information relevant to processes such as perceiving, remembering, reasoning . . . (and possibly) experiencing.

2. Cognitive processes are hybrid—they straddle both internal and external operations.

3. The external operations take the form of *action*, broadly construed: the manipulation, exploitation, and transformation of environmental structures—ones that carry information relevant to the accomplishing of a given task.

4. At least some of the internal processes are ones concerned with supplying the subject with the ability to appropriately use relevant structures in its environment.

As I shall understand it, therefore, the thesis of the extended mind is (1) an *ontic* thesis, of (2) *partial* and (3) *contingent* (4) *composition* of (5) *some* mental processes.[6]

1. It is *ontic* in the sense that it is a thesis about what (some) mental processes are, as opposed to an *epistemic* thesis about the best way of understanding mental processes. This ontic claim, of course, has an epistemic consequence: it is not possible to understand the nature of at least some of the mental processes without understanding the extent to which that organism is capable of manipulating, exploiting, and transforming relevant structures in its environment (Rowlands 1999). However, this epistemic consequence is not part of the thesis of the extended mind itself. Indeed, the epistemic claim is compatible with the denial of this thesis.[7]

2. The claim is that (some) token mental processes are, *in part*, made up of the manipulation, exploitation, or transformation of environmental structures. There is always an irreducible internal—neural and, sometimes, also wider bodily—contribution to the constitution of any mental process. No version of the extended mind will claim that a mental process can be composed entirely of manipulative, exploitative, or transformative operations performed on the environment.[8]

3. It is possible to understand the thesis of the extended mind as asserting a necessary truth about the composition of mental processes: that,

Box 3.1
Necessary and Contingent

To say that a (true) statement is necessary is to claim, roughly, that things have to be that way; things couldn't possibly have been otherwise. The statement, therefore, is not only true, it has to be true. To say that a (true) statement is contingent, on the other hand, is to say that while it is true, it might have been false. Things, in fact turned out the way described in the statement, but they might well have turned out differently.

In this book, I am going to understand the thesis of the extended mind as expressing a contingent truth. Some cognitive processes developed in such a way that, as a matter of contingent fact, they incorporate processes of manipulation, exploitation, and/or transformation of environmental structures. Cognitive processes didn't have to develop in this way. They could have developed as purely internal—neural—processes; but that's not what actually happened—at least not for all cognitive processes. Some may want to elevate the thesis of the extended mind into a necessary truth; but I am not one of them. And I don't think any arguments have ever successfully been advanced defending this stronger claim.

necessarily, some mental processes are partly constituted by processes of environmental manipulation and so on (see box 3.1).[9] It is possible but inadvisable. As we shall see, the underlying rationale for the thesis of the extended mind is provided by a fairly liberal form of *functionalism*.[10] And the entire thrust of liberal functionalism is to leave open the possibility of different ways of realizing the same (type of) mental process. By understanding the thesis of the extended mind as asserting a necessary truth, therefore, the proponent of this thesis is at risk of undermining his or her own primary motivation.

4. The thesis of the extended mind (henceforth simply "the extended mind") is a claim about the *composition* or *constitution* of (some) mental processes. Composition is a quite different relation from *dependence*. Thus, the extended mind is a stronger and more distinctive claim than one of environmental embedding; and it must be clearly distinguished from that of the *embedded* mind (see section 4). According to the latter, some mental processes function, and indeed have been designed to function, only in tandem with certain environmental structures; so that in the absence of the latter the former cannot do what they are supposed to do or work in the way they are supposed to work. Thus, some mental processes are dependent, perhaps essentially dependent, for their operation on the wider

environment. The extended mind, on the other hand, does not simply claim that mental processes are, in this way, *situated* in a wider system of scaffolding, a system that facilitates, perhaps in crucial ways, the operation of these processes. That would be a claim of dependence. Rather, it claims that things we do to this wider system of scaffolding in part compose or constitute (some of) our mental processes.[11]

Much of the distinctiveness and importance of the extended mind depends, I think, on understanding it as making an *ontic* (rather than epistemic) claim concerning the partial *constitution* of mental processes by processes of environmental manipulation (rather than merely dependence on such processes). This is how I shall understand the thesis of the extended mind. This seems to be the sort of understanding of the extended mind endorsed and defended by Clark and Chalmers in their eponymous (1998) paper (see box 3.2). However, in the version of the thesis I wish to defend, there is a marked difference of at least emphasis. Whether it is more than a difference of emphasis is unclear, but it is useful, at this point, to compare the version of the extended mind defined above with that defended by Clark and Chalmers.

Clark and Chalmers are often interpreted as claiming that the sentence "The Museum of Modern Art is on 53rd Street," located in Otto's notebook, is identical with Otto's belief that the Museum of Modern Art is on 53rd Street. This interpretation is, presumably, too simplistic. More accurately, the idea is that *when* the sentence in the notebook is being deployed by Otto in the right sort of way, then, and only then, can it count as among Otto's beliefs. The guiding principle here is, as Clark and Chalmers put it:

If, as we confront some task, a part of the world functions as a process which, *were it done in the head*, we would have no hesitation in accepting as part of the cognitive process, then that part of the world is (so we claim) part of the cognitive process (1998, 8)

This claim, however, is unacceptably vague. If the "part of the world" in question is the sentence in Otto's notebook, then we must ask: how can the sentence function as a process? This apparently muddled talk seems to mask two possible interpretations:

1. The sentence in Otto's notebook, when appropriately deployed by Otto, and so situated in a context composed of the right sorts of surrounding psychological states and processes (Otto's perception of the sentence, his desire to see the exhibition, etc.) is one of Otto's beliefs. This interpretation

Box 3.2
The Curious Case of Otto

Here is a classic—if it is correct to describe something barely a decade old as classic—thought experiment devised by Clark and Chalmers (1998). Otto is in the early stages of Alzheimer's disease. Otto has a friend, Inga, who is not similarly afflicted. Inga sees advertised in the newspaper an exhibition that she would like to see. The exhibition is taking place at the Museum of Modern Art. Inga thinks for a moment, recalls that MoMA is on 53rd Street, and sets off. Inga, it seems, has the belief that MoMA is on 53rd Street. And she had this belief even before she consulted her memory. Prior to the act of memory, of course, the belief was not *occurrent*. But most beliefs are like this: most of the beliefs we have we are not aware of having at any given moment. I believe that MoMA is on 53rd Street, but this is a belief I consciously entertain (usually) only when I am thinking about this thought experiment. Most of the time most of our beliefs exist in *dispositional* form: they exist in our tendencies or dispositions to do and say things in certain circumstances. Prior to her consciously accessing it, Inga's belief existed in dispositional form. And the basis of this disposition was that the belief was somewhere in Inga's memory, waiting to be accessed.

Otto, like many patients with Alzheimer's disease, relies on information contained in the environment to facilitate his day-to-day life. Otto carries a notebook around with him wherever he goes and, upon learning new information that he decides is sufficiently useful, he writes it down in his book. So whenever he needs previously acquired information, he looks it up. Otto's notebook, in effect, plays for him the sort of role usually played by biological (i.e., brain-based) memory. Otto reads about the exhibition at MoMA and, wanting to see it, looks in his notebook. This tells him that the museum is on 53rd Street, which he is where he duly goes.

According to Clark and Chalmers (C&C), "it seems reasonable to suppose that Otto believed the museum was on 53rd Street even before consulting the notebook" (1998, 12). This parallels the claim that Inga possessed the belief prior to her act of memory, for, according to C&C:

In relevant respects the cases are entirely analogous: the notebook plays for Otto the same role that memory plays for Inga. The information in the notebook functions just like the information constituting an ordinary non-occurrent belief; it just happens that this information lies beyond the skin. (1998, 12)

Inga sees the exhibition advertised in the newspaper, decides that she wants to see it, recalls that MoMA is on 53rd Street, and heads off in that direction. Similarly, Otto sees the exhibition advertised in the newspaper, decides he wants to see it, looks in his notebook and sees that MoMA is on 53rd Street, and heads off in that direction. The entry in the notebook that reads "The Museum of Modern Art is on 53rd Street" seems to function the same way

Box 3.2
(continued)

> in Otto's psychology as the corresponding belief functions in Inga's psychology. That is, the entry in Otto's notebook interacts with his desires (for example, to see the exhibition) in the same way that Inga's belief interacts with her desires. And it issues in the same actions: both Otto and Inga set off in the direction of 53rd Street. So, C&C ask: why shouldn't we regard the entry in Otto's notebook as one of his beliefs? They argue, notoriously, that there is no reason—no *justifiable* reason—to deny that the entry in Otto's notebook is one of his beliefs. Otto's beliefs exist not just in his head. They also exist in his notebook. But this is true not just of Otto: it is true of the rest of us as well.

identifies a token cognitive state—a belief—with an external structure—a sentence.

2. The process of manipulating and/or exploiting the sentence is a properly cognitive part of an overall cognitive process. The overall process in question would be that of *remembering* or *believing*. The manipulation involved would be that of opening the book to the relevant page and orienting the page so that the sentence is open to detection by Otto. The manipulation, therefore, transforms the information contained in the sentence from the merely *present* to the *available*—available to Otto and/or to his subsequent processing operations. In virtue of playing this role, the manipulation of the sentence forms a properly cognitive part of the overall process of remembering or believing.[12]

The second interpretation claims that manipulation of an external structure is a properly cognitive part of a larger cognitive process. But it stops short of identifying the structure thus manipulated with a cognitive state. The version of the extended mind defended in this book is that implicated in the second interpretation. And there are very good reasons, I think, for rejecting the first interpretation. For those of you not antecedently convinced, you'll find the reasons in box 3.3.

My version of the extended mind—as a form of process rather than structure externalism—has little use for cognitive states. It is framed purely in terms of cognitive processes. This, I think, is the best way to understand the extended mind: as a process-oriented account. Therefore, on my version of the extended mind, the entry "The Museum of Modern Art is on 53rd Street" is not identical with any belief of Otto, no matter how he uses this entry, and no matter what the psychological milieu in which it is situated.

Box 3.3
How Not to Understand the Extended Mind

In "The Extended Mind," Clark and Chalmers (1998) are commonly regarded as defending this claim:

(O) The sentence "The museum of Modern Art is on 53rd Street" is, in appropriate circumstances, identical with one of Otto's beliefs.

Roughly, the circumstances are appropriate when the sentence is being deployed by Otto in an appropriate way (where such deployment requires Otto to also be engaged in suitable internal processing operations). I am not convinced that Clark and Chalmers are committed to (O), or even that they intend it, but I shall put aside this issue of interpretation. This interpretation of their view is widespread. For example, in what is sure to be an influential recent review of Clark's (2008) book *Supersizing the Mind*, Jerry Fodor (2009) writes (in connection with the original argument of C&C): "Since the content of Otto's notebook is derived (i.e., it's derived from Otto's thoughts and intentions with a 't'), the intensionality of its entries does not argue for its being part of Otto's mind." In other words, the entries in Otto's notebook are not beliefs because, unlike beliefs, their intentionality is merely derived. This intended criticism of Clark and Chalmers makes sense only if we assume that they are claiming that the entries in Otto's notebook are identical with (some of) his beliefs. Perhaps they do indeed intend this claim. I hope not; because the claim is untenable. This does not, however, entail rejection of the extended mind thesis; there is another, far more plausible, way of understanding this thesis.

The thesis of the extended mind is a thesis about mental tokens, not types. EMT is, among other things, a thesis about the location of mental items, and it is not clear where, if anywhere, mental types are located. Therefore, (O) should be understood as asserting an identity between a sentence token—a physical inscription in Otto's notebook—and a token belief. The problem with this identification, I shall argue, is that the token sentence is the *wrong* sort of token to be identical with a token belief. (O) is, ultimately, incoherent.

In developing the problem, let us first recall two claims that are (partially) constitutive of the concept of a token. First, tokens are dated, unrepeatable entities. The eruption of Vesuvius in 79 AD is not token-identical with any subsequent eruption of that volcano. A token comes, goes, and never recurs. Second, tokens obey the transitivity of identity: if token x = token y, and token y = token z, then $x = z$. The problem with (O) is that it makes it impossible to satisfy both conditions.

Box 3.3
(continued)

Suppose, now, Oscar is deploying his notebook in a way deemed accept-able by C&C. Then, according to (O), the following claim is true:

(1) The sentence-token "The Museum of Modern Art is on 53rd Street" is identical with Otto's token belief that the Museum of Modern Art is on 53rd Street.

However, suppose that someone else is also deploying the notebook in a way deemed acceptable by C&C. For example, suppose Inga has also succumbed to the ravages of Alzheimer's and has decided to make use of Otto's book rather than going to the trouble of making one of her own. With suitable tinkering, I think we can make the example satisfy the sorts of conditions that C&C stipulate for Otto. Thus, we suppose that every time Otto made an entry in his book, Inga witnessed this and consciously endorsed the informa-tion Otto entered, and so on. We can suppose that the notebook is as easily and reliably accessible to Inga as it is to Otto, and so on. I won't push this point, however, for reasons to follow shortly: even if we deny that Inga can deploy the book in the right way, the same problems arises for Otto's repeated use of the book. In such a circumstance, it seems, (O) would commit us to the following:

(2) The sentence-token "The Museum of Modern Art is on 53rd Street" is identical with Inga's token belief that the Museum of Modern Art is on 53rd Street.

However, this means, by the transitivity of token-identity, that Otto's belief-token is identical to Inga's belief-token. This is not, it must be emphasized, a case of Otto and Inga sharing two token beliefs of the same type. It is a case of two distinct people having the same token belief. And this is, of course, impossible if tokens are dated, unrepeatable entities.

Perhaps C&C might try to preclude this possibility by denying that anyone but Otto can deploy the book in the right way. I am not sure this strategy would work (see above), but I shall not press this point here. Even if this strategy were effective, it does not rule out the following problem. Suppose Otto, at a given time t, deploys his notebook in a way that, according to (O), qualifies the sentence-token as identical with a belief. Thus:

(3) At time t, the sentence-token "The Museum of Modern Art is on 53rd Street" is identical with Otto's token belief that the Museum of Modern Art is on 53rd Street.

However, if Otto can do this at time t, then there is nothing preventing him from deploying the notebook in the relevant way at a distinct time, t^*. Thus:

Box 3.3
(continued)

(4)   At time t^*, the sentence-token "The Museum of Modern Art is on 53rd Street" is identical with Otto's token belief that the Museum of Modern Art is on 53rd Street.

It again follows from the transitivity of identity that Otto's token belief at t is identical with his token belief at t^*. Once again, this is not a case of Otto instantiating two distinct belief-tokens of the same belief-type. Rather, it is a case of him possessing one and the same belief-token on two distinct occasions. And this is, again, impossible: tokens are dated, unrepeatable entities. In other words, (O) has the unfortunate consequence that one and the same belief-token can be possessed by the same subject at different times (and arguably by more than one subject at the same or different times). This is incoherent, and (O) must, therefore, be rejected.

What has gone wrong? The sentence-token is a physical inscription in Otto's notebook. As such, it can be deployed by Otto on more than one occasion. But the sentence-token is token-identical with itself on all of these occasions of use. Therefore, by the transitivity of identity, Otto's belief-tokens must be token-identical with themselves on all occasions in which they occur. And this is incoherent. What is needed is fairly clear. We need a way of individuating tokens such that when Otto deploys the sentence-token at time t it qualifies as a distinct token from the one deployed at distinct time t^*. But what this means, in effect, is that we must reject the identification of the sentence- or inscription-token with a token belief possessed by Otto. That is, we must replace (O) with:

(O*)   Otto's deployment, at time t, of the sentence in his notebook is (when it meets appropriate conditions) part of the process of his believing that the Museum of Modern Art is on 53rd Street.

The process in question is, of course, a process-token. Thus, when Otto deploys the sentence in his notebook in the same way at a distinct time t^*, this automatically qualifies as (part of) a distinct process-token. The same would be true if Inga were to deploy the sentence in a way that met appropriate conditions (or ones deemed acceptable by C&C). On each occasion we have a distinct process-token, and the problem of incoherence is thereby avoided.

If the above arguments are correct, (O) should be rejected. However, the rejection of (O) is not equivalent to the rejection of the thesis of the extended mind. Although (O) provides a common interpretation of the claims of the extended mind, it is not, in fact, fruitful to understand this thesis as asserting the identity of mental state–tokens with external structure–tokens. A far more fruitful approach, one implicated in (O*) and untouched by the rejection of

Box 3.3
(continued)

(O), is to understand the thesis of the extended mind as a claim about the partial composition of token cognitive processes: when Otto deploys his notebook in the right sorts of way, then this is part—a genuinely cognitive part—of the overall process of believing or remembering the location of the museum. We might call this version of the extended mind thesis "process externalism," and contrast it with the sort of "structure externalism" implicated in (O)—which identifies mental state–tokens with environmental structure–tokens.

The thesis of the extended mind should not be understood as claiming that cognitive states can be identical with environmental structures. Properly understood, the thesis makes no claim about cognitive states at all. It is a thesis that concerns cognitive processes and it claims some of these processes are, in part, composed of processes of manipulating, exploiting, or transforming environmental structures. It is the things we do with external structures—our manipulation, exploitation, and transformation of them—that constitute properly cognitive parts of overall processes of cognition. This is compatible, of course, with the idea that environmental structures can form parts of cognitive processes. They do so, but not because they are identical with cognitive states. It is the manipulation of environmental structures that forms part of the cognitive process; and so these structures form part of the process only insofar as they are part of the process of their being manipulated.

4   The Embedded Mind

The thesis of the extended mind is, first and foremost, a thesis of the *composition* or *constitution* of cognitive processes: some cognitive processes are partly composed of environmental processes. As such, the extended mind parallels the third interpretation of the thesis of the embodied mind, according to which some cognitive processes are partly composed of wider bodily structures and processes. In both cases, this claim of composition is an ontic claim that should be distinguished from epistemic claims about how we *understand* cognitive processes. However, as we saw in connection with the thesis of the embodied mind (henceforth simply "the embodied mind"), there is another ontic way of interpreting this thesis: as a claim of *dependence* rather than composition or constitution. Interpreted in this way, the embodied mind claims that (some) cognitive processes are dependent for their successful functioning on wider bodily structures and processes.

Therefore, we might expect that there is also a corresponding way of interpreting the thesis of the extended mind. This expectation is, in effect, correct—but misleading. When interpreted in this way, what we end up with is not another version of the extended mind, but a quite distinct thesis: the thesis of the *embedded mind* (henceforth simply "the embedded mind"). Although often confused with the extended mind, the embedded mind is a very different thesis—far weaker and less interesting.

According to the *embedded mind*, cognitive processes are often (and on some versions essentially) embedded in the environment. The usual way of thinking about cognitive processes is in terms of what they do; in terms of their *function*. Take visual perception, for example. As we saw in the earlier discussion of Marr's theory of vision, a common way of understanding perception is as an input–output function from stimulus to visual representation. The stimulus is the retinal image—a pattern of light intensity distributed across the retina. The function of visual perception is to transform this into a visual representation of the world, a function that it completes in a series of stages. We should be careful to distinguish two things. On the one hand, there is the general idea that perception and other cognitive processes are best understood in terms of functions. This idea is known as *functionalism*—at least on one of the meanings of that widely used term. We shall look at functionalism in more detail in a later chapter. On the other hand, there is the identification of a particular role with which a cognitive process such as perception is to be defined. These claims are quite different. To say that perception is defined by its functional role—by what it does—is one thing. To say that perception is defined by this specific functional role is quite another. For example, you might accept that perception is defined by its functional role, but deny that the role is one of transforming retinal images into visual representations.

For now, let us just work with the general idea that a given cognitive process is defined by its functional role—whatever that role turns out to be. Fulfilling a certain role requires certain things to be done, and traditionally those things are regarded as being done by the brain. So, on the traditional, influential way of thinking about visual perception, it is the brain that has the task of transforming a retinal image into visual representation. This is where the idea of environmental *embedding* comes in. By relying on the environment in an appropriate way, the complexity of what the brain has to do in order to accomplish a cognitive task—that is, in order to fulfill the role that defines a cognitive process—can be reduced.

We've already encountered this general idea in the opening chapter. The complexity of the operations that my brain must perform in order to get me from A to B is reduced by my deployment of an external information bearing structure—a GPS or a MapQuest printout. The complexity of the operations my brain must perform in order for me to complete a jigsaw puzzle—mental image formation and rotation—are reduced by my picking and manually rearranging its pieces. In general, the guiding idea underlying the thesis of the embedded mind is that in accomplishing cognitive tasks, an organism can *utilize* structures in its environment in such a way that the amount of internal processing it must perform is reduced. Some of the complexity of the task is, thereby, off-loaded onto the environment, given that the organism has the ability to appropriately exploit that environment.

This is, again, an *ontic* thesis, but whereas the thesis of the extended mind was one of composition or constitution, the thesis of the embedded mind is one of *dependence*. According to this thesis, some cognitive processes are dependent on environmental structures in the sense that these processes have been designed to function only in conjunction, or in tandem, with these structures. In the absence of the appropriate environmental structures, an organism may be unable to accomplish its usual repertoire of cognitive tasks because the processes it typically uses to perform such tasks work only in conjunction with the missing structures. Or it may be able to accomplish these tasks, but in a less than optimal way—it takes longer, for example, or exhibits a greater frequency of mistakes. One can understand this thesis of dependence in various ways—as a contingent fact about the way (some) cognitive processes work, or as a necessary truth about the essential nature of (some) cognitive processes. But however tight we make the relation of dependence, it is *still* relation of dependence, not constitution.

The thesis of the embedded mind is an interesting thesis in its own right. However, there is a clear sense in which it leaves the traditional Cartesian picture of cognitive processes largely untouched. If you endorse the idea that at least some cognitive processes are environmentally embedded, you can still hold on to the idea that real cognition goes on in the brain. These brain processes might have been designed to fulfill their cognitive functions only in conjunction with help from the environment, but that does not mean that these processes take place anywhere else than the brain. Cognition may be dependent for its efficacy on things outside the brain, but it is still something that goes on in the brain and not outside it. As we have seen, to say that a cognitive process is environmentally *driven* does not entail that the process is environmentally *constituted*. To suppose that it does it to confuse causation and constitution (Adams and Aizawa 2001, 2010; Rupert 2004).

Because of this, the thesis of the embedded mind occupies a rather curious position in recent debate. While it is an interesting thesis in its own right, it is not as radical or—from the point of view of unseating the Cartesian picture of cognition—interesting as the thesis of the extended mind. Therefore, in recent debate, the thesis actually tends to be deployed largely by those who acknowledge the force of the arguments for the extended mind but want to limit their consequences (Adams and Aizawa 2001, 2010; Rupert 2004). In other words, the thesis of the embedded mind has tended to be used as a sort of neo-Cartesian fallback position for those who acknowledge that that are various ways in which the complexity of internal cognitive operations can be reduced by reliance on and use of appropriate structures in the environment but who nonetheless want to maintain that real cognition occurs only in the brain. We shall look in more detail at the role played by the embedded mind in the next chapter.

5   The Mind Enacted

Suppose you are a blind person holding a bottle (O'Regan and Noë 2001). You have the feeling of holding a bottle. But what tactile sensations do you actually have? Without slight rubbing of the skin, tactile information is considerably reduced, and information about temperature will soon disappear through the adaptation of receptors, and so on. Nonetheless, despite the poverty of sensory stimulation, you have the feeling of having a bottle in your hand. According to the traditional approach, the brain supplements, augments, and embellishes the impoverished information contained in sensory stimulation with what are, in effect, various inferences or "guesses" about the sort of thing most likely to be responsible for this stimulation. The result is the construction of an internal *haptic* (i.e., tactile) representation of the bottle.

However, according to Mackay (1967), there is an alternative explanation: information is present in the environment over and above that contained in sensory stimulation, and this information is sufficient to specify that you are holding a bottle.[13] More precisely, your brain is *tuned* to certain *potentialities*. For example, it is tuned to the fact that if you were to slide your hand very slightly along the bottle's surface, a change would come about in the incoming sensory signals that is typical of the change associated with the smooth, cool surface of glass. Furthermore, your brain is tuned to the fact that if you were to slide your hand upward far enough, the size of what you are encompassing with your hand would diminish (because you are moving to the bottle's neck). Your sense of holding a bottle is made up of these *anticipations* of how your experience would change if you were to perform certain types of action. In this, Mackay was drawing (explicitly) on an account of phenomenological presence developed by Edmund Husserl (1913/1982).

According to Mackay, again following Husserl, *seeing* a bottle is, at least in one respect, analogous to touching it. You have the impression of seeing a bottle if your brain has extracted knowledge concerning a certain web of contingencies. For example, you have knowledge of the fact that if you move your eyes upward toward the neck of the bottle, the sensory stimulation will change in a way typical of what happens when a narrower region of the bottle comes into foveal vision. You have knowledge of the fact that if you move your eyes downward, the sensory stimulation will change in a way typical of what happens when the bottle's label is fixated by foveal vision, and so on.

Mackay's discussion provides an important early illustration of what has become known as the *enactive* approach to perception, an approach that has received significant recent theoretical development by O'Regan and Noë (2001, 2002), Noë (2004), and Thompson (2007). I shall refer to this as the thesis of the *enacted mind* (henceforth simply "the enacted mind"). In this section, I want to examine the connection between this thesis and that of the extended mind. In doing so, I am going to focus on Noë's (2004) account. I am not entirely sure the same conclusions can be drawn for all major statements of the enactivist position, but to examine all these statements would be beyond the scope of this chapter.[14] Indeed, I suspect there is a way of understanding the enactivist position such that my version of the extended mind—organized around the idea of action on external information-bearing structures—qualifies as a version of this position. Nevertheless, my primary concern here is to distinguish the extended mind, as it was developed in section 3, from at least one deservedly influential statement of the enactivist position: that provided by Noë (2004). In doing so, we help clarify the content of both the mind extended and (this version of) the mind enacted.

Suppose you are looking at a cube. You can't, of course, see the whole of the cube at any given moment; you see only some of its surfaces.

Nonetheless, it appears to you that you are looking at a cube. Noë captures the basic idea of his enactive account in passages such as this:

As you move with respect to the cube, you learn how its aspect changes as you move—that is, you encounter its visual potential. To encounter its visual potential is thus to encounter its actual shape. When you experience an object as cubical merely on the basis of its aspect, you do so because you bring to bear, in this experience, your sensorimotor knowledge of the relation between changes in cube aspects and movement. To experience the figure as a cube, on the basis of how it looks, is to understand *how* its look changes as you move. (Noë 2004, 77)

Alternatively, consider your visual experience of a tomato. If you look at a tomato you experience it as three-dimensional and round, even though you only see its facing side. Suppose, further, that your view of the tomato is blocked by the pepper pot that stands in front of it. Nevertheless, you experience it *as* a tomato, and not as a pair of noncontiguous tomato parts. The tomato is *phenomenologically present* to you, despite the apparent limitations of the visual scene. Traditional accounts would explain this in terms of the construction of a visual representation of the tomato—your brain's *guess* concerning what is causing your visual impressions. Noë, however, demurs:

Our perceptual sense of the tomato's wholeness—of its volume and backside, and so forth—consists in our implicit understanding (our expectation) that the movements of our body to the left or right, say, will bring further bits of the tomato into view. Our relation to the unseen bits of the tomato is mediated by patterns of sensorimotor contingency. Similar points can be made across the board for occlusion phenomena. (Ibid., 63)

Abstracting from the details, the general idea seems clear. Visually perceiving the world is made up of two things:

1. Expectations about how our experience of an object will change in the event our moving, or the object of our vision moving relative to us (or some other object moving with respect to that object—for example, in front of it). Noë calls this *sensorimotor knowledge* or *knowledge of sensorimotor contingencies*. When our expectations are correct, this is because we have *mastered* the relevant sensorimotor contingencies.
2. The ability to act on the world—that is, to probe and explore environmental structures by way of the visual modality.

Prima facie, of course, the thesis of the extended mind and the enacted mind seem to have much in common. To see how much, recall the earlier characterization of the extended mind; in particular, the first three conditions. First:

• The world is an external store of information relevant to processes such as perceiving, remembering, reasoning . . . experiencing.

The enacted mind seems to make use of this claim in much the same way as the extended mind. The role traditionally assigned to visual representations can be taken over, at least in part, by the fact that the visual world is a stable store of information that can be explored at will by the visual modality. The sense of phenomenological presence implicated in our visual experience of a tomato—our sense that in addition to the aspect it presents to us it has other systematically related aspects—is underwritten by the fact that the tomato is a continuous, structured, and stable store of information, one to whose parts or aspects the visual subject is able to direct its attention at will. (In the same way, of course, the bottle is a stable store of haptically obtainable information that can be explored at will by the subject.) Second:

• At least some mental processes are hybrid—they straddle both internal and external operations.

Again, this also *seems* to be a claim endorsed by the enacted mind. A representationalist account will explain seeing in terms of the production within the subject of an internal visual representation. Visually perceiving, therefore, begins where sensation—the distribution of light intensity over the retina—ends; and it consists in the internal processes responsible for the production of the visual representation. The enactivist approach, on the other hand, thinks that at least some of the role traditionally assigned to visual representations can be taken over by the probing and exploration of visually accessible structures by way of visual modality. Clearly what is going on in the brain is going to be crucially important in this process. But, if the enactivist account is correct, it would be a mistake to suppose that it exhausts the process of visually perceiving the world. To the extent that visual representations are involved, they provide us, at most, with the gist of the visual situation; and the details have to be filled in by suitable probing and exploratory action.[15] If so, then the enacted mind seems to be committed to the hybrid conception of visual perception. Finally:

• The external operations take the form of *action*: manipulation, exploitation, and transformation of environmental structures—ones that carry information relevant to the accomplishing of a given task.

Probing and exploration of visual structures in the environment do, of course, seem to be forms of action in this sense. If the visual task in question is, for example, producing (i.e., enacting) experiences that reflect the structure, richness, and complexity of the visual environment surrounding the subject, then the enactive account denies that these features need to be reproduced internally—that is, it denies that they need to be reproduced as features of the visual representation. Rather, in its probing, exploratory activities, the perceiving subject *exploits* the structure, richness, and complexity contained in stable external stores of information, and then uses these to enact experiences that reflect this structural richness and complexity. Thus, the enacted mind also seems to conform to the third condition of our characterization of the extended mind.

On the surface at least, the enacted mind seems to follow closely the characterization I have given of the extended mind. It is, therefore, initially tempting to think of the enacted mind as simply a version of the extended mind. Indeed, I was once thus tempted and did so characterize the enacted mind (Rowlands 2002, 2003). I now suspect that this was premature. Not only are the extended mind and the enacted mind—at least as developed by Noë—different views; it is not even clear that they are compatible views. Thus, it is noticeable that the identified points of similarity between the extended mind and the enacted mind above all turn on the role allotted by the enacted mind to the probing and exploration of the world by the perceiving subject. However, on closer analysis I think we shall find that this role has been grossly overplayed in this sense: it is far from clear that the enacted mind, as developed by Noë, assigns any essential role to this sort of activity. In the remainder of this section, I shall argue that his enacted mind turns on *expectations* and *abilities* rather than exploratory *activities*. And there is no convincing reason for thinking that either of these is extended in the sense required to make the enacted mind a version of the extended mind (Rowlands 2009b).

Recall the two claims that, I have argued, are constitutive of the enacted mind. Visually perceiving the world is made up of two things:

1. Expectations about how our experience of an object will change in the event of our moving or the object of our vision moving (or some other object moving with respect to that object—for example, in front of it). This is *sensorimotor knowledge* or *knowledge of sensorimotor contingencies*.
2. The ability to act on the world—that is, to probe and explore environmental structures by way of the visual modality.

Claim (1) concerns sensorimotor *knowledge*: knowledge that consists in a related set of *expectations* about how our experience will change given the obtaining of certain environmental contingencies. Claim (2) concerns our ability to act on the world. Adjudicating the claim that the enacted mind yields an extended account of perception, then, amounts to answering this question: is there any reason for supposing that either our expectations or our ability to act (or both) are extended? Is there any reason for thinking that our expectations about how our experience will change in the event of certain contingencies are extended in the way that the extended mind claims (some) mental processes are extended? Is our ability to probe and explore environmental structures extended into, or distributed onto, the world? If the answer to both of these questions is "no," then we would have to reject the idea that the enacted mind yields an extended account of perceptual processes. I shall argue that the answer to both questions is, probably, "no." Therefore, appearances notwithstanding, the enacted mind probably does not yield an extended account of perceptual processes.

Claim (1): Sensorimotor Knowledge

There seems to be little reason why expectations about how our experience of an object will change in the event of our moving or the object of our vision moving should be extended. The idea that these sorts of expectations constitute our experience is one that originates in the phenomenological tradition; and they were certainly not introduced there as examples of extended mental processes. So, there is certainly no reason why these expectations *must* be extended ones. But is there any reason for supposing that they *might* be?

Noë (2004) claims that these expectations are a form of practical knowledge or *knowing how*. But, again, there is little reason for thinking that this sort of knowing how is extended. It is common, for example, to think of practical knowledge in *procedural* terms: that is, in terms of a list of instructions the following of which will, in theory, allow one to accomplish a given task. But there is no reason for thinking that these sorts of instructions are extended; and, typically, that is not the way they have been understood.

If we want to more closely align the mind enacted with the mind extended, one route does suggest itself: a serious injection of Heideggerian phenomenology. If, for example, we were influenced by what we might call the Heidegger–Dreyfus–Wheeler axis, we would want to deny that sensorimotor knowledge can be reduced to procedural knowledge.[16] Our manner of relating to the world, including in this case, the way in which we relate perceptually to the world, is ultimately nonpropositional: propositional modes of relating to the world are always derivative on a more basic way of *being-in-the-world*. I have a considerable amount of sympathy for this view. If this is what sensorimotor knowledge is, then of course it is extended. It is so for the simple reason that *being-in-the-world* is extended.

For Heidegger (1927/1962), *Dasein*—the being of humans—is essentially *being-in-the-world*. By this, he didn't mean that first there are humans and, in addition, there is this property of being-in-the-world that all humans possess essentially. His claim was that humans *are* being-in-the-world. That is, the being of each of us consists in a network of related practices. Each of these practices presupposes an instrumental network of related items. We might find ourselves tempted to describe this by saying that human practices are embedded in a wider system of instruments. However, this would be crucially misleading. To describe the relation as *embedding* presupposes that there is a distinction between the practices and the instrumental network that embeds them. And this is precisely what Heidegger wished to deny. The instruments are partly constitutive of the practices. Division I of *Being and Time* is the attempt to understand humans simply as a system of practices in this sense. So, each one of us incorporates both the practices and the instrumental network that is constitutive of those practices. But if this is the underlying vision then cognition is extended for the simple reason that everything we do is extended. We must eschew thinking of a human being as a biological entity with biological boundaries of the usual sort. The being of humans is simply practices—practices that take place in the instrumental networks that partly realize them. Any expectations we might possess concerning the likely trajectory of our experiences are derivative upon this more basic way of being-in-the-world. Given this Heideggerian vision, there cannot be any special issue of whether the mental things we do are extended. The claim that the expectations constitutive of our sensorimotor knowledge are extended, therefore, would emerge as trivially true. So too would the extended mind.

I leave it to the reader to judge the relative appeal of this Heideggerian move. In any event, it is not clear that it is a move that Noë is in a position to make—at least not without a lot of shuffling of assumptions. The Heidegger–Dreyfus–Wheeler axis emphasizes the nonpropositional, hence nonprocedural, nature of sensorimotor knowledge. However, although Noë's official position is that sensorimotor knowledge is a form of knowing how, all the actual examples he gives of this knowledge seems to be forms of knowing that. Recall the passage cited earlier:

Our perceptual sense of the tomato's wholeness—of its volume and backside, and so forth—consists in our implicit understanding (our expectation) *that* the movements of our body to the left or right, say, will bring further bits of the tomato into view. (Noë 2004, 63; emphasis mine)

This is knowledge *that* rather than knowledge *how*. Or take the other passage cited earlier:

When you experience an object as cubical merely on the basis of its aspect, you do so because you bring to bear, in this experience, your sensorimotor knowledge of the relation between changes in cube aspects and movement. To experience the figure as a cube, on the basis of how it looks, is to understand *how* its look changes as you move. (Ibid., 77)

Here, Noë does at least talk of understanding "how" the look of something changes as you move. But this is such an anodyne sense of understanding how that it seems interchangeable with understanding that. After all, what is it to understand *how* the look of something changes as you move? This seems to amount to nothing more than understanding *that* if you were to move thus, then the look of the object would change in such and such a way. In other words, the grammar of Noë's claim is, here, misleading: though he appears to be talking about understanding how, he is really talking about understanding *that* (Rowlands 2006, 2007).[17]

So, if sensorimotor knowledge, as Noë seems to understand this, were to be regarded as extended, we would have to make out the case that at least some tokens of declarative knowledge or understanding are extended. And not just any declarative knowledge: we would have to show this with regard to the declarative knowledge implicated in perception. The difficulties with this are, I think, formidable. Therefore, if there is a stronger connection between the enacted mind and the extended mind, we shall have to find it in the second constitutive feature of the former: the ability to act on the world—to probe and explore its structures by way of the visual modality.

Claim (2): The Ability to Act on the World

In assessing whether the ability to probe and explore the visual environment is extended, we need to draw a familiar distinction between *ability* and the *exercise* of that ability. There are two ways of understanding claim (2), one much stronger than the other. According to the weak version, visually perceiving the world only requires the *ability* to probe and explore the world by way of the visual modality. It does not require the actual *exercise* of that ability—it does not require the actual probing and exploring of the world. On the stronger version of the claim, visually perceiving the world requires not only the ability to probe and explore the world by way of the visual modality; it also requires exercise of that ability.

Consider, first, the weaker claim. Is there any reason for thinking that abilities to probe and explore the world are extended? Given the distinction between an ability and the exercise of that ability, there does not seem to be. My playing of the piano is a spatially and temporally extended process that centrally involves, as one of its constituents, the keys of the piano itself. But I can have the ability to play the piano even if I never come across another piano in my life and so never have the chance to exercise that ability. The distinction between the possession and the exercise of ability can be applied to abilities of all kinds—human or not. The fertilization of an egg by a sperm is a process that incorporates, as constituents, both sperm and egg. But the sperm has this ability even if, owing to the vicissitudes of fortune, it never finds itself in the right place at the right time. The obvious moral seems to be that although the exercise of ability might be an extended process, the same does not hold for the ability itself. Abilities are not extended in the sense required by the thesis of the extended mind.

It is true, of course, that some abilities might be *embodied*.[18] Here is John Haugeland discussing the ability to type:

[T]hat some particular pulse pattern [in my brain], on some occasion, should result in my typing an "A" depends on many contingencies, over and above just which pattern of pulses it happens to be. In the first place, it depends on the lengths of my fingers, the strengths and quicknesses of my muscles, the shape of my joints, and the like. Of course, whatever else I might do with my hands, from typing the rest of the alphabet to tying my shoes, would likewise depend *simultaneously* on particular pulse patterns and these other concrete contingencies. But there need be no way to "factor out" the respective contributions of these different dependencies, such that contents could consistently be assigned to pulse patterns independent of which fingers they're destined for. (Haugeland 1995, 253)

I think one should readily agree with Haugeland on this point. Many abilities are embodied in the sense that whether or not you have them is a matter not just of what is going on in your brain but also of dispositions built into your body whether through training or biological endowment. My ability to surf is not simply a matter of my brain encoding the relevant form of practical knowledge but also of my body having acquired, through a long process of training, the necessary bodily dispositions or tendencies. Without these dispositions, what is going on in the brain would not add up to the ability to surf. Although not all abilities are embodied, it seems undeniable that some of them are. However, as we have seen, the extended mind is a quite different thesis from the embodied mind. Even when both are understood as *ontic* theses of *composition*, composition by bodily structures is quite different from composition by environmental structures. The enacted mind's appeal to abilities to probe and explore the world by way of the visual modality might point us in the direction of an *embodied* view of perception. But this, by itself, does not yield an extended account of perception.[19]

The same sorts of considerations also point to the conclusion that some abilities are environmentally *embedded*. The bodily dispositions I have acquired in the course of learning to surf themselves have to be tailored to specific environmental contingencies. For example, the ability to surf on a 7'11" Mini-mal does not translate into the ability to surf on a 5'11" Thruster. However, as we saw earlier, the extended mind is distinct from, and considerably stronger than, the claim that mental processes are embedded. The claim that mental processes have environmental constituents— that they are composed, in part, of processes that take place in the world outside the head—is a much more striking claim than merely that they are *dependent*, even essentially dependent, on the wider environment. One can accept that many abilities—though by no means all—seem to be complex constructions out of brain activity, acquired or innate bodily dispositions, and environmental feedback. This still does not give you an extended account of abilities.

According to the stronger interpretation of claim (2), visually perceiving the world requires not only the ability to probe and explore the world by way of the visual modality; it also requires exercise of that ability. It goes without saying, of course, that the exercise of many abilities consists in processes that are extended into the world and include items in the world among their constituents. So, the stronger interpretation of (2) might certainly entail the extended mind. The problem, however, is that this stronger interpretation seems grossly implausible.

The immediate problem, of course, lies in accounting for *novel* visual phenomena. Suppose you encounter—to return to Noë's example— a tomato that you have never seen before. According to condition (1), perceiving the shape of the tomato consists in grasping the relevant sensorimotor contingencies. That is, it involves understanding how your visual experience will change contingent on your moving relative to the tomato, or the tomato moving relative to you, or an object occluding the tomato, and so on. But suppose we now add on the stronger version of condition (2): perceiving the shape of the tomato involves the actual exercise of the ability to probe and explore the world by way of the visual modality. But this entails that prior to exercising the ability one does not see the shape of the tomato.

The obvious response is to appeal to prior experience. You do not need to actually exercise the ability to probe and explore the environment, because although you might not have seen this particular tomato before, you have seen tomatoes of a similar shape. Therefore, on the basis of this prior experience, you can anticipate how your experience would change contingent upon certain events, such as your moving relative to the tomato.

This response, however, faces two problems: the first intrinsic to it, the second pertaining to the possibility of regarding the enacted mind as yielding an extended account of perception. The first problem concerns the possibility of perceiving novel visual shapes. For any object with a shape that you have hitherto not encountered, the stronger version of (2) entails that you do not actually perceive that shape until you have acted on it— visually probed and explored it—and witnessed how your experience changed as a result. Failing this, you will fail to perceive the novel shape. The same, according to this strong interpretation of the enactive account, is true of any novel visual property of an object.

The worry here, of course, is that the enactive account is confusing perception with subsequent cognitive operations. In essence, the worry is that the enactive approach runs together the distinction between *perception* and *judgment*.[20] It certainly seems that something *in the vicinity* of seeing must be going on prior to the probing and exploratory activity. There is no probing and exploratory activity *simpliciter*. That is, probing and exploratory activity is not something one does willy-nilly. On the contrary, the activity is guided by some visually salient feature of the situation. So, when we explore the visual potential of a novel shape, for example, what is it that guides our exploration? The obvious response is that what guides our exploration is our perception of the shape. We certainly see something, and the most natural candidate for what we see is the shape. We may not know exactly what shape it is; that is what the subsequent exploration is to tell us. But this latter issue is a matter of judgment, not perception.

The second problem is more germane to our concerns. Noë does seem to endorse the stronger interpretation of claim (2). In a passage cited earlier, for example, he talks of perception being "constituted by our possession *and* exercise of bodily skills" (Noë 2004, 25).[21] However, sometimes his claims seem to suggest that the actual exercise of a sensorimotor ability is required only during the process of learning to perceive a visual property. Thus: "only though self-movement can one test and so learn the relevant patterns of sensorimotor dependence" (ibid., 13).

However, if the exercise of one's ability to probe and explore the environment is only required for *learning* how to perceive a visual property, whereas simply the ability will suffice for actually perceiving a property one has previously encountered, then this means that only learning how to perceive a visual property will be an extended process. Perceiving an already encountered property will require only the relevant expectations concerning how one's experience will change given certain contingencies, and the ability to probe and explore the relevant portion of the environment. And if the arguments developed here are correct, there is no reason to think that either of these is an extended process.

We can represent the situation in the form of a dilemma. If the enacted mind claims that the actual exercise of one's ability to visually probe the world is required for perception, then it is implausible. If, on the other hand, it claims that exercise of this ability is required only during the learning phase, then it yields only an extremely attenuated version of the extended mind: an extended account of learning to perceive, but not of perception itself. As far as its account of the latter goes, the enacted mind supplies us with a solidly internalist account oriented around the possession of expectations and abilities. This is, of course, not necessarily a bad thing. Many would regard this anodyne internalist interpretation of the enactive mind as counting in its favor rather than as a strike against it. However, it does suggest that if there is to be a non-Cartesian science of the mind—radically different from its Cartesian forebears—then the enactive mind, at least as this has been developed by Noë, is not going to be at the heart of it.

Thus, it seems that any attempt to return the enactive mind to the heart of the non-Cartesian science is, in one way or another, going to have to try and undermine the distinction between perceiving and learning to perceive; and it has to do this in such a way that perception turns out to be a lot more like learning than learning is like perception. Interestingly, an attempt to undermine the distinction between learning and perception can be found in both Hurley and Noë 2003 and Hurley 2010.[22] Here, the learning–perception distinction is represented as the training–post-training distinction. The attempt to undermine this distinction is based on trying to shift attention away from what Hurley calls the "sufficiency question" to what she calls the "explanatory question." With regard to perceptual experience, the sufficiency question would be: "What in the system suffices for a visual experience, *P*, with a given content?" The corresponding explanatory question would be: "Why is this neural state the neural correlate of the visual experience *P*?" Thus, Hurley proposes that we switch focus from the issue of the *most local mechanism* of perceptual experience to the issue of what provides the *best explanation* of the quality and character of the experience. Whereas the local mechanism that suffices for a perceptual experience may be internal to the perceiving subject, Hurley argues, the best explanation of the quality and character of the experience will have to advert to "a characteristic extended dynamic." That is, the best explanation of the quality and character of the perceptual experience will advert to a distributed process incorporating brain, body, and the active probing or exploration of the world.

Unfortunately, however, I do not think this attempt will work. To see why, consider a distinction I drew in my Rowlands 2003: the distinction between the *possession* of a property and the *location* of things that possess that property. Consider, for example, the property of being a planet. Possession of this property by an object requires that it stand in a certain relation to things outside it—a sun that it orbits, for example. It is standing in this relation that makes something a planet; and an explanation of why something is a planet would, therefore, have to refer to these things. But it does not follow from this that a planet is located wherever its central sun is located. Issues of property *possession*, and explanation of that property possession, do not translate into issues concerning the *location* of the token items that possess this property.[23] Thus, we might agree with Hurley that the best explanation of the quality and character of an experience might appeal to a characteristic extended dynamic. And we might agree that this is the best explanation because this dynamic is indeed responsible for the possession by the experience of this quality or character. However, it does not follow from this that the experience is extended.[24] In other words, even if we accepted Hurley's attempt to switch the focus of concern, this move will yield, at most, only an *embedded* account of perceptual processes. It will not yield an *extended* account.[25]

6   The Mind Embodied, Extended, and Amalgamated

As things stand, the embedded mind is a neo-Cartesian fallback position employed by those who accept the force of the arguments for the extended account but seek to limit their consequences. However, it is far from clear that the enacted mind, at least as represented by Noë, significantly diverges from an environmentally aware form of internalism. That is, short of an injection of Heideggerian phenomenological ontology, the enactive account still yields only an embodied and/or embedded account of cognitive processes. With the possible exception of perceptual learning, it does not yield an extended account. Therefore, if the arguments of this chapter are correct, at the heart of a non-Cartesian cognitive science, we find the mind embodied and the mind extended. The four Es with which we began this chapter have, effectively, shrunk to two.

However, the embodied mind and the extended mind are united by one central idea: both are ontic theses of the (partial) composition of (some) cognitive processes. Accordingly, it is this idea that lies at the heart of the non-Cartesian conception of the mind. Some cognitive processes are composed, in part, of structures and processes that are located outside the brain of the cognizing subject. Cognitive processes are an *amalgam* of neural structures and processes, bodily structures and processes, and environmental structures and processes. We can subsume the theses of the embodied mind and the extended mind into one: the *amalgamated mind*. The new science will be based on the idea of mental processes as amalgamations.

The idea that cognitive processes are extended can easily conjure up the wrong sorts of images. The root of the difficulty is that extension is a spatial concept and, so, is closely tied to that of *location*. And the issue of the location of cognitive processes can easily sidetrack us into concerns that we should not have. Thus, the idea that cognitive processes are extended can easily tempt us into thinking of mental processes as somehow stretching outside of the brain, and thus having a definite spatial location but simply one that incorporates expanses of the extracranial world. This is, I think, precisely how *not* to think about extended cognition. In general, cognitive processes have a location that is, at best, vague, and may be genuinely indeterminate. That is, there might be no fact of the matter with regard to where a given token cognitive process occurs. It is not, as the metaphor of the extended mind might tempt us to suppose, that cognitive processes have determinate extended boundaries—like an elastic band that has been stretched outside the brain or skull. It is rather that they have no determinate boundaries at all. The thesis of the extended mind might more accurately be called the thesis of the *spatially indefinite* mind. But, let's face it, that's nowhere near catchy enough.

The thesis of the *amalgamated mind* is a little better in this regard. What is important for the new science is the *composition* or *constitution* of cognitive processes and not, in the first instance, their *location*. Claims about the precise location of cognitive processes do not follow, in any straightforward manner, from claims about their composition. That would depend on whether the things that compose cognitive processes have precise spatial location. However, claims about where such processes are *not* located do follow. Thus, the thesis of the amalgamated mind—the claim that (some) token cognitive processes are amalgamations of neural, bodily, and/or environmental structures and processes—entails that not all cognitive processes are located inside the heads of cognizing organisms. But what is of primary importance to this thesis is the issue of composition, not location.

Thus, *AM*, the thesis of the *amalgamated mind*—cognitive processes as amalgamations of the neural, bodily, and environmental—subsumes both theses of the embodied and the extended mind. Amalgamation of these apparently disparate realms is based on the concepts of *exploitation*, *manipulation*, and *transformation*. When the extracranial structures and processes thus amalgamated are bodily ones, the idea of exploitation is likely to be at the forefront of the possibility of amalgamation. The brain *exploits* the distance between the organism's ears in its processing of the distance and direction of sound sources. However, when the extracranial structures and processes thus amalgamated are also extrabodily, then manipulation and transformation can come to the fore. In *manipulating* environmental information-bearing structures, the organism can *transform* the information they contain from the merely present to the available. In doing so, it can now exploit that information in its subsequent processing operations.

The concept of amalgamation thus incorporates both the thesis of the embodied mind and that of the extended mind. The possibility of such incorporation will come as a surprise to many—who have supposed, for reasons we will explore later, that the theses of the embodied and extended mind are mutually inimical. The next chapter begins defense of the amalgamated mind.

4   Objections to the Mind Amalgamated

1   The Amalgamated Mind: Challenges

The thesis of the amalgamated mind is the combination of the theses of the embodied mind and the extended mind. Both of these are versions of a more general idea: cognitive processes are partly composed of, or constituted by, extraneural processes. They are made up, in part, of bodily and/or wider environmental processes. The thesis of the amalgamated mind (henceforth simply "the amalgamated mind") is this claim of extracranial composition. Since the amalgamated mind incorporates both theses of embodiment and extendedness, the principal challenges facing it can be divided into three categories:

1. Challenges to the thesis of the extended mind.
2. Challenges to the thesis of the embodied mind.
3. Challenges to the combination of these theses.

According to the third type of challenge, even if there is nothing wrong with the embodied mind and the extended mind taken individually, these two theses cannot be combined together in the way envisioned by the amalgamated mind since they are, in fact, mutually incompatible.

I shall discuss the challenges in this order.

2   The Extended Mind and Its Discontents

The thesis of the extended mind has recently been the target of a number of objections, broadly divisible into four kinds:

1. *The differences argument*   This type of objection points to the significant differences between internal cognitive processes and the external processes that the thesis of the extended mind also claims are cognitive. This casts doubts on the claim that both processes should be regarded as examples

of a single psychological kind. This sort of objection has been vigorously championed by Rupert (2004) and also by Fodor (2009).

2. *The coupling-constitution fallacy* This type of objection claims that the thesis of the extended mind confuses real cognition with its extraneous causal accompaniments. More precisely, it confuses those structures and processes constitutive of cognition with structures and processes in which cognition is (merely) causally embedded. We have already encountered this type of objection on several occasions. It is an objection that has been developed by Adams and Aizawa (2001, 2010) and also, in a somewhat different way, by Rupert (2004).

3. *The cognitive bloat objection* According to this objection, the admission of extended cognitive processes places us on a slippery slope. Once we permit such processes, where do we stop? Our conception of the cognitive will become too permissive, and we will be forced to admit into the category of the cognitive all sort sorts of structures and processes that clearly are not cognitive.

4. *The mark of the cognitive objection* According to this objection, the thesis of the extended mind should be rejected on the grounds that it is incompatible with any plausible mark of the cognitive. A mark of the cognitive is a criterion or set of conditions that specifies when a process is to count as cognitive (and perhaps also when it is not to count as cognitive). The objection is that any plausible criterion of the cognitive will disqualify the sorts of extended processes invoked by the thesis of the extended mind from counting as cognitive. This objection is developed by Adams and Aizawa (2001, 2010).

In the next few sections of this chapter, I shall argue that the first three objections all reduce to the *mark of the cognitive objection*. They do so either in that they presuppose this objection or can be answered by way of the provision of a satisfactory mark or criterion of the cognitive.

3 The Differences Argument: Parity and Integration in the Extended Mind

The thesis of the extended mind is often thought to be grounded in the concept of *parity*: roughly speaking, the *similarity* between the external processes involved in cognition and internal processes that are widely accepted as cognitive. The *extended mind*'s reliance on this notion of parity is often thought to be embodied in, and demonstrated by, Clark and Chalmers's deployment of what they call the *parity principle*:

If, as we confront some task, a part of the world functions as a process which, *were it done in the head*, we would have no hesitation in accepting as part of the cognitive process, then that part of the world is (so we claim) part of the cognitive process. (Clark and Chalmers 1998, 8)

Critics of the *extended mind* have, seemingly without exception, understood the parity principle as introducing a *similarity-based criterion* of when an external process or structure is to be understood as cognitive—that is, as a genuinely cognitive part of a cognitive process. Very roughly, on this understanding of the parity principle, if an external process is sufficiently similar to an internal cognitive process, then it too is a cognitive process.

It is this interpretation of the role of the parity principle—as introducing a similarity-based criterion for when cognition can legitimately be regarded as extended—that underwrites the *differences argument*. For example, in one recent development of this argument, Fodor criticizes Clark and Chalmers on the grounds that the alleged parity between the cases of Otto and Inga is merely apparent, and rests on Clark and Chalmers inaccurately describing the scenario:

Surely it's not that Inga remembers that she remembers the address of the museum, and having consulted her memory of her memory then consults the memory she remembers having, and thus ends up at the museum. . . . It's untendentious that Otto's consulting "outside" memories presupposes his having inside memories. But on pain of regress, Inga's consulting inside memories about where the museum is can't require her first to consult other inside memories about whether she remembers where the museum is. . . . There is, after all, a built-in asymmetry between Otto's sort of case and Inga's sort. Otto really does go through one more process than Inga. . . . Inga's "consulting her memories" her memories is a fake, and a particularly naughty fake because . . . it makes Inga's case look more like Otto's than it can possibly be. (Fodor 2009, 15)

In other words, Clark and Chalmers's argument does not work because the parity between internal and external on which it relies is only apparent and not real.

In a similar vein, Rupert, in connection with an argument for extended memory developed by me (Rowlands 1999), outlines his strategy as follows:

I argue that the external portions of extended "memory" states (processes) differ so greatly from internal memories (the process of remembering) that they should be treated as distinct kinds; this quells any temptation to argue for HEC [hypothesis of extended cognition] from brute analogy (viz. extended cognitive states are like wholly internal ones; therefore, they are of the same explanatory cognitive kind; therefore there are extended cognitive states). (Rupert 2004, 407)

Later on, we shall look at one specific application of this strategy. For present purposes, however, let's just focus on the general strategy rather than its specific applications. The assumption underlying both Fodor's and Rupert's objections is that the function of the parity principle is to introduce a similarity-based criterion of when a cognitive process such as remembering can be extended into the world: *if* an external process is sufficiently similar to internal cognitive processes, *then* it too is a cognitive process. Fodor and Rupert then argue that since external processes involved in memory are, in fact, *not* sufficiently similar to internal cognitive processes, then they do *not* qualify as cognitive processes. Presumably this is intended as an inductive argument: since the internal and external processes involved in cognition are not sufficiently similar, the parity principle provides no reason to regard the latter as cognitive.[1]

The differences argument, however, fails to properly understand the arguments for the extended mind.[2] This thesis does not, in fact, rely on a similarity-based criterion of when an extended process may legitimately be regarded as cognitive. The notion of parity is indeed, I shall argue, an important one for the extended mind. However, equally important is the notion of *integration*: the meshing of disparate types of process that, *precisely because* of their disparate character, can enable a cognizing organism to accomplish tasks that it would not be able to achieve by way of either type of process alone (Menary 2006, 2007; Sutton 2010).

From this *integrationist* perspective, the *differences* between internal and external processes are as important as, or even more important than, their similarities. The reason cognition extends into the environment is precisely because, with respect to the accomplishing of certain cognitive tasks, external processes can do things that internal processes cannot do (or, depending on how you want to understand the thesis of the extended mind, simply, in certain cases, *do* not do). External structures and processes possess quite different properties from internal ones; and it is precisely this difference that affords the cognitive agent the opportunity to accomplish certain tasks that it would not be able to accomplish purely by way of internal cognitive processes. Without these differences, the external processes would be *otiose*.

For example, in *The Body in Mind* (Rowlands 1999), I emphasized the relative *permanence* and *stability* of external forms of memory storage, and I examined the implications of this for the development of biological memory strategies during the process of enculturation. It is because this

permanence and stability have no real echo in internal, biological processes that the development of external forms of memory was both useful
and had marked implications for the character of biological memory (see
also Donald 1991). More recently, O'Regan and Noë (2001, 2002) and Noë
(2004) have emphasized the importance of the permanence and stability
of the external world in constituting visual perception. The world, by
providing a stable and relatively permanent structure that can be probed
and explored at will by the visual modality, obviates the need for at
least certain sorts of visual representations as these were traditionally
understood.[3]

In *The Body in Mind* I also emphasized the distinctive *structure* of external
systems—for example, the recursive, combinatorial structure peculiar to
linguistic systems—structure that has no real echo in internal, biological
processes. I argued that if an organism is capable of appropriately utilizing
worldly structure in the performance of its cognitive tasks, then this sort
of structure need not be replicated internally. Thus, once again, the importance of the world, and by extension the processes occurring in it, derives
precisely from its possessing structure that internal processes lack, and so
allows us to do what we cannot do in the head alone.[4]

Therefore, it is a mistake to suppose that the case for the extended
mind is built on parity alone. Equally important are the differences
between internal and external processes. It is precisely the different properties of external structures that allow the cognitive agent to accomplish
things that it either could not, or in fact does not, accomplish by way of
internal processes alone. Given the central role played by the notion of
integration in the thesis of the extended mind, one cannot base, as does
the differences argument, an objection to this thesis simply by citing
differences between internal and external processes. The thesis of
the extended mind, properly understood, both *predicts* and *requires* such
differences. Understood on its own terms, therefore, the differences
argument fails.

The importance of the role of integration in the extended mind should
not, however, blind us to the role of parity. The extended mind requires
both parity and integration. And it requires both of these to be properly
understood and allotted their proper place and appropriate role. Suppose
we tried to develop a case for the extended mind based purely on the
notion of cognitive integration. This would leave the thesis open to another
objection. If the thesis of the extended mind requires significant differences between internal processes and the external processes that it regards
as cognitive, what reason is there for supposing that the latter are really

part of cognition rather than a merely external accompaniment to real, internal cognitive processing? That is, using a distinction between the extended mind and the embedded mind we developed in the previous chapter, given that there are significant differences between internal cognitive processes and extended processes involved in cognition, why not simply suppose that the latter are part of the extraneous scaffolding in which the real, internal cognitive processes are *embedded*? In other words, reliance on the differences between internal and external processes might give you the thesis of the embedded mind. But it will not, it seems, give you the thesis of the extended mind (Rowlands 2009a).

Given the integrationist's emphasis on the differences between the internal and external processes involved in cognition, it is not possible to establish the cognitive status of the latter simply by analogical extension from the former. Therefore, if we are to defend the cognitive status of the extended processes, we need some other way of defending the claim that these external processes are cognitive ones. One way of doing this—and it is not clear that there is another way—would be to provide an adequate and properly motivated criterion or mark of the cognitive: a criterion that would allow the thesis of the extended mind to justify the claim that the external processes involved in cognition are indeed cognitive processes, rather than merely an extraneous scaffolding in which cognitive processes are embedded. In short, the integrationist response deflects the differences argument only by leaving the thesis of the extended mind vulnerable to the mark of the cognitive objection.

In this context, the provision of an adequate and properly motivated mark of the cognitive would accord due importance to the differences between internal and external processes but, at the same time, reintroduce a sufficient degree of parity between internal and external to avoid the charge that we have no reason for supposing that the latter are really cognitive. The parity reintroduced here is of an appropriate sort. It is not parity that obtains between particular processes: we have to safeguard the idea that internal and external processes can be quite different (for that is, in many cases, the *point* of the external processes). Rather, it is parity with respect to certain abstract, general features of cognition that will be identified by the mark of the cognitive. These are features that are sufficiently abstract to be possessed by both internal and external processes, no matter how different these may be with regard to more concrete features. It is these abstract features that warrant the claim that the external processes involved in cognition are, in fact, cognitive (Rowlands 2009a,b,c).

4   The Coupling-Constitution Fallacy

The *coupling-constitution fallacy* objection can take slightly different forms. According to Adams and Aizawa:

This is the most common mistake that extended mind theorists make. The fallacious pattern is to draw attention to cases, real or imagined, in which some object or process is coupled in some fashion to some cognitive agent. From this, they slide to the conclusion that the object or process constitutes part of the agent's cognitive apparatus or cognitive processing. (Adams and Aizawa 2001, 408)

Rupert expresses a similar objection, albeit in more cautious terms. Referring, again, to my version of the extended mind, he writes:

Rowlands, however, does not make clear why the use of an internally represented code applied to the contents of an external store implies HEC, rather than what it would seem to imply: HEMC. (Rupert 2004, 410)

HEC is the hypothesis of extended cognition, which Rupert correctly distinguishes from HEMC, the hypothesis of embedded cognition. What reason, Rupert asks, do we have for regarding the external processes as part of cognition rather than simply a form of extraneous scaffolding in which *real*—internal—cognitive processes can be causally embedded? That is, what reason do we have for thinking that the arguments for the thesis of the extended mind support anything more than the thesis of the embedded mind?

A charge of confusion can be interpreted in two distinct ways. On the one hand, it might mean that proponents of the extended mind have proceeded in their arguments blithely unaware that there is a distinction between cognition and its extraneous causal accompaniments. That is, these proponents are blithely unaware that there is a distinction between the *constitution* of cognitive processes and the extraneous structures with which such processes might *causally* interact. Such a charge is, frankly, ridiculous. Far from blithely *confusing* constitution and causal coupling, the most natural way of understanding the arguments for the extended mind is precisely as *arguments* for reinterpreting what had traditionally been regarded as extraneous causal accompaniments to cognition as, in fact, part of cognition itself. And, in general, to *argue* for the identification of X and Y, when X and Y had hitherto been regarded as distinct, if causally related, categories, is not to *confuse* X and Y.

Thus, consider my arguments for the extended mind, since these occasioned Rupert's charge of *confusing* extended cognition with embedded cognition. In *The Body in Mind*, I argued that, in certain cases, the external processes involved in cognition—bodily manipulation and exploitation of information-bearing structures in the cognizing organism's environment—possess certain abstract, general features of processes commonly regarded as cognitive, while also differing in the sorts of concrete ways required by the integrationist underpinning of the extended mind. Thus, these external processes are employed in order to accomplish cognitive tasks. They involve information processing—the manipulation and transformation of information-bearing structures, and so on. This processing results in the making available to organisms of information that was previously unavailable; and so on. That is, I *argued* for the cognitive status of external processes of these sorts by trying to show that they satisfy a certain criterion of the cognitive.

The same is true, to take just one more example, of Clark and Chalmers's arguments for the *extended mind*. In the case of Otto, for example, they *argue* that the entries in his notebook qualify as a subset of his beliefs because they play a functional role relevantly and sufficiently similar to that played by beliefs when instantiated in an unimpaired brain. Thus, their arguments are an attempt to show that what we normally take to be a mere extraneous causal accompaniment to the domain of cognition should, in fact, be regarded as part of that domain itself.

There is, however, another more charitable way of understanding the charge of confusion. Now, the charge is not that defenders of the extended mind proceed blithely unaware that there is an important distinction between constitution and causation. Rather, it is that they are aware of the distinction but, in their arguments, for one reason or another, flout it anyway. For example, it might be argued that in *The Body in Mind*, my arguments for extended cognitive processes rested on a criterion of the cognitive that was never rendered sufficiently explicit and/or was importantly inadequate. Against Clark and Chalmers it might be argued that their arguments rest on a criterion of the cognitive as consisting in similarity with what is antecedently accepted to be cognitive, and that this criterion is, for one reason or another, inadequate.

These are reasonable charges, and they deserve to be answered. However, they are double edged. Suppose my arguments, for example, had been developed using an insufficiently explicit or otherwise inadequate criterion of the cognitive. Then, *if* I were in possession of an explicit, adequate, and properly motivated criterion of the cognitive, and if the sorts of external processes I identified in *The Body in Mind* were to satisfy this criterion, then I would have made it clear why my view entails the thesis of the extended mind rather than merely that of the embedded mind. In such circumstances, there would be no substance to the charge that I confuse—in *either* of the two senses—causation and constitution.

Therefore, more generally, like the differences argument, the coupling-constitution fallacy objection is derivative from the mark of the cognitive objection. If defenders of the extended mind can provide an adequate criterion of the cognitive and can demonstrate that the external processes they regard as cognitive satisfy this criterion, then there is no substance to the charge that they confuse constitution and mere coupling. In the next chapter I shall supply and defend what, I shall argue, is an explicit, adequate, and properly motivated criterion of the cognitive.

5   Cognitive Bloat

The *cognitive bloat objection* is, in essence, a slippery slope argument usually raised in connection with Clark and Chalmers's discussion of Otto's notebook. To recap, Otto is in the early stages of Alzheimer's and so keeps a notebook with him in which he writes down various facts that can help him with his day-to-day living, facts such as that the Museum of Modern Art is on 53rd Street. At least on one interpretation, Clark and Chalmers argue, notoriously, that the sentences in Otto's book can constitute a subset of his beliefs. The entries in Otto's book are literally beliefs that Otto possesses because they have a functional role in Otto's truncated psychological economy that is sufficiently and relevantly similar to the role played by beliefs in the psychological economy of Otto's unimpaired friend, Inga.

The cognitive bloat objection uses this claim as a starting point. If we are willing to allow that the sentences in Otto's notebook are beliefs, why stop there? Why not also allow that status for the entries in the telephone directory of which Otto makes frequent use? Why cannot these be numbered among Otto's beliefs? Indeed, why stop even there? Why does Otto not believe everything contained on the Internet, given that he is able to use this in a way akin to which he uses his notebook?

Clark and Chalmers try to preclude this problem of bloat by advocating a *conscious endorsement* criterion on beliefs. The entries in Otto's notebook count as beliefs, whereas the entries in Otto's telephone book do not, because Otto has, at some point, consciously endorsed the former but not the latter. However, this condition is questionable: beliefs can be formed subliminally, as well as through conscious experience, and, presumably, we would not regard a subliminal mode of formation as automatically excluding them from the class of cognitive states.[5]

In the previous chapter, I rejected Clark and Chalmers's claim that the entries in Otto's notebook form a subset of his beliefs. Instead, I formulated the thesis of the extended mind exclusively in terms of cognitive processes rather than cognitive states. Otto's process of remembering the location of the Museum of Modern Art could be a process that incorporated his manipulation of his notebook. But it does not follow from this that the entries in the book qualify as cognitive states. This latter claim should be rejected. Therefore, since the problem of bloat faced by Clark and Chalmers is one that pertains to cognitive states such as belief, and since I have rejected formulation of the thesis of the extended mind in terms of cognitive states, one might think that my version of the thesis is immune to this objection.

Sadly, however, this is not so: a parallel problem of bloat arises for cognitive processes. Suppose I am using a telescope.[6] Let us assume that the telescope is a *reflector*, and therefore works by transforming one mirror image into another. Mirror images are information-bearing structures— their properties are systematically determined, by way of a mapping function that is itself determined by the specific properties of the mirror and by the properties of the visual environment. Therefore, the operation of the telescope is based on the transformation of information-bearing structures. I use these transformations to achieve cognitive tasks I could not have achieved without them—the perception of distant objects. So, the processes occurring inside the telescope are information-processing operations used to accomplish a cognitive task. So why, if the thesis of the extended mind is true, do these processes not count as cognitive? Relevantly similar examples can be easily generated. How can we rule out, for example, processes occurring inside my calculator, or my computer, from counting as cognitive ones? They too are information-processing operations that I employ in the accomplishing of cognitive tasks. If Clark and Chalmers's version of the extended mind faces a problem of bloat for cognitive states, then it seems my version will face a parallel problem for cognitive processes.

I shall argue—although this argument must be postponed until later— that the cognitive bloat objection can be rebutted by way of an adequate criterion of the cognitive. The key to this rebuttal lies in the role played by the concept of *ownership* in qualifying a state or process as cognitive. The processes occurring in the telescope, computer, or calculator are not, at least as they figure in the cognitive bloat objection, *owned* by anyone. And anything that is to count as cognitive, I shall argue, must be owned by someone or some thing. Defense of this claim must be postponed until I have defended the criterion of the cognitive.

6 The Mark of the Cognitive Objection

The *mark of the cognitive objection* can take two forms. In its more cautious form, it claims that adjudication of the claims of the *extended mind* requires possession of an adequate criterion of the cognitive, and we possess no such criterion. In its more sanguine form, it claims that we do possess such a criterion, and it precludes the claims of the extended mind. I shall argue that neither the cautious nor the sanguine form of the objection can be sustained. I shall do this by providing what I shall argue is an explicit, adequate, and properly motivated criterion of the cognitive and showing that, far from contradicting the claims of the extended mind, it actually supports those claims.

The provision of an adequate criterion of the cognitive, therefore, would defuse both the mark of the cognitive objection and, if the arguments of this chapter are correct, the three other objections to the extended mind. In the next chapter I shall provide such a criterion.

7 Objections to the Embodied Mind

Now that we have reviewed the major objections to the thesis of the extended mind, it is relatively easy to see that each of these objections, with suitable modification, can also be applied to the thesis of the embodied mind. Note that these objections apply only to, and indeed are specifically tailored toward, the interpretation of the embodied mind thesis I endorsed in the previous chapter. That is, they apply to the embodied mind thesis only as understood as an *ontic* thesis of (partial) bodily *constitution* rather than the alternative interpretations—as an ontic thesis of bodily *dependence* or an *epistemic* thesis concerning the best way to understand cognitive processes. Indeed, these objections, in their different ways, all pose the question: what reason is there for thinking of the arguments for embodied cognition as establishing the ontic–constitution thesis rather than one of the weaker alternatives?

1. *The differences argument* There are significant differences between traditional—neural—cognitive processes, and the wider bodily processes invoked by the thesis of the embodied mind. This casts doubt on whether they can both be viewed as cases of a single psychological kind.

2. *The coupling-constitution fallacy*   The thesis of the embodied mind confuses cognition with its extraneous causal accompaniments. That is, it confuses those structures and processes constitutive of cognition with structures and processes in which cognition is (merely) causally embedded.

3. *Cognitive bloat*   Admitting wider bodily processes into the domain of the cognitive places us on a slippery slope. Where will it all end? Our conception of the cognitive will become unduly permissive, and we will be forced to regard all sorts of clearly non-cognitive processes as cognitive.

4. *The mark of the cognitive objection*   The claim that wider bodily processes of the sort invoked by the embodied mind are cognitive violates any plausible mark or criterion of the cognitive.

Once again, and for the same reasons, the mark of the cognitive objection is the crucial one. All the other objections either presuppose the mark of the cognitive objection or can be resolved by the provision of a suitable criterion of the cognitive.

With regard to the *differences argument*, the thesis of the embodied mind will accept that there are significant differences between cognitive processes as these are traditionally understood and the wider bodily processes that it invokes and claims as cognitive. Given that these wider processes are not neural, significant differences are inevitable. However, if the thesis of the embodied mind can demonstrate that these wider bodily processes, when they are appropriately combined with relevant neural processes, can satisfy an adequate criterion of the cognitive, then these differences would in no way count against the claim that the wider bodily processes are cognitive ones.

According to the modified *coupling-constitution fallacy* objection, the thesis of the embodied mind confuses cognitive processes with wider structures in which these processes are embedded. In other words, it understands itself as arguing for the *constitution* of cognitive processes by wider bodily processes, but it really amounts to nothing more than the thesis that cognitive processes are causally *embedded* in wider bodily structures and processes. Again, however, if the thesis of the embodied mind can show that these wider bodily processes, when conjoined with the relevant sorts of neural processes, can satisfy an adequate criterion of the cognitive, then this charge would have no substance. By the provision of such a criterion, the thesis of the embodied mind would have shown that the wider bodily processes that we might have thought of as merely extraneous casual scaffolding should, instead, be regarded as among the cognitive operations performed by an organism.

Proper discussion of the *cognitive bloat* objection will have to be postponed until after the provision of what I shall argue is an adequate and properly motivated criterion of the cognitive. I shall provide such a criterion in the next chapter. The basic idea, however, is the same as the one advanced with the extended mind: an adequate criterion of the cognitive will contain an ownership condition: any process that is to count as cognitive must be owned by a cognizing organism or subject. This ownership condition, I shall argue, undermines the charge of cognitive bloat.

All these objections, therefore, ultimately trace back to the mark of the cognitive objection. What we have to show in order to defend the thesis of the embodied mind is that when we combine neural processes with wider bodily ones, then the resulting *combination* of processes satisfies an adequate and properly motivated criterion of the cognitive. We do *not* need to show that the wider bodily processes themselves satisfy this criterion. The thesis of the embodied mind is not the thesis that the wider bodily processes on their own, or in themselves, qualify as cognitive. That would be a silly thesis. Rather, the claim is that, when conjoined with the relevant sorts of neural processes, these wider bodily processes can satisfy the mark of the cognitive. Similarly, as we saw earlier, it is no part of the thesis of the extended mind to claim that processes occurring outside the body of the cognizing organism can, by themselves, count as cognitive. What qualifies as cognitive, according to the thesis of the extended mind, is the combination of neural processes plus processes of manipulating environmental structures.

In the next chapter, I shall provide and defend a mark or criterion of the cognitive. I shall argue that this mark accurately captures the sense of "cognition" involved in traditional—internalist—examples of cognitive science. And I shall further argue that, far from undermining the claims of the theses of the mind embodied and the mind extended, this criterion actually supports those claims.

8   Reconciling the Mind Embodied and the Mind Extended

The third type of problem facing the new science of the mind concerns not the theses of the mind embodied and the mind extended taken in isolation, but the possibility of combining these in any sort of consistent way. The problem is that each thesis rests on its own set of assumptions, and the assumptions underlying the thesis of the embodied mind and

Box 4.1

Functionalism

According to functionalism, mental phenomena are identified according to their *causal* or *functional role*. Consider an analogy. A carburetor is a physical object located somewhere in the innards of a car's engine (or older cars anyway—fuel injection systems have replaced them in more recent models). What is a carburetor? Or, more precisely, what makes something a carburetor? The answer is that a carburetor is defined by what it does. Roughly, it is something that takes in fuel from the fuel inlet manifold, takes in air from the air inlet manifold, mixes the two in an appropriate ratio, and sends the resulting mixture on to the combustion chamber. It is fulfilling this role that makes something a carburetor, and anything that fulfills this role in a car thereby counts as a carburetor. Most carburetors tend to look pretty similar. But this is at best a contingent fact, because it doesn't matter what a carburetor looks like as long as it fills this role. The details of its physical structure and implementation are of secondary importance compared to the role it fills, for it is filling this role that makes something a carburetor, and not the details of its physical structure or implementation. Of course, not every physical thing is *capable* of playing the role of a carburetor—a lump of Jell-O, for example, is not. So, the details of the how the functional role is physically implemented are not irrelevant. But as long as you have a suitable physical structure—one that is capable of fulfilling the role of a carburetor—then it doesn't matter what it is as long as it, in fact, fulfills this role.

Functionalism takes a similar view of the nature of mental properties. That is, such properties are defined by what they do—by their functional role. What is it that mental phenomena do? Fundamentally, they relate to each other, to perception, and to behavior in various complex, but in principle analyzable, ways. Take a belief, for example, the belief that it is raining. This is a belief that is typically caused by perception of certain environmental conditions, rain being the most obvious. Of course, perception of other environmental conditions might also produce the belief; for example, someone, unknown to you, using a hose outside your window. But rain is the most typical cause of the belief. The belief can, in turn, go on to produce certain sorts of behavior. Because of your belief you might, for example, carry an umbrella with you when you leave the house. However, the belief has these sorts of ramifications for your behavior not in isolation but only in combination with other mental states. You will carry the umbrella because you believe it is raining, but only if you also want to stay dry. Your wanting—your *desire*—to stay dry is necessary for your behavior too. And this belief-desire combination will produce your behavior only if you also believe that the umbrella will keep you dry; only if you believe that it is not too windy to use an umbrella; indeed, only if you believe that what you have picked up is an

Box 4.1
(continued)

umbrella; and so on. What emerges is a complex network of mental states, perception, and behavior. According to functionalism, each mental state is defined by its place in this network: by the relations in which it stands to perception, to other mental states, and to behavior. To specify the place of a mental state in this network is, according to functionalism, to define that state. Of course, any such definition would be grotesquely long. Indeed, if you spent your whole life attempting to give a functional definition of even one mental state, you might well not have time to finish the task. But, its practicalities aside, the strength of functionalism consists in giving us a general vision of what mental phenomena are. The vision is of mental phenomena forming a vast causal system—a system of interrelated causal connections—where each mental property is individuated by way of its place in this system: by way of its causal connections to other mental states, to perceptual stimuli, and to behavioral responses. (See also box 1.1.)

those underlying the thesis of the extended mind are not merely very different; they are, many think, actually incompatible. If this is correct, and if the new science is based on ideas of embodiment and extendedness, the new science appears to be in conceptual tatters. To see why, let us turn to the relevant assumptions made by each thesis, beginning with the extended mind.

The most important assumption underlying the thesis of the extended mind seems to be *functionalism* about mental states and processes (Clark 2008a,b). Indeed, the functionalism presupposed by the thesis of the extended mind is of a peculiarly *liberal* sort. As we saw earlier, Clark and Chalmers's use of Otto in developing their case for the extended mind makes clear their functionalist commitments. What is decisive in determining whether or not the entry in Otto's notebook qualifies as a belief is the way it interacts with perception, behavior, and other mental states. Thus, when combined with his desire to see the exhibition, the entry in his notebook causes Otto to set off in the direction of 53rd Street. In general, Clark and Chalmers argue that the entries in Otto's notebook have a functional role in Otto's psychology that is sufficiently similar to the functional role of belief in Inga's psychology that the notebook entries should be counted as among Otto's beliefs. Though there are differences between the entries in Otto's notebook and more standard cases of belief, these differences are shallow ones—insufficiently significant to disqualify the entries from counting as beliefs.

This commitment to functionalism, however, is not peculiar to Clark and Chalmers's development of the extended mind. My case for the extended mind developed in *The Body in Mind* was based on the idea that cognitive processes could be defined in terms of what they do and the way they do it. Roughly, the idea was that cognitive processes are ones whose function is to enable organisms to accomplish cognitive tasks (e.g., perceiving the world, remembering perceived information, reasoning on the base of remembered information), and they do this by way of the manipulation, transformation, and exploitation of information-bearing structures. As a matter of contingent fact, I argued, some of the information-bearing structures involved were ones external to the body of the cognizing organism, and therefore, the manipulative processes involved were similarly external. So, to this extent, my case for the extended mind was also a functionalist one.

Indeed, not only are most arguments for the extended mind functionalist ones, there is a way of understanding functionalism according to which the thesis of the extended mind emerges as a straightforward, almost trivial, consequence.[7] Functionalism, it is widely supposed, is based on a principled indifference to the details of the physical structures that realize mental processes. What is crucial to a mental state or process is its functional role, not its physical realization. This indifference to physical realization is principled in this sense: the structure or mechanism in question has to be capable of realizing the functional role that defines a mental state or process; but this is all that is required of it. As long as it is capable of doing that, nothing else about the mechanism matters. In other words, the structure or mechanism is only indirectly relevant; it is relevant insofar as it realizes or underwrites a functional role, and only insofar as it does this. For the functionalist, if it walks like a duck, and talks like a duck, then it is a duck. *How* it manages to walk and talk like a duck is not directly relevant.

The thesis of the extended mind is, in effect, based on a further consequence of functionalism—less familiar but ultimately no less obvious. For the functionalist, not only are the details of the physical structures and mechanisms only indirectly relevant, so too is their *location*. For functionalism, the only thing that is directly relevant to whether or not something qualifies as a mental state or process of a certain sort is whether it plays the required functional role. It doesn't matter what mechanism realizes or accomplishes this role—as long as it does so. And, crucially, it doesn't matter *where* this mechanism is located when it realizes or accomplishes this role—as long as it does, in fact, realize this role. According to functionalism, when consistently understood, the location of the mechanisms that realize functional roles is no more relevant than the physical details of those mechanisms. Both are only indirectly relevant. What is always crucial, according to functionalism, is whether or not a given functional role is realized, not *how* and not *where* this role is realized. *How* something manages to walk and talk like a duck does not matter for the functionalist; neither does it matter *where* it walks and talks like a duck.

This understanding of functionalism is sometimes referred to as *liberal*, where this is opposed to *chauvinistic*. There are many different explanatory levels at which functional description of a process might be useful. Therefore, for some versions of functionalism, it does, in fact, matter how something might walk and talk like a duck. This more chauvinistic conception of functionalism is presupposed by Rupert (2004), in an influential critique of the thesis of the extended mind. This commitment is clear in the way he prosecutes his differences argument. Rupert argues that there are significant differences between internal cognitive processes and the sorts of environmental processes invoked and claimed to be cognitive by the extended mind. These differences are significant enough to preclude the latter being regarded as part of the same psychological kind as the former.

For example, in attacking the extended conception of memory I developed in *The Body in Mind*, Rupert (2004) argues that there are significant differences between the fine-grained profile of internal memory operations and external memory stores of the sort invoked in the case of Otto. For example, internal (neural) memory operations seem subject to what is known as the *generation effect*. The ability of a subject to remember the second term of a paired associate upon being presented with the first is augmented if the subject is allowed to generate meaningful connections between each associate. Rupert argues that this generation effect will fail to occur in at least some extended memory systems. For example, it will fail to occur in a notebook-based system where there are connection sentences between paired associates but where, crucially, these sentences have been entered into the notebook by the experimenter rather than the subject. Rupert does accept that the effect might occur if the subject both creates the meaningful association and records this in the notebook—and this, of course, is far closer to Clark and Chalmers's case of Otto. However, he argues that this is simply a contingent feature of the system. Such differences, Rupert claims, undermine any attempt to regard internal and extended memory systems as forming part of a single explanatory kind.

I think there are several points that can be raised against Rupert's argument. Most obviously, suppose someone's internal, biological memory failed, for whatever reason, to exhibit the generation effect. Every other aspect of his memory was functioning normally. If you ask him facts about the world, he is, if he was aware of those facts, able to reply correctly. If you ask him to describe events from his childhood, he is able to do so. In short, his memory is what we would regard as a perfectly normal one, except for one thing: it fails to exhibit the generation effect. Would we really want to say, in such a case, that he does not really remember? This would be implausible. The generation effect is a peripheral feature of human remembering whose absence, by itself, is nowhere near decisive enough to disqualify a process from counting as one of remembering (Wheeler 2008).

However, my purpose here is not to evaluate Rupert's argument but to identify its guiding presupposition. And this seems to be a more chauvinistic form of functionalism than the thesis of the extended mind can afford to accept. Rupert's argument is based on the idea that a coarse-grained functional profile is not, by itself, decisive in determining the identity conditions of a psychological kind. Fine-grained functional details, of which the generation effect would be one example, are also crucial determinants of these identify conditions.

The latter claim, however, is not one that the thesis of the extended mind can accept. That thesis presupposes a liberal form of functionalism, according to which gross functional role is crucial. Rupert's objections presuppose a far more chauvinistic conception of functionalism, according to which fine-grained functional details are also crucial. To this extent, Rupert's objections are question-begging (Wheeler 2008). Matters would be different if we possessed some independent reason for preferring the chauvinistic version of functionalism presupposed by Rupert. Partly in anticipation of this sort of response, Rupert argues that any psychological kind general enough to subsume both internal and extended memory would be so lacking in detail as to be explanatorily useless. However, this seems merely to beg further questions. If it would, in fact, be implausible to deny that a person who exhibited every feature normally associated with memory-recall except the generation effect was able to remember, then the generation effect does seem to be an accidental rather than a defining feature of memory—which is, of course, precisely what the liberal conception of functionalism entails. And if this is correct, we have no reason for withdrawing the attribution of remembering to the extended system.

The thesis of the extended mind, therefore, is predicated on a liberal conception of functionalism that sees gross functional profile as decisive in determining the type-identity conditions of psychological kinds. Any objection to the thesis that presupposes a more chauvinistic form of functionalism is, therefore, question-begging. However, charges of question-begging can cut both ways. It is one thing to argue that, in the case of memory, the generation effect is a peripheral aspect of memory that is not decisive in deciding whether or not a process counts as one of remembering; it is quite another to argue that there are general reasons for preferring liberal over chauvinistic forms of functionalism. This is so for two reasons. First, perhaps there are other aspects of memory—different from the generation effect—that are more important in qualifying a process as one of remembering; these processes might not be captured within the broadbrush way of identifying functional kinds adopted by liberal approaches. Second, perhaps a liberal conception of functionalism is simply more appropriate to some kinds of cognitive process, whereas a chauvinistic form is more appropriate to others. If, so the dispute between liberal and chauvinistic forms of functionalism would have to be adjudicated on a case-by-case basis. The question, then, is: how do we so adjudicate? On what basis do we decide between the claims of liberal and chauvinistic functionalism? On what criteria do we draw to make such adjudications?

There is, however, a more pressing problem. If the extended mind does indeed rest on a form of liberal functionalism, then, in the eyes of many, this makes it perilously close to being incompatible with the embodied mind. For it is commonly thought, at least by its protagonists, that the latter requires rejection of any liberal form of functionalism (Clark 2008a). Thus, in the previous chapter, we saw how Shapiro understands his embodied mind thesis as being opposed to what he calls ST, the separability thesis—the thesis that minds make no essential demands on bodies and that therefore a humanlike mind could very well exist in a nonhumanlike body. Shapiro understands ST as, in essence, an expression of a liberal form of functionalism. As we have seen, for liberal functionalism, details of the physical implementation of a cognitive process are of only derivative importance: what is crucial is whether or not the relevant functional role is realized. Therefore, if a nonhumanlike body were to realize the functional roles definitive of humanlike cognitive processes, that, and that alone, would be decisive in determining whether the nonhumanlike body possessed a humanlike mind.

However, although Shapiro's embodied account is incompatible with liberal functionalism it is perfectly compatible with a more chauvinistic form. To see why, recall Shapiro's analogy of the submarine instruction manual. What this analogy in fact undermines is not a functionalist account of cognitive processes itself, but a particular—and peculiarly liberal—conception of what this account must look like. A more sophisticated form of functionalism, it might be thought, might accept that functional roles cannot be understood in isolation from the bodily structures that they include and depend on. The relevant submarine instruction manual would, then, look something like this. It contains a series of instructions on how to pilot the submarine, but these make noneliminable reference to features of that submarine. So, an instruction for increasing depth might look something like this: "Pull out the red-colored knob in the column on the far left. Keep this knob out until the blue bulb in the second column from the left starts flashing. Then push it back in." You can neither fully understand nor successfully employ this manual unless you are already in the process of piloting the submarine, or at least physically placed to do so. But, nevertheless, the instruction manual can be regarded as a functionalist program of a certain sort. The manual—the program—remains, and does so independently of the existential fortunes of the submarine; it is just that without the submarine, the program can be neither employed nor properly understood.

The form of functionalism described here is compatible with Shapiro's body centrism, but is not sufficiently abstract to be compatible with the standard arguments for the extended mind. In a nutshell, Shapiro's body centrism can be rendered compatible with a form of functionalism, but only if this form is sufficiently chauvinistic to include explicit reference to bodily structures and mechanisms. And, as we have seen, the thesis of the extended mind presupposes a liberal form of functionalism. Without this, it is vulnerable to the sorts of objections raised by Rupert (2004). Of course, if there could be a more general manual, sufficiently abstract to subsume instructions for submarines and other forms of vehicle, then the rapprochement of embodied mind with extended mind would be back on the table. However, the thesis of the embodied mind is, in effect, that there is no such general-purpose manual.

9   Desiderata for Further Development of the Amalgamated Mind

This chapter has identified two clear imperatives for the further development of the amalgamated mind. First of all, there is the imperative that centers on the issue of functionalism. This is crucial for the amalgamated mind thesis in two different but related ways. First of all, the extended mind's reliance on a liberal form of functionalism can leave it vulnerable to charges of question-begging. Second, and more worryingly, the reliance of the thesis on liberal functionalism seems to make it incompatible with the thesis of the embodied mind, a thesis that can accept functionalism only in its more chauvinistic forms. The first imperative facing the amalgamated mind, therefore, is to resolve these problems.

In the chapters to come, I propose to satisfy this imperative by, insofar as this is possible, taking functionalism out of the equation. Thus, in chapters 7 and 8, I am going to develop an argument for the theses of the embodied mind and the extended mind—and hence for the amalgamated mind—that does not rely on functionalism. This is not to say, of course, that the argument I shall develop is necessarily incompatible with functionalism. However, it does not rely on functionalist assumptions, whether liberal or chauvinistic. Indeed, it provides us with the means to adjudicate, in particular cases, the competing claims of liberal and chauvinistic forms of functionalism. Moreover, since the argument is one that supports both the thesis of the embodied mind and the extended mind, and does so for precisely the same reasons, the issue of the compatibility of the two theses is resolved.

The second imperative facing the amalgamated mind is the provision of an adequate and suitably motivated mark or criterion of the cognitive. This is required for two reasons. First, it is needed to defend the thesis of the extended mind against the charge that the arguments used to support it in fact only support the thesis of the embedded mind (as well as subsidiary concerns pertaining to cognitive bloat, causal-constitutive confusions, etc.). Second, it is needed to defend the thesis of the embodied mind from the (corresponding) charge that the arguments used to support it only support the claim that cognitive processes depend on wider bodily structures and processes rather than being constituted by, or composed of, such structures and processes. That is, it is needed to show that the arguments for the compositional interpretations of the theses of the extended and embodied mind establish no more than the dependence interpretations.

These two requirements are connected in a way that is not obvious but is deeply significant. In the next chapter, I shall provide a mark or criterion of the cognitive of the required sort. This criterion is made up of four conditions, the satisfaction of which, I shall argue, are *sufficient* for a process to count as cognitive. Three of the conditions are relatively unproblematic. The fourth, however, is distinctly tricky. The fourth condition is an *ownership* condition on cognitive processes: any process that is to qualify as cognitive must be owned by some cognitive subject or organism.

There are no cognitive processes without a subject. Developing an adequate account of the conditions under which a subject can *own* its cognitive processes is a deceptively difficult task, one to which much of the second half of this book will be devoted. The project, here, will to be to develop an account of in what the ownership of a cognitive process *consists*. In answering this question, however, I shall, in effect, develop a novel argument for the amalgamated mind. This is an argument that (a) does not depend on functionalism, and (b) unifies the embodied mind and the extended mind under a single guiding principle. If successful, it provides the strongest imaginable support for the amalgamated mind.

Thus, the criterion of the cognitive I am going to develop in the next chapter provides the link between both problems facing the amalgamated mind. The criterion allows us to reject the arguments directed at the thesis of the embodied mind and the thesis of the extended mind taken individually. And satisfying the fourth condition of the criterion—the ownership condition—requires the development of an argument for the amalgamated mind that subsumes both embodied and extended arms of this view—subsumes them in equal measure and for the same reasons. This argument will make it clear why both the embodied mind and the extended mind are essentially versions of the same idea. Thus, if all goes well, the criterion of the cognitive will kill two birds with one dialectical stone.

5   The Mark of the Cognitive

1   Criteria: What Are They Good For?

In what sense, and to what extent, does a science need to understand its subject matter? The answer to this question may seem obvious. Of course a science needs to understand what it is supposed to be investigating. How else could it investigate it? However, matters are not as obvious as they seem. Does physics, for example, require a precise—or even adequate—understanding of what makes something physical in order to proceed? Does biology require a precise definition of what makes something biological? The answer to both seems to be "no." Physics has survived various significant shifts in our understanding of what it is to be physical. And the general idea that biology is the science of living things has learned to deal with the fact that there is no consensus on what makes something living. At most, we might think that an understanding of what it is to be physical or what it is to be biological is something that slowly *emerges* from the progress of the relevant sciences. If so, it is not something that is required in order for each science to conduct its business.

Among cognitive science practitioners one can, I think, discern two types of attitude. On the one hand, there are pragmatists who think that cognitive science is simply in the business of modeling cognitive processes, at varying levels of abstraction. Deeper questions of self-interpretation—what exactly is it that I am doing?—are left to philosophers, and are strictly tangential to the practice of cognitive science itself. The other attitude, more plausibly I think, regards a deepening understanding of the concept of cognition as something built into the cognitive scientific enterprise itself—as something that slowly emerges from the enterprise rather than guides it from the outset. In this, they echo a tradition that sees science not just as an activity concerned with interpreting the world, but also as one that has the possibility of self-interpretation built into it as one of its basic ingredients (Heidegger 1927/1962). But the idea that cognitive science requires a proper understanding of what cognition is before it can set about its legitimate business is one that finds few, if any, defenders.

This chapter will be concerned to develop a criterion of cognition. Very roughly, this is a criterion that tells us when a process counts as a cognitive one. However, this is—emphatically—*not* because I think cognitive science in general needs one in order to be able to conduct its business. Rather, although cognitive science in general does not need a criterion of cognition, the amalgamated mind most certainly does. As we saw in the previous chapter, if the amalgamated mind is to have any genuine substance, then it cannot be allowed to collapse into claims about environmental and bodily embedding or dependence; for these are claims that can be easily assimilated into the old science. But if it is to avoid collapsing into claims of environmental or bodily dependence, the amalgamated mind must be able to make the case that the bodily and environmental exploitation and manipulation that it invokes are genuinely cognitive parts of overall cognitive processes that contain an irreducible neural element. The goal, therefore, is to show that manipulation and exploitation of bodily and environmental structures can satisfy a plausible criterion of the cognitive. If they can do this, then processes of manipulating or exploiting bodily and environmental structures will have every right to be regarded as *genuinely cognitive components of* an overall cognitive process, rather than merely *causal contributors to* an overall cognitive process.

2 Criteria of the Criterion

A mark of the cognitive is a criterion that specifies when a process qualifies as cognitive. A criterion that can do this provides what is known as a *sufficient* condition for a process to count as cognitive. One might also want the criterion to specify when a process does *not* count as cognitive. If it can do this, then it provides what is known as a *necessary* condition for a process to count a cognitive. I am not going to pursue a criterion of this latter sort. The mark of the cognitive I am going to develop and defend in this chapter provides only a sufficient condition for a process to count as cognitive—at least I shall claim no more than this. For reasons that will become clear, this is all the amalgamated mind needs in order to respond to the objections we have identified in the previous chapter. As we shall also see shortly, there is another reason, stemming from the way in which a mark of the cognitive is best motivated and defended.

Given that the mark of the cognitive will provide a sufficient condition for a process to qualify as cognitive, the next question is: how does it do this? It does so by listing a set of conditions such that, if a process were to satisfy them, that would be enough for the process to count as cognitive. The conditions collectively make up a criterion of cognition. If the arguments of the previous chapter are correct, it is clear why the thesis of the *extended mind* requires a criterion of the cognitive: all the recognized objections to the thesis seem to depend, directly or indirectly, on its perceived failure to provide such a criterion. It is also clear why the thesis of the *embodied mind* requires such a criterion: without it, the thesis is vulnerable to the charge that the arguments for it establish only the claim that cognitive processes are dependent on wider bodily structures and processes and not the claim that they are, in part, constituted by such structures and processes. What is not yet clear, however, and even ignoring for the moment questions of its specific content, is precisely what *sort* of thing the criterion should be. In particular, questions can be raised about both the *scope* and *character* of the desired criterion.

Consider, first, the issue of *scope*. The term "cognition" can, in effect, be spelled with a big or small "c." With a big "C," the sense of the term is fairly narrow. In this sense, cognition is routinely opposed to perception (and, of course, sensation). That is, in this sense, cognition is restricted to postperceptual processing. However, there is a broader sense of the term, "cognition" with a little "c," where it is understood to include perceptual processing. Reference to cognition in this chapter, and indeed the rest of the book, should be understood to be reference to cognition in the more general sense: "cognition" with a little "c." And the proposed criterion of "the cognitive" is one that attempts to demarcate items that are cognitive in this broader sense from items that are not.

Consider, now, the issue of the *character* of the criterion. What sort of thing would the mark of the cognitive have to be? Here, two quite distinct projects need to be distinguished. On the one hand, there is the philosophical project of *naturalizing* the mind. If we were engaged in this project, we might take ourselves—intelligibly but, I think, mistakenly—to require a reductive definition of the expression "the cognitive" in terms that are entirely noncognitive (or, initially at least, less than fully cognitive). On the other hand, there is the cognitive-scientific project of understanding how cognitive processes work. This project consists in functional decomposition of these processes into progressively simpler constituents. To engage in this project, we do not require a naturalistic reduction of cognition—in the form of a definition of "cognition" in noncognitive terms. Rather, we simply require a means of demarcating, with a reasonable but not necessarily indefeasible level of precision, those things in which we are interested from those things in which we are not.

I shall propose and defend a criterion of this latter sort. This sort of criterion, I shall argue, is sufficient to defuse the standard objections to the theses of the extended mind and the embodied mind—the theses that together make up the amalgamated mind. The idea underpinning the criterion is that if we want to understand what cognitive processes are, we had better pay close attention to the sorts of things cognitive scientists say are cognitive and then try to identify the general principles—the general conception of cognition—that explains why they say what they say. This is not to say that we must restrict ourselves to the pronounce-ments of cognitive scientists. Cognitive scientists, like the rest of us, can be mistaken, and they can be confused. It is possible that in certain cases, the general conception of cognition we find in cognitive-scientific practice may be incompatible with specific determinations of cognitive status or lack thereof. In part, the purpose of a criterion of the cognitive is to allow us to render consistent the general conception of cognition that is embodied in cognitive-scientific practice with specific judgments about which processes are cognitive. That is, the goal of this process is to render consistent general principles and specific judgments insofar as this is possible. In doing so, as John Rawls puts it in a different but structurally similar context, we *work from both ends* with the goal of achieving *reflective equilibrium* between our specific judgments of cognitive status and the general conception of cognition that underlies those judgments.

Our starting point, however, must be cognitive-scientific practice itself, and the specific judgments, made by cognitive scientists, concerning what processes count as cognitive. Thus, the criterion of the cognitive I propose here will be motivated and defended, in the first instance, by way of a careful examination of cognitive-scientific *practice*.

3   The Criterion

Before we get to the motivation and defense of the criterion, however, let us first look at what the criterion is. I shall argue that when we examine cognitive-scientific practice, what we find is an implicit mark or criterion of the cognitive that looks like this:

A process *P* is a *cognitive* process if:
1. *P* involves *information processing*—the manipulation and transformation of information-bearing structures.

2. This information processing has the *proper function* of *making available* either to the subject or to subsequent processing operations information that was, prior to this processing, unavailable.
3. This information is made available by way of the production, in the subject of *P*, of a *representational* state.
4. *P* is a process that *belongs* to the *subject* of that *representational state*.[1]

Before motivating and defending this criterion, it is necessary to make a few introductory remarks, both in general and about each of its conditions.

General Remarks

The criterion is, as I emphasized earlier, presented only as providing a *sufficient* condition for a process to count as cognitive. If a process satisfies these four conditions, it is a cognitive process. It does *not* follow that if a process does not satisfy these conditions, it is not a cognitive process. There may be other ways in which a process can count as cognitive. However, these potential other ways are not embodied in or recognized by current cognitive-scientific practice, and this, as I have also stressed, is to be the starting point for motivation and defense of the criterion.

Condition (1)

The idea that cognition involves information processing is now commonplace. Indeed, it is a central plank of the conception of cognition embodied in the cognitive science tradition. In its classical form, cognitive science was understood to involve the postulation of internal configurations of an organism or system: configurations that carry information about extrinsic states of affairs. The concept of information employed is, in essence, that elaborated by Claude Shannon (1948), or a close variant thereof. According to Shannon, information consists in relations of conditional probability. On the version championed by Shannon, a receptor *r* carries information about a source *s* only if the probability of *s* given *r* is 1 (cf. Dretske 1981). Other, less sanguine versions associate the carrying of information with an increase in conditional probability, although not necessarily to the value of 1. That is, *r* carries information about *s* only if the probability of *s* given *r* is greater than the probability of *s* given not-*r* (Lloyd 1989).

Whichever explication of the concept of information is employed, the underlying vision of cognition is unaffected. Cognitive processes are understood as a series of transformations performed on information-bearing structures. These transformations will be effected according to certain rules or principles—principles that effectively define the character of the type of cognitive process in question. Shortly, we shall examine one influential example of this general vision.

Condition (2)

The second condition relies heavily on the concept of *proper function*. I shall understand this in what is known as an *etiological* sense championed by Millikan, among others (Millikan 1984, 1993). The proper function of something is what it is *supposed* to do, or what it has been *designed* to do. The proper function of the heart is to pump blood; the proper function of the kidneys is to process waste, and so on. Invoking the idea of proper function in the criterion of cognition is to remind us that the concept of cognition is, in part, a *normative* one. Cognitive processes can function well or badly, properly or improperly; they are defined in terms of what they are *supposed* to do, not what they *actually* do. This distinction between what a cognitive process does and what it is supposed to do can manifest itself in at least four ways:

i. Although the proper function of a cognitive process, *P*, is to make available information that was previously unavailable, it might not fulfill this function in particular cases. Indeed, it might never fulfill this function, owing either to faults in the mechanisms that realize it, or to faults in the mechanisms that are supposed to receive the information it supplies. Similarly, a defective heart that is never able to pump blood is still a heart with the proper function of doing so. And if a heart is connected to arteries that are blocked, then it will not fulfill its proper function.

ii. In addition to performing its proper function, *P* might also do all sorts of things that are not its proper function—because these things do not explain why the mechanism has proliferated and is extant today. Similarly, the heart, in addition to pumping blood, also makes noise and produces wiggly lines on an electrocardiogram. These other causal effects of the heart, however, are not part of its proper function. The reason, very roughly and there is devil in the details, is that hearts that made noise but did not pump blood would not have been selected for; but, conversely, hearts that pumped blood without making noise would have been selected for.

iii. *P* might have the proper function of making information available to a subject or subsequent operations only in the presence of environmental contingency *C*, and *C* may sometimes fail to obtain; in principle, it may never obtain. Similarly, the function of the sperm cell is to fertilize the female egg, but the vast majority of sperm cells fail to fulfill this function, largely owing to inopportune circumstances.

iv. *P* may have the proper function of making information available only in combination with a number—perhaps a vast number—of other processes. In such circumstances, *P*'s fulfilling its proper function is dependent on these other processes fulfilling their proper functions. Similarly, kidneys cannot process waste without being connected up, in the right way, to a circulatory system that produces this waste.

Whether something qualifies as a cognitive process is a matter of what it is supposed to do, and not simply a matter of what it does. Defective cognitive processes are still cognitive processes. This is why the second condition of our criterion invokes the idea of function. However, when the idea of function is applied to cognitive processes, this involves a further distinction that has no real echo in the case of hearts, kidneys, and sperm cells. There are, broadly speaking, two sorts of general function that a cognitive process might have. Both functions involve the making available of information. What distinguishes them is to what they make this information available. Some cognitive processes make information available to the cognitive organisms or cognizing subject. Remembering is a cognitive process that, if successful, makes information available to *me*. So too do perception, reasoning, and so on. However, some cognitive process make information available not to a cognitive organism such as myself, but only to further nonconscious processing operations. For example, on Marr's (1982) theory of vision (discussed earlier, and soon to be discussed again), the transformation of the retinal image into the raw primal sketch makes information available not to the subject of vision (for example, you or me) but only to the subsequent nonconscious processes whose function is to transform the raw primal sketch into the full primal sketch.

The distinction between making information available to a subject and making it available to subsequent processing operations is an important one and, indeed, will play a crucial role in the arguments to be developed in the second half of this book. The distinction corresponds to that between what are known as *personal* and *subpersonal* cognitive processes. Processes that make information available to a subject are personal-level processes, and this is true even *if* they also make information available to subsequent processing operations.[2] However, processes that make information available only to subsequent processing operations are subpersonal cognitive processes. This distinction corresponds to two different ways in which a cognitive process might belong to a representational subject, and will be discussed in more detail later on.

Condition (3)

It is currently fashionable in some quarters to suppose that cognitive science can do away with the idea of representation. I think this fashion is seriously confused, but perhaps that is to be expected when one is dealing with a multiply ambiguous concept such as representation. However, recall that this criterion is presented only as a *sufficient* condition for a process to count as cognitive, and not a *necessary* condition. So, if you believe that cognition does not require representation, that is fine with me—at least for the purposes of the arguments to be developed in this chapter. There are, however, important strategic or dialectical reasons for me to formulate the criterion of cognition in terms of the idea of representation.

First of all, as we shall see, certain objections to the thesis of the extended mind—versions of the differences argument—are based on the assumption that cognition involves representation (indeed, representation of a quite specific sort). To deny this at the outset would, therefore, invite charges of question-begging. Second, the invocation of mental representations has, at least until recently, been a staple of cognitive-scientific theorizing. The denial that representations are required for cognition is still controversial, and in developing my argument for the theses of the extended and embodied mind, I want to rely on as few controversial assumptions as possible. I am going to use the criterion of cognition to argue for the theses of extended and embodied cognition, and so to defend the new science in general. So, in developing the criterion of cognition, I want to give the objector everything he or she could reasonably want. I am going to focus on the most respectable, conservative, even reactionary versions of cognitive-scientific practice it is possible to find, and I am going to defend the criterion of cognition on the basis of this sort of practice. And then I am going to argue that the theses of the extended and embodied mind *still* follow. In other words, the criterion of cognition, I shall argue, has conservative origins—origins that even the most dyed-in-the-wool defender of tradition would have to accept—but radical consequences.

Now that I have explained *why* the criterion of cognition invokes the idea of representation, some further clarifications are required concerning *what* this invocation involves. The third condition takes no stand on whether representation is, ultimately, a *naturalistic* phenomenon. Many suppose that it is possible to supply broadly naturalistic conditions of representation, and that a state will count as representational if, and perhaps only if, it satisfies these conditions. This naturalistic assumption is neither mandated by, nor incompatible with, condition (3).

There are three further distinctions we need to observe in the formulation of condition (3). The first is the distinction between *representational* and *semantically evaluable*; the second is that between *derived* and *nonderived* representation; and the third is that between *personal* and *subpersonal* representations.

(a) *Representational versus semantically evaluable* As I shall use the expression, a state is semantically evaluable if and only if it has *truth conditions*: that is, it is the sort of thing that can be true or false. The notion of a representational state is not coextensive, still less synonymous, with the notion of a *semantically evaluable* state. It would be implausible to suppose that all representational states are semantically evaluable: such states must possess *adequacy conditions*, but they need not possess *truth conditions*. Mental models, or cognitive maps, possess adequacy conditions but not truth conditions (McGinn 1989a,b). That is, mental models or cognitive maps can be accurate or inaccurate, but they cannot be true or false. They cannot be true or false because the concept of truth is essentially bound up—for familiar Davidsonian reasons—with the logical connectives (*not*, *and*, *or*, and variants thereof); and mental models do not relate to these connectives in the same way as sentences. Thus, for example, the negation of a sentence is another *specific* sentence; but to the extent that it makes sense to speak of the negation of a map or model, this can mean nothing more than a distinct, but nonspecific, map or model. Similarly, the disjunction of two sentences is another sentence; but the disjunction of two maps or models is not another map or model. Once we understand the connection between truth and the logical connectives, I take it that this point is incontrovertible, though often oddly neglected. However, nothing much will turn on it in the arguments to follow. But it is perhaps worth emphasizing that the commitment to representational states in condition (3) does not involve commitment to the idea that these representations are sentence-like, and so does not entail commitment to a *language of thought*.

(b) *Derived and nonderived content* The type of representational state invoked in (3) is, in a sense to be clarified shortly, a *nonderived* one. That is, it is a representational state that possesses nonderived *content*. Derived content is content, possessed by a given state, that derives from other representational states of a cognizing subject or from the social conventions that constitute that agent's linguistic milieu. Nonderived content is content that does not so derive. A form of content's being nonderived is not equivalent to its being irreducible or *sui generis*: nonderived content can, for example, "derive" from, and be explained in terms of, the history or information-carrying profile of the state that has it. It is *what* content is derived from that is crucial. Nonderived content is content that is not derived from *other* content; it is not content that is irreducible or *sui generis*.

The existence of nonderived content is controversial. However, there are at least *three* reasons for understanding the representational state invoked in condition (3) as being a state that possesses nonderived content.

First, the claim that nonderived content is central to cognition has been used to attack the thesis of the extended mind. For example, Adams and Aizawa (2001) attack Clark and Chalmers's claim that the sentences in Otto's notebook constitute a subset of his beliefs precisely on the grounds that these sentences possess only derived content. These sentiments are echoed by Fodor (2009). We shall return to this attack later, where I shall argue that it is unsustainable. However, at this stage, I might be regarded as unacceptably slanting discussion in favor of the extended mind were I to allow that the representational states invoked in condition (3) need possess only derived content. Recall that the strategy to be prosecuted in this chapter is to give the objector to the amalgamated mind everything he or she could reasonably request, to develop a criterion of cognition on this basis, and then argue that the theses of the embodied and extended mind still follow. Insisting that the representational states invoked in condition (3) are nonderived is required to give the objector everything he or she could reasonably want.

Second, the strategy I am going to employ in defending the criterion of cognition turns on an examination of cognitive-scientific practice. I shall argue that the criterion can be extracted, in a relatively straightforward way, from this practice. As we shall see, however, the postulation of non-derived representational states (states that possess nonderived content) is a staple of such practice.

Third, there are certain reasonable expectations concerning what a criterion of the cognitive will allow us to do. The goal is, of course, to understand what cognition *is*.[3] And the strategy is to do this by way of the provision of a criterion that allows us to demarcate, with a reliable though not necessarily infallible level of precision, those processes that count as cognitive from those that do not. Derived content, however, is content that derives from the operation of cognitive processes. So to allow that the representational state specified in (3) need be one that possesses only derived content would, it seems, undermine the primary rationale for the criterion.

One final, but important, point of clarification regarding the notion of the "nonderived" is required, and this can best be made with respect to Marr's model of vision we examined earlier. Marr's account begins with the retinal image. Visual processing transforms this successively into the raw primal sketch, full primal sketch, and 2½D representation. Does the content of the full primal sketch derive from that of the raw primal sketch? In one sense, it obviously does. The full primal sketch has the content it has only because the raw primal sketch has the content it has, and this content was transformed by various rules of visual processing. However, this is not the sense of derived presupposed in the condition of nonderived content. If this counted as derived content, then there would be almost no nonderived content in cognitive theorizing. At most, the beginning of processing streams would consist in structures with non-derived content. All structures downstream would possess only derived content.

With this in mind, recall the dialectical situation. I am agreeing to the condition of nonderived content because such content has been used as an objection to the extended mind, and I don't want to be accused of stacking the deck at the outset. However, if we adopt a conception of nonderived content such that it can be possessed only by structures at the very beginning of processing streams, then almost nothing turns out to have nonderived content. But then it becomes unclear, to say the least, how nonderived content can be used as an objection to the extended mind. In other words, those who wish to object to the extended mind on the grounds of nonderived content (e.g., Adams and Aizawa, Fodor) are committed to denying that the content of the full primal sketch is derived simply because it comes from that of the raw primal sketch. And, as I have been at pains to emphasize, I am simply giving the objectors to the extended mind what they ask for. Thus, the relation between the content of two subpersonal states within the same processing stream, one of which causally succeeds the other, cannot be regarded as a relation of derivation in the required sense. If we are to make a case that the content of one of these states is derived, we must look to factors outside the processing stream.[4]

(c) *Personal and subpersonal* The distinction between *derived* and *non-derived* representations is not equivalent to the distinction between *personal* and *subpersonal* states. Personal and subpersonal states can, in principle, have both derived and nonderived content (although the conditions under which the latter would possess derived content would be extremely unusual). More important, for the purposes of this book, is the claim that both personal and subpersonal states can possess nonderived content; they can both be representational in a nonderived sense. This claim is disputed by some, but any disagreement with the position advanced here is likely to be a matter of stipulation rather than substance. Thus, I shall assume that subpersonal states can be representational; but I shall not assume that they are representational *in the same way* that personal states are. I shall assume, equivalently, that subpersonal states can possess a content of sorts; but I shall not assume that it is *the same sort of* content as that possessed by personal states. The dispute concerning whether subpersonal states are representational or possess content almost invariably turns on the issue of whether the (allegedly) representational properties, hence content, possessed by subpersonal states are the same sort of thing as the representational properties or content possessed by personal states. And the denial of the status of representation or content to the former derives from the claim that the two are insufficiently similar. The content of my claim that subpersonal states can be representational is given by the claim that they satisfy broadly naturalistic criteria of representation of a familiar sort. This is compatible with being noncommittal on the issue of whether representation is, in general, a naturalistic phenomenon. If personal-level representation turns out to not be naturalistic, then it remains true that subpersonal representation almost certainly is. The primary reasons for denying naturalistic status to personal-level representation turns on the relation between such representation and consciousness—the failure to naturalistically explain the latter being thought to legislate against the possibility of a naturalistic account of the former (e.g., McGinn 1991). However, since subpersonal states are not conscious, these sorts of considerations have no echo at the level of subpersonal states.

The relevant naturalistic criteria of representation applied to subpersonal representations will almost certainly look something like this: Subpersonal representational states must (i) carry information about the world, (ii) have the function of carrying such information, or the function of allowing the cognizing organism to achieve a given task in virtue of carrying this information, (iii) be capable of misrepresenting the world, (iv) are decouplable from the world, (v) have an appropriate structure that permits combination with other states, and (vi) play an appropriate role in guiding the organism's behavior. One need not, of course, accept all of these conditions; and each condition is susceptible to a variety of interpretations. They are provided merely as the sorts of conditions a naturalistic account of representation will supply. I take no stand on the precise character of these naturalistic conditions for one very simple reason. The strategy I am going to follow is to defend the criterion of the cognitive presented above by way, in the first instance, of a careful examination of cognitive-scientific practice. And the postulation of subpersonal representational states is a staple of traditional cognitive-scientific practice.

Condition (4)

As we shall see, perhaps the most difficult implication of taking the thesis of the amalgamated mind seriously lies in understanding the sense in which cognitive processes *belong* to cognizing subjects or organisms. I am going to argue that cognitive processes can belong to a subject in two different ways, one pertaining to the personal level, the other to the subpersonal level. The personal level, I shall argue, is primary. Cognitive processes occurring at the subpersonal level belong to the subject to the extent that they make an appropriate contribution to cognitive states and processes occurring at the personal level. This idea is straightforward, but surprisingly difficult to render precise. I shall attempt to do so in terms of the concept of *integration*: subpersonal cognitive processes belong to the subject to the extent that they are appropriately integrated into the personal-level states and processes possessed by a representational subject. The key, then, is to provide an account of how a personal-level cognitive process can belong to a representational subject. This is the task of the second half of the book.

I am going to motivate and defend conditions (1)–(3) separately from condition (4). Conditions (1)–(3), I shall argue, can be extracted from examination of various standard models of cognitive-scientific practice. Condition (4) is also implicit in this practice, but the bulk of its defense will be based on more general grounds of plausibility. Defense of (4) will be postponed until the next chapter.

4   Defending the Criterion: Cognitive-Scientific Practice

I shall defend conditions (1)–(3) of the criterion by showing that they can be extracted, in a relatively straightforward manner, from examination of cognitive-scientific practice. The guiding thought is that if we want to identify a mark of the cognitive, then we had better pay close attention to the sorts of processes that cognitive scientists regard as cognitive, and then try to identify the general features of processes of these kinds. However, to avoid the charge that the criterion is motivated by amalgamated mind aforethought, the cognitive-scientific practice in question must be *internalist* cognitive science—and the more typical or paradigmatic the form of internalism the better. In this respect, they simply do not come any more typical and paradigmatic than David Marr's (1982) theory of vision. Although many of the details of this theory are now starting to look decidedly quaint, the general approach instigated by Marr has, as I argued earlier, both dominated and shaped internalist-inspired theorizing in cognitive science.

To recap: for Marr (1982), visual perception begins with the formation of an informationally impoverished retinal image. The function of properly perceptual processing (which is cognitive with a small "c" but not with a large "C") is to transform this retinal image into, successively, the raw primal sketch, the full primal sketch, and then the 2½D sketch—the culmination of properly perceptual processing. At each stage in the operation, one information-bearing structure is transformed into another. The retinal image, reputedly, contains very little information, but it does contain some. The retinal image is made up of a distribution of light-intensity values across the retina. Since the distribution of intensity values is nomically dependent on the way in which light is reflected by the physical structures that the organism is viewing, the image carries some information about these structures. The first stage in visual processing consists in transforming the retinal image into the raw primal sketch. In the raw primal sketch, information about the edges and textures of objects has been added. Application of various grouping principles (e.g., proximity, similarity, common fate, good continuation, closure, and so on) to the raw primal sketch results in the identification of larger structures, boundaries, and regions. This more refined representation is the full primal sketch. And so on.

Abstracting from the details, a very definite picture of visual perception emerges. First of all, perception involves information processing: the transformation of information-bearing structures—condition (1) of the criterion. The retinal image is transformed into the raw primal sketch. Further processing operations then transform this into the full primal sketch, and so on. The result of these transformations is the making available of information, to subsequent processing operations, that was previously unavailable—condition (2). Thus, in the transformation of the retinal image into the raw primal sketch, new information becomes available for subsequent processing—information that was not present in the retinal image. And in the transformation of the raw primal sketch into the full primal sketch, further information becomes available, information that was not available in the raw sketch. The culmination of the perceptual process is the 2½D

sketch. This sketch carries information that is available for further processing operations—the postperceptual operations that result in the formation
of *3D object representations* (which are, in turn, available to play a further
role in belief formation, etc.). The general picture is clear: at each stage in
the operation, it is possible to identify a new structure, one that carries
novel information that is available to subsequent processing operations.
Marr's theory, thus, provides a graphic illustration of condition (2).

At each stage in the operation, we find a new representational item.
The retinal image, though informationally impoverished, does carry some
information about the environment. The goal of visual processing is to
successively transform this into an item sufficiently rich in informational
content to provide the basis of visual perception and postperceptual judgments. Each stage of the process, therefore, culminates in an item that
carries more information about the environment than its predecessor.
Once we leave the retinal image behind, each successive item is *normative*
in at least the following minimal sense: given that the item is instantiated
with the properties it has, the world is *supposed* to be a certain way. With
the retinal image, there is no distinction between the way the world is
and the way it is supposed to be: the retinal image is caused by whatever
causes it. However, the raw primal sketch contains new information—
information contributed by the first stage of perceptual processing. This,
in effect, is the brain's "guess" about the way the world would have to be
in order to have produced the retinal image being processed. As such,
given the "guess," the world is supposed to be a certain way; and if it is
not, the "guess" was mistaken. At each successive stage of processing,
therefore, we find an item that carries information and makes normative
claims on the world. Such items are basic representational states. Moreover, the content they carry as representational states does not derive
from the content of representational states that lie outside the particular
processing stream. That is, whereas the content of the 2½D sketch derives
from that of the full primal sketch, which, in turn, derives from that of
the raw primal sketch, the content involved in the successive transformations that constitute this processing straw does not derive from the
content of representational states that lie outside this stream. This is an
innocuous sense of "derived" that cannot be what is at issue when objectors to the extended mind insist on cognitive processes containing nonderived content (see the earlier discussion of the distinction between
derived and nonderived content). The content embodied in this particular
processing stream is, therefore, *nonderived* content in the sense required
by condition (3).

5   Extending Perception

Conditions (1)–(3) of the proposed criterion of the cognitive can, therefore, be painlessly extracted from an examination of a paradigmatic internalist approach to cognitive-scientific practice. Therefore, these conditions can hardly be accused of being devised for the purposes of advocating the theses of the embodied mind and extended mind. Nevertheless, (1)–(3) can also be extracted, in an equally effortless and straightforward manner, from extended models of cognition.

Let us begin with the extended model of perception I defended in *The Body in Mind* (Rowlands 1999). The basis of this model was a creative reinterpretation of the work of Gibson. Whether you think the resulting account remains sufficiently Gibsonian to merit the epithet (for what it's worth, I do) does not matter for our purposes.

To recap once again: according to Gibson (1966, 1979), the environment is filled with rays of light traveling between the surfaces of objects. At any point, light will converge from all directions. Therefore, at each physical point in the environment, there exists a set of solid visual angles composed of differential light intensities and wavelengths. We can, therefore, imagine an observer as a point surrounded by a sphere that is divided into tiny solid angles. The intensity of light and the mixture of wavelengths vary from one solid angle to another. This spatial pattern of light is the *optic array*. Light carries information because the structure of the optic array is nomically determined by the nature and position of the surfaces from which it has been reflected.

The optic array is an *external information-bearing structure*. It is external in the quite obvious sense that it exists outside the skin of a perceiving organism and is in no way dependent on this organism for its existence. By acting on the optic array, and thus transforming it, the perceiving organism is able to make available to itself information that was, prior to this action, present—at least conditionally—but not immediately available. When an observer moves, the entire optic array is transformed, and such transformations contain information about the layout, shapes, and orientations of objects in the world. The transformation of the array makes available to the organism information that was, prior to the action, present in only a conditional or dispositional form.

Specifically, by effecting transformations in the ambient optic array— by transforming one array into another systematically related array— perceiving organisms can identify and appropriate what Gibson calls the *invariant* information contained in the array. This is information contained not in any one static array as such, but in, and *only* in, the transformation of one optic array into another. In the absence of such transformations, invariant information is present, but only in conditional form: conditionally upon certain types of transformation being systematically related to certain changes in sensory input.

The manipulation of the optic array—the transformation of one optic array into another—is the transformation of one information-bearing structure into another, and thus satisfies condition (1) of the criterion of cognition. The result of this transformation is the making available, either to the organism or to subsequent processing operations, of information—invariant information—that was previously unavailable, and thus satisfies condition (2).

Now we come to the creative reinterpretation of Gibson's theory employed in the extended model of perception developed in *The Body in Mind*. The reinterpretation was based on distinguishing what Gibson said about his theory, or is widely thought to have said about his theory, from what his theory actually requires. Gibson's account of perception is widely thought to be hostile to the postulation of representations and to the concept of representation more generally. Whether or not this widespread perception is correct (I think it is not), the extended model of perception developed in *The Body in Mind* was based on the claim that Gibson's account did not *require* any general hostility to representations (even if Gibson, arguably, thought that it did). Rather, what Gibson's position actually requires is best expressed in terms of two cognate ideas, one epistemological, the other metaphysical.

The *epistemological* idea is that one cannot understand the internal information-processing task facing an organism unless one understands the extent to which the organism is capable of manipulating, exploiting, and transforming relevant information-bearing structures in its environment. The *metaphysical* claim is that visual perception does not start at the retina, but consists, *partly*, in operations that transform ambient information-bearing structures. It is these claims, I argued, that delineate the content of Gibson's work and underwrite its significance, and not any hostility to representation per se (Rowlands 1995, 1999).

The extended model of perception developed in *The Body in Mind* was, therefore, a Gibsonian account purged of any gratuitous hostility toward representations. On this model, the transformation of one optic array into another consists in the manipulation of information-bearing structures. This can be supplemented, when circumstances dictate, with the manipulation of intracranial information-bearing structures. The culmination of processes of this sort is the production, in the subject, of a representational state: the visual recognition that the world is such-and-such (condition 3). And this recognition has been achieved by way of processes—the manipulation and transformation of information-bearing structures—that straddle the boundary of the skin.

The processes described in the extended model of perception developed in *The Body in Mind*, therefore, satisfy conditions (1)–(3) of the criterion or mark of the cognitive. The arguments of *The Body in Mind*, in other words, operate on the basis of a criterion of the cognitive that was never made sufficiently explicit in that work, but was (arguably) there in implicit form. It is the satisfaction of these conditions that, pending satisfaction of condition (4), explain why these processes of manipulation and transformation of external structures should be regarded as cognitive and not as merely extraneous causal accompaniments to the supposedly real, internal processes of cognition. The argument is, emphatically, not that they count as cognitive because they are closely causally coupled with internal cognitive processes. And the argument is not that they count as cognitive because they provide a milieu in which cognitive processes are embedded. Rather, they count as cognitive because, pending satisfaction of condition (4), they conform to the mark or criterion of the cognitive. To the extent that the objections to the idea of extended cognitive processes all turn, in one way or another, on the mark of the cognitive objection, the model of extended perception I described in *The Body in Mind* is, pending satisfaction of condition (4), immune to those objections.

6   Extending Cognition

Consider, now, the extended account of memory I developed in *The Body in Mind*. This account was structured around four principles, two of which are pertinent to our current concerns. These are:

(A) An organism can process information relevant to memory task T through the manipulation of physical structures in its environment (Rowlands 1999, 122).
(B) In certain circumstances, acting on, or manipulating, external structures is a form of information processing (ibid., 123)

In suitably fleshing out these principles we find, I shall argue, an implicit commitment to the criterion of the cognitive advanced above.

Consider our reliance, highlighted by Luria and Vygotsky (1930/1922), on external information-storage structures in the constitution of memory.

The Peruvian *kvinu* officer who employs a system of knots to store information employs his biological memory in a very different way from that of the envoy of a culture in which external forms of information storage have not been invented (Rowlands 1999, 134–136). The latter must rely on biological memory to retain information, and must do so afresh for each item of information he needs to retain. But the *kvinu* officer need deploy his biological memory only in the remembering of the "code" that allows him to tap into the information contained in each knot. Once he does this, a potentially unlimited amount of information becomes available to him through his abilities to manipulate and exploit such external structures.

The knot is an information-bearing structure that exists outside the skin of the subject who deploys it: it is, in this sense, external to the subject. Deployment of knots can take various forms: one can tie them, one can modify them, one can read them, and one can use the information they contain as an aid in the construction of further knots. These are all ways in which the knots can be manipulated or exploited. When one ties a knot, for example, or modifies a knot that one has already tied (in order, for example, to register some change in pertinent information), then one is, I argued, manipulating or transforming an information-bearing structure. Thus, the deployment of knots by the *kvinu* officer satisfies condition (1) of the criterion of the cognitive.

The result of this manipulation or transformation of knots is the making available to the cognitive subject of information that was previously unavailable. Indeed, not only does the knot do this: it is its proper function to do this. We are, of course, dealing with a case of remembering, rather than the transformation, of novel information by a distinct individual. So, the relevant scenario would look something like this. The person who ties the knot would otherwise have forgotten the information that the knot contains, owing to, let us suppose, other demands on his biological memory resources. But when he picks up the knot again—the next day, for example—the information it contains is once again available to him. In this case, the knot has the proper function of making available to the subject information that would have been, without the tying of the knot, unavailable. It thus satisfies condition (2) of the proposed criterion of the cognitive.

The way in which this process of manipulating or exploiting knots makes information available to the subject is in the form of the production in that subject of a representational state: a perception of the knot and subsequent doxastic representations of the informational content contained therein. It is, of course, no part of the thesis of the amalgamated mind to claim that processes entirely external to (i.e., outside the skin of) a cognizing subject can count as cognitive. According to this thesis, cognitive processes are entirely internal or are coupled wholes composed of operations occurring both inside and outside the subject's skin. That is, according to the amalgamated mind, cognitive processes always contain a noneliminable internal element. According to most versions of the amalgamated mind, it is here and only here—in the internal component—that we find representational states that possess nonderived content (but see Rowlands 2006 for an alternative). Manipulation of the knot, an external information-bearing structure, thus makes information available to the subject by way of its production in that subject of representational states that possess nonderived content. Therefore, this manipulation of an external information-bearing structure satisfies condition (3) of the proposed criterion of the cognitive. Note, since this will prove important shortly, that there is nothing in the thesis of the amalgamated mind that requires us to claim that the knots, or any other form of external information-bearing structure, possess non-derived content. The nonderived content need be possessed only by the internal states produced in a subject through its deployment of these sorts of external information-bearing structures.[5]

Therefore, the kinds of manipulation, exploitation, and transformation of external information-bearing structures described for the process of remembering satisfy conditions (1)–(3) of the criterion of the cognitive in precisely the same way as the manipulation of internal information-bearing structures described by Marr for the process of perceiving. Therefore, if (1)–(3) do indeed partly delineate what it is for a process to qualify as cognitive, then with respect to these conditions at least, external operations of the sort invoked by the thesis of the extended mind seem to qualify as cognitive in the same way that classical internal operations qualify as cognitive.

7   The Objections Revisited

This, then, is the strategy that should be, and arguably largely has been, employed by the defenders of the amalgamated mind (understood as the combination of extended mind and embodied mind). Cognitive processes are hybrid ones that straddle both neural processes and wider bodily and environmental processes. Pending satisfaction of condition (4), these hybrid processes satisfy the criterion of cognition advanced above, and therefore count as cognitive. They qualify as cognitive because they (1) involve manipulation or exploitation of information-bearing structures, where this manipulation or exploitation (2) has the function of making information available to a subject or subsequent processing operations, which it does so by way of (3) the production in that subject of a representational state. Because, pending satisfaction of condition (4), they satisfy this criterion, these processes of manipulating or exploiting extracranial structures qualify as cognitive processes.

Their satisfaction of this criterion also makes it clear why there are no purely extracranial cognitive processes. We can divide the thesis of the amalgamated mind into two claims. First, a process of manipulating, transforming, or exploiting an external structure never counts as cognitive unless it is combined with an appropriate internal (i.e., neural) process. Second, once combined in this way, the external process can be regarded as cognitive to the same extent, and for the same reasons as the internal one. The criterion explains both of these claims. The external process on its own never counts as cognitive because cognition, I have assumed of the sake of argument, always involves representational states with non-derived content. This, it is commonly supposed, can only be found on the inside.[6] Cognitive processes always involve the production in a subject of a representational state—for this is how they satisfy condition (3). Therefore, conditions (1)–(3) of the criterion collectively entail that all cognitive processes are purely intracranial or a combination of intra- and extracranial processes. There are, therefore, no purely extracranial cognitive processes. Second, once combined with an appropriate internal process, the external process counts as cognitive because, pending condition (4), it satisfies the criterion of cognition: it consists of (1) manipulation or transformation of information-bearing structures, where this has the proper function of (2) making available to the subject or subsequent processing operations of information that was, prior to this manipulation or transformation, present but not available, which it does by way of (3) the production in the subject of a representational state.

If the arguments developed in the preceding sections are correct, the hybrid processes invoked by the amalgamated mind can satisfy at least the first three conditions of the criterion of the cognitive. To this extent, they qualify as cognitive processes—pending satisfaction of condition (4). However, I have also argued that the other objections to these theses collapse into the mark of the cognitive objection. Thus, there is no reason for thinking that the wider bodily and environmental processes provide merely an external causal scaffolding or milieu within which the real, internal processes of cognition can do their work. The hybrid amalgamations of processes together satisfy conditions (1)–(3) of the mark of the cognitive and, therefore, pending satisfaction of condition (4), qualify as cognitive in their own right.

At this point, any further objections to the thesis of the extended mind tend to coalesce around the role of representation. Condition (3) claims that the information made available to a cognitive subject is done so by way of the production in that subject of a *representational* state. This representational state, I have assumed, must possess *nonderived* content. This renders the criterion—and the thesis of the amalgamated mind predicated upon it—immune to some further objections associated with Adams and Aizawa (2001) and Fodor (2009).

A perceived reliance on derived representations forms the basis of one of one of Fodor's objections to Clark and Chalmers's version of the extended mind:

[I]f something literally and unmetaphorically has content, then either it is mental (part of the mind) or the content is "derived" from something that is mental. "Underived" content (to borrow John Searle's term) is the mark of the mental; underived content is what minds and only minds have.

Items external to the brain, Fodor seems to think, do not possess non-derived intentionality—their content is determined by convention rather than nature. Thus, the sentences in Otto's notebook are not mental items because, while being about something (e.g., the location of the Museum of Modern Art), this aboutness or intentionality is merely derived from the (inner) mental states of Otto, or anyone else who uses the book.

Here, Fodor is reiterating a point made by Adams and Aizawa: "If you have a process that involves no intrinsic content, then the [nonderived content] condition rules that the process is noncognitive" (2010, 70). This is a version of their mark of the cognitive objection. As we have seen, Clark and Chalmers have been widely interpreted as arguing that the sentences in Otto's notebook constitute a subset of his beliefs—and these sentences are, of course, examples of external visuographic storage structures that possess only derived content in the sense introduced earlier. For reasons discussed earlier, I reject Clark and Chalmers's claims that the sentences in Otto's book are to be numbered among his beliefs. However, my own development of an extended account of remembering also accords a central role to external *visuographic* information-bearing structures—of which language is the most familiar and important—in the constitution of memory, and so I might also be thought vulnerable to Adams and Aizawa's objection. However, in fact, when the thesis of the extended mind is properly understood, neither I nor Clark and Chalmers are vulnerable to this objection. So, in the argument to follow, I shall assume that Clark and Chalmers are correct in claiming that the entries in the notebook are among Otto's beliefs. This is an assumption because both Fodor's and Adams and Aizawa's objections are framed in terms of this claim; I make the assumption purely for the sake of the argument to follow and, in particular, to show why these objections do not work.

According to Adams and Aizawa, if a process is to count as cognitive it must involve states that possess nonderived content (2001, 2010). I agree, or at least have made this assumption in advancing my criterion of the cognitive. However, what is puzzling is that they think this provides an objection to the thesis of the extended (or, for that matter, the amalgamated) mind. As I have been at pains to emphasize, the thesis of the extended mind does not claim that extracranial processes—processes of environmental manipulation, exploitation, and transformation, for example—can, *by themselves*, be cognitive. It is not that a cognitive process might ever consist in processes entirely and exclusively outside the skin, or even outside the skull, of a cognizing organism. On the contrary, the thesis of the extended mind claims that cognitive processes are either purely internal or are hybrid processes straddling both internal and external components. They are never purely external. The thesis of the extended mind is a claim about the character of the external or extended processes when, and only when, they are appropriately combined with the relevant sorts of internal processes: the claim is that these external or extended processes are genuinely cognitive components of the overall cognitive process—a process that straddles both internal and external elements. The external processes are not merely noncognitive accompaniments that facilitate the "real" process of cognition that occurs inside the head or in which the "real" process of cognition is causally embedded.

Therefore, the thesis of the extended mind is not only compatible with but actually insists on the claim that the external processes involved in cognition are dependent on internal cognitive processes for their status as cognitive: the former could not count as cognitive without the latter. However, the extended mind thesis is then defined by the claim that once these external processes are appropriately combined with internal cognitive process of the requisite sort, the label "cognitive" can be as legitimately applied to the overall process—the hybrid combination of internal and external processes—as it can to the internal process itself. And this book cashes out this claim in terms of the idea that both the overall process and its external component satisfy the mark or criterion of the cognitive.

Adams and Aizawa object to the thesis of the extended mind on the grounds that Otto's notebook entries possess merely derived content. But, when the thesis of the extended mind is properly understood, this is irrelevant. According to this thesis, the external component of the overall hybrid process would not on its own count as cognitive. And the overall process certainly does contain components that possess nonderived content. Thus, although the sentences in Otto's book do not—we might accept—possess nonderived content, Otto's perceptions of these sentences certainly do (Menary 2006, 2007). So too does his belief that sentence s communicates content c. That is: the sentences in Otto's book may not possess nonderived content, but his perceptual and doxastic apprehensions of them certainly do. This point can also be explained in terms of our criterion of the cognitive. According to condition (3) of the criterion, a cognitive process must make information available to an organism or subsequent processing operations by way of the production, in the cognizing organism, of a representational state. When Otto forms a perceptual or doxastic representation of the entry in his notebook, this condition is satisfied, and it is satisfied irrespective of the status of the notebook entries themselves. Whether they are representations that possess only derived content is completely irrelevant to the thesis of the extended mind.

Otto's perceptual representation—an internal, nonderived, state of Otto—is part of the overall hybrid cognitive process: the overall process in the context of which, and *only* in the context of which, Otto's notebook entries can qualify as beliefs (if we believe the widespread interpretation of Clark and Chalmers's version of the extended mind). However, since this hybrid process clearly does involve states with nonderived content, Adams and Aizawa's requirement that cognition involve nonderived content would seem to be satisfied. Accordingly, it is puzzling why they think they have provided an objection to the thesis of the extended mind.

Matters are even clearer on my process-oriented version of the extended mind that eschews the identification of cognitive states and notebook entries. The process of manipulating an external information-bearing structure does not count as cognitive on its own, but only when it is suitably combined with a relevant internal (i.e., neural) process. However, once it is combined in this way, the external process of manipulation satisfies the mark of the cognitive and hence counts as a genuinely cognitive part of the overall (amalgamated) cognitive process. Since any cognitive process always contains a noneliminable internal component, it will also, for that reason, be made up of states that possess nonderived content. No case has been made for the extended mind to answer.

Of course, matters would be substantially different if Adams and Aizawa could show that *every* part of a cognitive process must involve a state that possesses nonderived content—or, conversely, that the possession of derived content by a state automatically precluded that state from qualifying as cognitive. However, this is an extremely implausible claim, and one that Adams and Aizawa explicitly, and correctly, deny:

Although we have good reasons to believe in the existence of intrinsic content, we have no good reasons to think that cognitive states must consist entirely of intrinsic representations or that cognitive states must be, in their entirety, content bearing. This is why we said that "it is unclear to what extent each cognitive state of each cognitive process must involve non-derived content." (Adams and Aizawa 2010, 69)

They are, of course, entirely correct in this denial. Most cognitive processing does not involve states with nonderived representational content, for the simple reason that most cognitive processing does not involve representational states at all. Rather, with respect to the cognitive operations of a subject, we have compelling reasons to accept a general picture of small islands of representational states in a large sea of nonrepresentational processing. This is equally true whether you are an externalist or internalist.

Thus, to return to our paradigmatically internalist model of visual perception, the transformational operations postulated in Marr's theory of vision do not represent anything. The intermediate states that these operations produce might be regarded as representational; but the processes that produce them are not. For example, the application of principles such as *common fate* and *good continuation* (among others) to the raw primal sketch produces the full primal sketch. However, what does the application, to the raw primal sketch, of common fate or of good continuation represent? What content does it possess? The answers are, respectively: nothing and none. The raw primal sketch possesses content (of a sort), and when the operative principles are applied to it, the full primal sketch can possess content—again of a sort. But operations according to which the one is transformed into the other do not represent anything at all. (This fact is often obscured by the misguided assimilation of cognitive transformations to inference rules. They may be describable in terms of inference rules, but they are not themselves forms of inference.) Cognitive states are representational; but the processes whereby one cognitive state is trans-formed into another are not. Nonetheless, it would be implausible to deny them the status of cognitive: if Marr's transformational operations do not count as cognitive, it is difficult to see what does. And their status as cogni-tive is, of course, preserved in the criterion of the cognitive proposed here. The processes are cognitive because, when they are fulfilling their proper function, and when they are combined with other processes of the requi-site sort, they are capable of yielding representational states, thus making information available to the subject or subsequent processing operations that was previously unavailable. If our criterion of the cognitive is correct, a cognitive process must be the sort of thing that, in isolation or in com-bination with other processes, can be normally capable of yielding a state with nonderived content. But it is simply false to claim that anything that is to count as cognitive must possess nonderived content.

Given Adams and Aizawa's apparent acquiescence on this point, there-fore, it is mystifying why they think they have made any case for the thesis of the extended mind to answer. The sorts of hybrid processes posited by the thesis clearly always involve states that possess nonderived content. The criterion of cognition defended here, in effect, elevates this into a necessity. According to the criterion, the culmination of cognitive process-ing is the making available of information (to an organism or subsequent processing operations) by way of the production, in the cognizing subject, of a representational state. In the case of Otto, this requirement would be satisfied by way of his perceptual or doxastic representations of the con-tents of his notebook. When the thesis of the extended mind is properly understood—as entailing the possibility of hybrid, or amalgamated, rather than purely external cognition—then the nonderived content condition is one that it clearly meets. Therefore, the Adams and Aizawa objection has no substance.

There is, perhaps, one option remaining for Adams and Aizawa. Consider the sorts of hybrid processes postulated by the thesis of the extended mind—processes that straddle both internal and external com-ponents. The crucial difference between components, they might argue, is that the external component *never* contains states with nonderived content. Nonderived content might always be involved in these hybrid processes, but it always attaches to the internal operations and never to the external ones. That is why the external processes are never more than merely accompaniments to cognition.

There are two ways one might respond to this. One can challenge Adams and Aizawa's premise; or one can grant the premise and show that the conclusion still does not follow. I have, in effect, challenged the premise elsewhere (Rowlands 2006). Here, however, for the sake of argument, I propose to grant Adams and Aizawa's premise and argue that their desired conclusion still does not follow.

Imagine an unlikely but certainly conceivable internalist proposal concerning the implementation of the functional roles that constitute cognition. This implementation is hybrid in a manner that parallels the extended mind's conception of (some) cognitive processes. That is, the neural processes involved turn out to be localized in two causally coupled but functionally and structurally isolable regions—brain region R (for representational) and region P (for processing). Region R provides the neural realizations of representational states. Region P supplies the neural basis of transformational operations performed on those states. The two regions are causally coupled in the sort of intimate manner required to underwrite their successful cooperation. Region R contains states with nonderived content; but region P does not, for the simple reason that it does not contain states with *any* sort of representational content.[7]

If the details of the neural implementation turned out as described above, then it would be implausible to deny the transformational operations occurring in region P the status of cognitive, simply because this region contains no states with nonderived representational content. That is, would we want to claim that these transformational processes are merely extraneous causal accompaniments to the "real" process of cognition that occurred in the region R? That would be a strange and deeply implausible form of legislation. And it is, of course, a form of legislation precluded by the criterion of cognition defended here. According to this criterion, the processes are cognitive because, when they are fulfilling their proper function, and when they are combined with other processes of the requisite sort, they are capable of yielding representational states, thus making information available to the subject or subsequent processing operations that was previously unavailable. A cognitive process must be the sort of thing that can, in isolation or in combination with other processes, be normally capable of yielding a state with nonderived content. But it is simply false to claim that *anything* that is to count as cognitive must possess nonderived content. Some processes that are clearly cognitive never possess nonderived content—for the simple reason that they never possess content at all. It is the role in contributing to the production of states that possess nonderived content that is crucial in determining the cognitive status of a process: whether or not it actually is a state that possesses such content is irrelevant.

8 Conclusion

In this chapter, I identified a mark or criterion of the cognitive: a sufficient condition for a process to qualify as cognitive. I defended this criterion by showing that it is presupposed by, and makes sense of and systematizes, paradigmatically internalist models of cognition. I then argued that according to this criterion, hybrid processes of the sort invoked by both the extended mind and the embodied mind qualify as cognitive. However, discussion so far is provisional and incomplete. I have argued only that the hybrid processes in question satisfy the first three conditions of the criterion; I now need to show that they satisfy the fourth.

According to the fourth condition, anything that is to count as a cognitive process must belong to the subject of the representational state adverted to in condition (3). That is, the process must be owned by a cognitive subject. Accordingly, I shall call this the *ownership condition*. Whereas the first three conditions are relatively straightforward, the ownership condition is, I shall argue, deeply problematic. It is not, however, problematic in a way that would provide succor to the internalist opponent of the new science. On the contrary, it is problematic for both parties in equal measures. Satisfying the ownership condition will take us on an extensive exploration of the notion of consciousness, and the ways in which it can be both embodied and extended; that is the subject of the second half of this book. In the next chapter, however, I shall examine the ownership condition and explain why it is so problematic.

6 The Problem of Ownership

1 Ownership and the Problem of Bloat

The previous chapter presented and began the defense of a mark or criterion of the cognitive. The criterion is formulated in terms of *processes*: it provides conditions sufficient for a process to count as cognitive. A state can also qualify as cognitive, but only by way of the contribution it makes to the cognitive processes instantiated in an organism. Thus, the primary role for states in the criterion is as representational items. And the significance of this is that they are produced by cognitive processes and, as representational items, can function to make information available either to the organism or to subsequent processing operations.

According to condition (4) of the criterion, if a process is to qualify as cognitive it must belong to, or be owned by, a subject. There are no subjectless cognitive processes. For our purposes, the notion of a subject can, I think, be understood quite broadly. For example, I do not wish to rule out the possibility that the subject in question might be a group rather than an individual.[1] Nevertheless, even when understood liberally, the appeal to a subject might be thought problematic. In particular, it might be thought to make the criterion *circular*. After all, it is not any sort of subject that can own a cognitive process: the subject in question must be a *cognitive* subject. But a cognitive subject, it seems, is a subject of cognitive processes. Therefore, the criterion presupposes, rather than explains, an understanding of what it is for a process to be cognitive.[2] However, this circularity is only apparent. What this shows, in fact, is that the criterion is *recursive* rather than circular. All I mean by "cognitive subject" is any organism that satisfies conditions (1)–(4) of the criterion. More precisely, S is a cognitive subject if it owns (i.e., is engaged in) information-processing operations (i.e., the manipulation and/or exploitation of information-bearing structures), where these operations have the proper function of making available, either to the subject or to subsequent processing operations instantiated by the subject, information that was hitherto unavailable, and where this proper function is realized by way of the production in the subject of a representational state that possesses nonderived content. That is: a "subject" in the sense required by condition (4) is an individual that owns processes that satisfy conditions (1)–(3). This is *all* that I mean by the term "subject."

The real problem, I think, is not explaining what a cognitive subject is but rather explaining the sense in which such a subject can *own* (or instantiate) its cognitive processes; that is, the problem is one of explaining the sense in which a cognitive process can legitimately *belong* to a subject.[3] I am going to spend much of this chapter convincing you that this is a problem—a deep and difficult problem. More than that, I shall try to convince you that it is a problem for *any* account of cognitive processes—whether orthodox internalist or some other version of the amalgamated mind. The problem of ownership is an equal opportunity problem that does not discriminate between Cartesians and anti-Cartesians. Providing a solution to this problem is the task of the reminder of this book. A useful way to begin examination of the problem is by way of a problem that was, in the previous two chapters, largely sidestepped in a blur of promissory notes: the problem of *cognitive bloat*.

The problem of *cognitive bloat* is usually thought of as one that arises in connection with cognitive states rather than processes. Specifically, the charge of cognitive bloat typically arises in connection with Clark and Chalmers's claim that the entries in Otto's notebook, when appropriately combined with various neural processes undergone by Otto, constitute a subset of his beliefs. If we are willing to allow that the entries in Otto's book can qualify as beliefs, why stop there? Given that Otto makes regular and reliable use of the entries in his telephone directory, for example, why not say that these entries also number among his beliefs? Or given that Otto makes regular and reliable use of the Internet, why not claim that his beliefs include the contents of the World Wide Web?

Given that the version of the extended mind I am defending in this book is formulated in terms of processes, and given that the usual problem of bloat is formulated in terms of states, it might be thought that the version of the extended mind I am defending is immune to the problem of bloat. I would, after all, deny that the entries in Otto's notebook are beliefs. However, the problem is not so easily sidestepped. There is a version of the problem of bloat that applies to cognitive processes rather than states. In this opening section, I am going to identify this version of the problem.

To return to an earlier example, suppose I am using a telescope.[4] The telescope is, let us suppose, a *reflector*, and therefore works by transforming one mirror image into another. Mirror images are information-bearing structures—their properties are systematically determined by way of a mapping function that is itself determined by the specific properties of the mirror and by the properties of the visual environment. Therefore, the operation of the telescope is based on the transformation of information-bearing structures, and so it satisfies condition (1). The processes occurring inside the telescope are, in combination with other processes, of the sort normally capable of yielding a representational state. This is true even when the content of this state is nonderived. Thus, in combination with other processes—ones occurring inside *me*—the processes can yield a representational state—for example, my visual perception of Saturn's rings. This is a representational state with nonderived content. Therefore, the processes occurring inside the telescope satisfy condition (3). And the proper function of the processes occurring inside the telescope is making information available, both to me and to subsequent processing operations within me (for example, processes of inference), of information that was previously unavailable (for example, the current orientation relative to Earth of Saturn's rings), and thus satisfy condition (2). Therefore, the processes occurring inside the telescope satisfy conditions (1)–(3) of our criterion of cognition. If these conditions were sufficient for cognition, then the intratelescopic processes would have to be classified as cognitive.

Relevantly similar examples can be easily generated. How can we rule out, for example, processes occurring inside my calculator, or my computer, from counting as cognitive ones? They (1) seem to involve the transformation of information-bearing structures. They are also (3) the sort of process that, when combined with other processes, can produce representational states. Thus, when combined with operations occurring inside my brain, the processes occurring inside the calculator can produce a representational state in me—for example, when I read off the result of their operations from the screen. And (2) the proper function of these processes is, it seems, to make available to me information—information that I might subsequently employ in further processing operations—where this information was not available prior to the operations of the calculator or computer. Therefore, the processes occurring inside the calculator and computer seem to satisfy conditions (1)–(3), and, without further constraints, would therefore count as cognitive.

This is the problem of *cognitive bloat*, applied to cognitive processes rather than states. At root, the problem is a reflection of the idea that the concept of cognition comprises three separable aspects: *why*, *how*, and, crucially, *who?* The *why* and *how* aspects of cognition concern how cognitive processes do what they are supposed to do and why they do it. The *why* of cognition—its function, broadly understood—is to make previously unavailable information available, either to subsequent processing operations or to the organism itself. They do this—the *how* of cognition—by producing, perhaps in combination with other processes of the same general sort, representational states. And the production of such a state is the result of information-processing operations—the manipulation and transformation of information-bearing structures. The first three conditions of the criterion of the cognitive capture these *why* and *how* aspects of cognition. However, in addition to the *why* and the *how* aspects of cognition, there is also an irreducible *who* aspect. Whatever else is true of cognitive processes, whatever the specific details of their form and function, such processes always belong to someone or something. There are no *subjectless* cognitive processes: they always have an *owner*—an owner that is the subject of states and processes that satisfy conditions (1)–(3) of the criterion. Condition (4)—the ownership condition—attempts to capture this idea. And if we fail to adequately capture this idea, we are immediately faced with the problem of bloat as it applies to cognitive processes: the processes in my telescope and in my computer count as cognitive.

There are, it seems, two ways in which the thesis of the extended mind might try and deal with this problem. The first is to *embrace* its conclusion: the processes occurring in my telescope and my computer are, intuitions notwithstanding, cognitive. The second is to show that the thesis of the extended mind can *avoid* this conclusion: the thesis is not committed to the claim that these processes are cognitive. There is, however, also a more subtle option. The two outlined responses are not, in fact, incompatible. They are not incompatible because the concept of a cognitive process covers two quite different kinds of process. On the one hand, there are *personal*-level cognitive processes. On the other, there are *subpersonal* cognitive processes. This distinction is captured in condition (2) of the criterion. This condition talks disjunctively of cognitive processes that have the function either of making information available to a subject or of making information available to subsequent processing operations, where in both cases such information would have been unavailable without the completion of the relevant cognitive processes. Processes that have the function of making information available to the subject of these processes are personal-level cognitive processes. This is true whether or not they also make information available to subsequent processing operations. Processes that have the function of making information available *only* to subsequent processing operations are subpersonal cognitive processes. The advertised subtle option, therefore, is based on the idea that we might be able to embrace the problem of bloat with respect to subpersonal-level processes, but avoid it with respect to personal-level processes. The possibility of personal-level bloat is far more objectionable than that of subpersonal bloat. Furthermore, embracing the relatively anodyne claim of subpersonal bloat, I shall argue, makes it possible to reject the far more objectionable personal-level version. This is the strategy that I shall pursue in this chapter.

In more detail, I am going to argue for four claims. First, the problem of ownership is just as much of a problem for the Cartesian internalist as it is for the defender of the extended mind. Focusing unduly on the problem of cognitive bloat does have the drawback of masking this fact. However, I shall try and show that the idea that the Cartesian internalist has an unproblematic grip on the conditions under which a cognitive process is owned by a subject, whereas the defender of the amalgamated mind does not, is an idea that cannot be sustained.

Second, I shall argue that the processes occurring in the telescope, computer, or calculator are, when the appropriate conditions are met, subpersonal cognitive processes. The "appropriate" conditions are those identified in the criterion of cognition. However, the processes occurring in the telescope, computer, or calculator are not personal-level cognitive processes. That is, I am going to embrace the problem of bloat for subpersonal cognitive processes, but reject it for personal-level processes. This is not to say that processes occurring in the telescope, computer, or calculator could *never* be personal-level cognitive processes. But the conditions under which this could happen would be very unusual. Typically, and almost always, intratelescopic processes and their ilk are not personal-level cognitive processes.

Third, the distinction between personal and subpersonal cognitive processes forces us to qualify the ownership condition. There are two quite different ways in which a cognitive process might be owned by a subject. Personal-level ownership of a cognitive process is quite different from subpersonal ownership. That is, the conditions that must be met for a subpersonal cognitive process to be owned are quite different from the conditions that must be met for a personal-level cognitive process to be owned. Typically, the ownership of subpersonal cognitive processes is understood in terms of a certain sort of *causal integration*. Subpersonal cognitive processes belong to an individual when they are appropriately integrated into the overall cognitive life of that individual. And when that subject is the possessor of personal-level cognitive processes, this means that the subpersonal processes are appropriately integrated when they make an *appropriate* contribution to the personal-level cognitive processes undergone by the subject. Spelling out the precise nature of the integration required for a subpersonal process to make an "appropriate" contribution to the unfolding of personal-level processes is a fiendishly difficult technical problem. I shall assemble some general arguments for thinking that the ownership of subpersonal processes is best understood in terms of the idea of causal integration. But, I shall not attempt the tricky technical task of providing a criterion that specifies which forms of integration are sufficient for ownership. Instead, my concern is with a more basic problem. This brings us to the fourth, and ultimately most important, task of this chapter.

Fourth, I am going to *begin* the task of explaining what it is for a subject to own his, her, or its personal-level cognitive processes. Beginning the task, in this chapter, involves canvassing and examining an initially plausible account of ownership of personal-level cognitive processes. Despite its initial plausibility, however, this account will ultimately turn out to be merely derivative. Its derivative character, however, is important; and it points us in the direction of the fundamental roots of ownership of personal-level cognitive processes.

Developing this account is, in effect, the subject of the rest of this book. And I have high hopes for it. I shall argue that when properly developed, the theses of the embodied and extended mind—and so also the amalgamated mind, understood as the conjunction of the two—emerge smoothly and elegantly from this account, as obvious, indeed entirely quotidian, consequences.

2   Ownership: Integration versus Containment

If we are to properly understand cognition, we must understand not only its *why* and its *how*, but also its *who* dimension. There are no subjectless cognitive processes. If this is correct, then the ownership condition is one that must be satisfied by intracranial as well as extended cognitive processes. That satisfying the condition appears less problematic for intracranial processes stems from tacit adoption of an untenable model of ownership: the assumption that ownership of a cognitive process by a subject can be explained in terms of its *spatial containment* within the boundaries of that subject. Roughly, the idea is that a cognitive process P belongs to subject S just in case P occurs *inside* S. This criterion of ownership is, I shall argue, indefensible. Indeed, I doubt that spatial containment is a plausible criterion of ownership for *any* of the primary bodily processes we undergo; *a fortiori* it is not true of cognitive processes.

To see this, consider, as an example of a noncognitive biological process, *digestion.*[5] It may seem obvious that what makes a digestive process mine, and not anyone else's, is the fact that it occurs inside of me and not anyone else. This claim, however, should be resisted: spatial containment is only a fallible guide to the ownership of digestive processes. For a digestive process to be mine, it is neither necessary nor sufficient that it occur inside my body. Consider, first, the issue of *necessity*. Imagine a case whereby one's digestive processes become *externalized*. Suppose, for example, one cannot produce enough of the relevant enzymes in one's digestive tract. The solution, drastic and implausible, but nonetheless a solution, is to reroute one's tract into an external device where the relevant enzymes are added, before routing the tract back into one's body where it finishes its work in the usual way. The most natural way of understanding this scenario is, I think, as a case where *my* digestive processes pass outside my body and receive the required external aid. The processes do not stop being mine just because they are, for a time, located outside my body. We shall examine the intuitions underlying this claim momentarily.

If this is correct, then the specific character of the external device is largely irrelevant—as long as it permits this proper function to be realized. Suppose, for example, that the external device were the body of someone else. That is, suppose my digestive tract were temporarily rerouted through the tract of someone else. We will suppose that the food contents of each tract are (somehow!) kept separate, but that the coupling allows the other person's digestive enzymes to pass over into my tract, thus aiding in the digestion of food that I ingested. Afterward, my tract passes back into my body where it culminates in the usual manner. This would appear to be a case where *my* digestive processes are spatially located inside someone else's body, and indeed make use of someone else's digestive enzymes. We can make the same points about *sufficiency*. If, for example, the position were reversed, and someone's digestive tract rerouted through mine, then a process of digestion would, temporarily, be taking place inside my body: but this digestive process would not be mine.

Underlying both the lack of necessity and sufficiency are two related intuitions. First, a digestive process is defined by way of its proper function: breaking down ingested food and releasing energy for subsequent respiratory processes. Second, a digestive process is mine if it fulfills this proper function with respect to me: it is *my* food that is being broken down, and energy is being released for *my* respiratory processes. Digestive processes are defined by way of the proper functions, and a digestive process is mine if it fulfills its function with respect to me. If this is correct, then the connection between ownership and location of a digestive process is merely contingent. The ownership of digestive processes seems to be determined not by spatial containment but by a kind of *integration*. For a digestive process to be mine, it is necessary and sufficient for it to be integrated into my other biological processes in the right way. It is integrated into my *ingestive* processes to the extent that it consists in the breaking down of food that I have taken in. And it is integrated into my other *respiratory* processes to the extent that it releases energy that enables these processes to continue. The criterion of appropriate integration is determined by proper function: a digestive process is appropriately integrated into my other biological processes when it is fulfilling its proper function with respect to *those* processes.

This, I think, provides the right model for understanding ownership of subpersonal cognitive processes. The failure of spatial containment as a criterion of ownership of subpersonal cognitive processes follows from a general commitment to *functionalism*—the idea that a cognitive process is defined by what it does.[6] Just as details of physical implementation are not decisive in determining the identity conditions of psychological kinds, neither, and for the same reason, are details of physical location decisive in determining ownership of instances of those kinds. Once you accept functionalism, you cannot cling to a conception of cognitive ownership based on spatial containment. Where the process is—that is relevant only to the extent that it impinges on what the process does (and, crucially, with respect to whom it does it).

Rather than spatial containment, the ownership of subpersonal cognitive processes is more plausibly understood in terms of the essentially functionalist idea of *integration*. Ownership of a subpersonal cognitive process is to be understood in terms of the function of that process and, crucially, with respect to *whom* it fulfills that function. Digestion is a functional process, and crucial in determining ownership of a digestive process is the individual with respect to whom it fulfills this function. Similarly, the most plausible way of understanding the ownership of subpersonal cognitive processes is in terms of the idea of functional integration. Crucial in determining ownership will be the individual with respect to whom a given subpersonal cognitive process fulfills its (proper) function, rather than the individual in which the process is spatially contained.

This sort of claim is, in fact, a familiar one, and has been the subject of well-known thought experiments in recent decades. With regard to the issue of necessity—whether it is *necessary* for a cognitive process to be mine that it occurs inside my body—there are various thought experiments that involve my mental life being somehow taken outside my body (brain transplants, memory downloads, etc.). With regard to the issue of sufficiency—whether it is *sufficient* for a cognitive process to be mine that it occurs inside my body, we find well-known variations on the "alien transplant scenario." Suppose, for example, I am abducted by aliens who modify the organization of a certain part of my brain. The function of this modification, let us suppose, is to cause me to undergo various alien thought-transitions—alien, now, not in the sense of being put there by aliens but in the sense of being completely unconnected with the rest of my psychological life. This part of my brain is activated whenever the aliens flip the relevant switch on their mother ship. The processes occurring in this part of my brain are spatially contained within me, and in one clear sense they are, of course, *my* brain processes: that is, they are brain processes, and they occur in my brain. But, in another equally clear sense, these alien thought-transitions are *not* mine. They are not mine because they are not appropriately integrated into the rest of my psychological life. Spelling out what counts as "appropriate integration" is, of course, going to be the tricky part—but, I strongly suspect, tricky in the sense of fiddly and technical rather than intractable. If the cognitive processes in question are subpersonal ones, then it is plausible to suppose that we can spell out the relevant notion of integration in causal terms. But if the cognitive processes are personal ones, it is likely that our account will have to incorporate concepts of rational consistency and coherence. But either way, what we are talking about is a certain sort of integration into the psychological life of the subject. It is in this sort of *integration* that we are going to find the roots of the idea of ownership and not in the idea of spatial containment within the body of a cognizing organism. And the idea of integration is nothing more than the general functionalist idea that ownership of a cognitive process is determined by the place of that process in a causal-*cum*-normative network of related cognitive processes.

It is condition (2) of the criterion of the cognitive that attempts to capture this idea. According to this, the proper function of a cognitive process is to make available, either to an individual or to subsequent processing operations performed by that individual, information that was, prior to the process, merely present but not available. The difference between a personal and a subpersonal cognitive process is determined by whether the process makes information available to an individual or *only* to subsequent processing operations: if the latter, then the process is a subpersonal one. This, of course, does *not* solve the problem of ownership, but merely pushes it back a step. Now we have to work out in virtue of what the subsequent processing operations belong to one individual rather than another. That is, the question of ownership now arises for *these* processes. (That, of course, is why the ownership condition is a separate, additional condition.) What it does do, however, is give us a way of thinking about the question of ownership for subpersonal processes. According to the criterion, such processes belong to an individual when they have a proper function of making information available to the processing operations performed by that individual (but not to the individual itself). This is an expression of the general functionalist idea that a cognitive process belongs to an individual when it fulfills its proper function with respect to that individual.

3   Integration: Personal and Subpersonal

In the case of cognitive processes, specification of the appropriate sort of integration is, notoriously, complicated by the possibility of a distinction that has no real echo in the case of biological processes such as digestion: the distinction between personal and subpersonal cognitive processes. In the case of digestive processes, it is undoubtedly possible to draw *a* distinction between personal and subpersonal processes. But this amounts to nothing more than the distinction between the digestive process as a whole, and its constituent parts. Digestion, as a whole, is something the organism does. The various components of digestion—peristalsis, the release of enzymes, and so on—are processes performed by subsystems of the organism. This is a legitimate distinction, although it may be difficult to apply with precision in particular cases. However, it is not the same as the personal–subpersonal distinction as this is applied to cognitive processes.

With respect to cognitive processes, the personal–subpersonal distinction is often understood as one between processes that are conscious, or under the conscious control of the subject, and those that are not. To a considerable extent, this tracks the distinction between processes performed by the organism and those performed by its subsystems. However, the congruence of the two distinctions is not perfect. Neither is it always entirely clear how the distinction applies in particular cases. For example, our ability to keep track of the visual world is facilitated by the presence of a low-level mechanism that automatically directs our attention to visual transients. This mechanism is not subject to our conscious control. However, the performance of its proper function does not seem restricted to any particular bodily subsystem. Saccadic eye movements are one of its most obvious effects. However, these effects can also involve gross movements of the eyes, face, head, and neck. Tracking visual transients often seems to be something that *we* do, as opposed to being something done by any particular bodily part or structure.

Condition (2) of the criterion of cognition attempts to capture the distinction between personal and subpersonal cognitive processes in a somewhat different, though compatible, way. Personal-level cognitive processes are ones whose proper function is to make information available to a subject. Subpersonal cognitive processes are ones whose function is to make information available *only* to subsequent processing operations.

The locution "personal" should not be taken too literally. There is no requirement that the subject or owner of cognitive processes be a *person* in anything like the sense sometimes countenanced by philosophers: for example, an agent capable of both reflecting on and morally evaluating its mental states and actions. Organisms that are not regarded as persons in this sense—or related senses—can be persons in the sense invoked in the personal–subpersonal distinction. In the sense employed in this distinction, there is an internal connection between something's being a person and something's owning cognitive processes: a person just *is* the owner of cognitive processes. And, clearly, this sense of person is far wider than common philosophical uses. Indeed, I have argued elsewhere (Rowlands 2006, 140–143) that there is not *one* personal–subpersonal distinction, but many such distinctions. The distinctions are relative and coreferring: what counts as a personal at one level of description can be subpersonal relative to another, and vice versa. Descriptions of the operations of mechanisms, relative to those of the submechanisms that make them up, can count as personal-level descriptions in some explanatory contexts.

The distinction between personal and subpersonal levels of description is, therefore, not as unproblematic as is sometimes thought. However, when the personal level corresponds to something like what philosophers have in mind when they talk about persons—for example, rational agents capable of evaluating their goals and actions—then it is typical to find attempts to spell out the idea of integration in terms of rational consistency and coherence. The alien thought-transitions described earlier are not integrated into the person's psychology because they are not rationally or logically consistent with the rest of that person's psychological life. I shall,

shortly, cast doubt on the idea that the whole story concerning the ownership of cognitive processes can be understood in terms of this sort of integration. When the issue of ownership is properly understood, these sorts
of integrationist attempts to understand it, I think, are necessarily incomplete. The attempts are, nonetheless, typical. At levels below this, where
we are not dealing with an agent toward which this *intentional stance*
(Dennett 1987) is appropriate, then issues of rational consistency and
coherence do not arise (although issues of normativity obviously still can).
Then the idea of integration will be spelled out in causal terms: being
integrated into a subject's psychological life is a matter of standing in the
right sorts of causal relations to the processes and states that realize this
psychological life.

However, although the personal and subpersonal levels are undoubtedly
distinct, and although the concept of integration appropriate to each is
quite different (at least when the personal level approximately converges
on traditional conceptions of the person), there is a clear sense in which
the personal level is more basic. Obviously, this sense of "basic" is not an
ontic one. Ontically, there is a personal level only because there are subpersonal mechanisms performing subpersonal processes. Without that,
there could be no such thing as a person and no such thing as personal-
level processes such as thinking, remembering, reasoning, and perceiving.
However, the personal level is basic in another sense: if there were no
personal level, there would be no reason for thinking that there are any
subpersonal *cognitive* processes going on.

This claim may seem controversial, but any controversy quickly dissi-
pates when we recall just how broadly I am using the notion of a "person."
"Person," in this context, approximates to "organism capable of detecting
changes in its environment and modifying its behavior accordingly." The
idea of the cognitive has its home in the context of organisms of this sort.
We are organisms of this sort, but so are many other things. So, there is
nothing in this claim that entails that only humans or higher mammals
are capable of cognition. On the contrary, the claim is simply that any
process that is to qualify a cognitive must belong to an organism of this
sort. This, of course, is the import of the ownership condition. If a process
did not belong to an organism of this sort, then there would be no reason
for regarding it as cognitive. We might be able to describe the process in
information-theoretic, and even information-processing, terms. But unless
they ultimately belonged to an organism capable of detecting changes in
its environment and modifying its behavior accordingly, there would be
no reason for regarding these processes as cognitive rather than as *merely*

information-theoretic or information-processing operations. For an organism that was not capable of doing this, there would be no reason to regard the processes occurring in it as any different in kind from, say, digestion.

Indeed, we can make a stronger claim. Not only must a process belong to an organism in order to qualify as cognitive, it must, at some point, and perhaps in combination with many other processes of a similar sort, make some contribution to the ability of the organism to detect changes in its environment and modify its behavior on the basis of this. We can make this stronger claim because this is precisely what the idea of "belonging" amounts to in this context. That is, a subpersonal cognitive process belongs to an organism when it makes some appropriate contribution to the organism's detection of the environment and/or subsequent behavior modification. These are personal-level abilities—something that the organism does *in virtue of* its various subsystems rather than something that can be attributed to the subsystems themselves. Therefore, ultimately, a subpersonal process will count as cognitive because, at some point, and, perhaps in combination with many other subpersonal processes that are also cognitive, it makes some contribution to the personal-level cognitive life of the subject. Of course, specifying the precise nature of this contribution in the form of necessary and sufficient (or even merely sufficient) conditions for a subpersonal process to be integrated into the personal-level cognitive life of a subject is no easy matter (to say the least). There is, however, every reason for supposing that it can be done if we assume, as it seems we must assume, that personal-level cognitive processes supervene on subpersonal cognitive processes.

If this is correct, however, it leaves us with another problem. If the strategy is to explain the ownership of subpersonal cognitive processes in terms of the ownership of personal-level cognitive processes, then we must now supply an account of ownership for the latter. It is to this task that we now turn.

4 Ownership: Criteriological versus Constitutive Problems

An account of ownership might take one of two forms. Both are, in their own way, legitimate. The first attempts to provide a criterion of ownership: a set of conditions necessary and sufficient (or perhaps just sufficient) for a personal-level cognitive process to be owned by a subject. We can call this, for obvious reasons, the *criteriological* approach. I shall be concerned, however, with a distinct project. The question I am looking to address is this: what *constitutes* ownership of cognitive processes? The criteriological question is one of specifying the conditions under which a cognitive process can be owned by a subject. The *constitutive* question, on the other hand, is one of explaining what the ownership of such processes consists in.

Typically, attempts to answer the criteriological question appeal to norms of logical consistency and rational coherence. Roughly, a personal-level cognitive state or process belongs to a subject to the extent that it is rationally or logically integrated into the psychological life of that subject. Even understood as attempts to answer the criteriological problem, these attempts are problematic. In particular, they suffer from a type of *doppel-gänger* objection. It seems metaphysically possible for there to exist two distinct individuals that are psychological duplicates.[7] If so, considerations of rational or logical consistency on their own cannot suffice to answer questions of ownership for a given psychological state or process: these considerations would license ownership equally to both individuals. This is not, it is important to realize, an epistemic problem. That is, it is not a problem about how you *ascertain* to which individual a given process belongs. Rather, it is a metaphysical problem: a problem of identifying in virtue of what a given process belongs to one subject rather than another. The worry is that considerations of logical or rational consistency by them-selves supply no fact of the matter that license attribution of a psychologi-cal state or process to one individual rather than another. If the possibility of two psychological duplicates is indeed a genuine metaphysical possibil-ity, then it seems we are going to have to factor in some further consider-ations. Spatial considerations are obvious ones—but we have already seen the problems in thinking of ownership in terms of spatial containment. Causal considerations are also obvious contenders. But this raises further formidable problems—such as how to appropriately combine consi-derations pertaining to the space of reasons with those of the space of causes, determining priority principles when these conflict, and how to respond when the rather nasty problem of deviant causal chains rears its ugly head.

I should emphasize that I am not claiming that these problems are insurmountable. Some may fancy their chances here; personally, I don't. My point, however, is that even if these problems can be eliminated in a way that everyone would accept, we have still made no headway on a more basic problem. The integrationist approach to explaining the ownership of cognitive processes turns on identifying what we can regard as a fixed frame of reference. Bluntly put, we need to know *what* is to be integrated into *what*. We have certain psychological items, for which there is a question of their ownership. We seek to answer this question by appealing to their logical or rational integration into the psychological life of a subject. But this strategy will work only if the question of ownership of that psychological life has already been answered. That is, in order for the integrationist to even proceed, let alone succeed, we need to be able to identify something that can be regarded as unproblematically belonging to the subject, and then work out the conditions under which its cognitive processes can be legitimately regarded as integrated into this. This is what I mean by a fixed frame of reference: items for which the question of ownership is unproblematic. Historically, of course, this allegedly unproblematic fixed frame of reference has been provided by a specification of the *inputs* and *outputs* for an organism.

We have already seen this general strategy at work in our earlier discussion of digestion. There, I suggested that a digestive process qualifies as mine if and only if its function is to break down food that I have ingested, and release resulting energy to power respiratory processes that are mine. Here, ingestion provides the input to digestion, and respiration provides the output. This strategy is entirely typical. However, it is going to work only if the question of ownership for ingestive and respiratory processes is unproblematic or has already been settled. If, however, there is a question of ownership for such processes, then we cannot hope to explain the ownership of digestive processes in terms of them until we have settled this question.

In the same sort of way, the strategy that tries to explain ownership of cognitive processes in terms of the idea of integration is going to identify a fixed frame of reference—for which there is no question of ownership—in terms of which the integration of cognitive processes can be effected. Traditionally, this frame of reference has been supplied by the input, in the form of sensation or perception, and the output, in the form of action or motor response. However, this strategy will work only if the question of the ownership of these items is unproblematic. However, the question of ownership arises for these sorts of process too. The idea that the ownership of input and output for an organism is unproblematic does not survive the demise of the attempt to understand ownership in terms of spatial containment. The broadly functionalist account of ownership that replaces the spatial criterion, and underwrites the idea that ownership is a matter of appropriate integration, has one obvious but unavoidable consequence. It is not simply that cognitive processes must be appropriately integrated into input and output in order to be owned by a subject. Just as fundamentally, input and output must be integrated into cognitive processes in order to be owned by a subject. Therefore, any attempt to employ the integrationist approach in answering the question of ownership simply begs the question of ownership for sensation and action.

If this is correct, then it makes the most sense to regard the integrationist attempt as attempting to answer a criteriological problem: given the assumption of a fixed frame of reference—the existence of states or processes for which the question of ownership is unproblematic—what are the conditions necessary and/or sufficient for a cognitive process to be integrated into this framework? This question is perfectly legitimate, but it raises an even more basic question that the integrationist approach cannot answer: what does an organism's ownership of its cognitive processes consist in? This question does not assume a fixed frame of reference and then try to integrate into this, but, instead, tries to understand what it is for an organism to own both its cognitive processes and the inputs and outputs to these processes. The question of what it is for an organism to own its cognitive processes cannot be separated from the question of what it is to own its detection of the environment, and what it is to own its subsequent behavioral responses. To answer the constitutive question is to answer all three of these questions.

The rest of the book will focus on the constitutive question. It would, of course, be nice to solve the various criteriological problems too. However, not only would this require a book in itself, but doing so is not necessary for the defense of the amalgamated mind to be developed here. Once we see how to solve the constitutive problem, I shall argue, the theses of the embodied and the extended mind will emerge as natural—indeed obvious—consequences, in much the same way that the thesis of the extended mind emerged from liberal functionalism. Both theses, I shall try to show, are straightforward implications of our *ownership* of cognitive processes, when this is properly understood. Showing this is the principal task of the rest of this book.

5 Ownership and Agency

To recap: the story so far is a rather winding one, and looks something like this. According to condition (2) of our criterion of cognition, a cognitive process has the proper function of making previously unavailable information available. However, it can do this in two ways: by making information available to the *subject*, or by making this information available to *subpersonal operations*. In the latter case, however, this simply postpones the question of ownership: what makes *these* processes belong to *that* subject? As we have seen, spatial containment does not provide a realistic criterion of ownership. These subpersonal processes belong to a subject only to the extent that they are themselves appropriately integrated into the subject. And they will be thus integrated only if they, eventually, make a difference to processes to which the subject has conscious access and over which it has conscious control. A subpersonal process is *integrated* into a subject to the extent that it, together with perhaps many other subpersonal cognitive processes, will ultimately have an impact on consciously accessible, personal-level cognitive processes. The qualification *together with perhaps many other subpersonal processes* is not insignificant. Many subpersonal processes, taken in isolation, need have no impact whatsoever on consciously accessible, personal-level cognitive processes: either because they are transient or because they are otherwise insignificant. However, in combination with other processes at the same level, subpersonal cognitive operations must reflect representational transitions that occur at the conscious level to the extent that the whole system of conscious and unconscious states and processes must form an at least relatively coherent whole. Once we fall below a certain threshold level of coherence, then we shall encounter, at the conscious level, certain thought- and attitude-transitions that we regard as alien.

If this is correct, then we should regard ownership of subpersonal cognitive processes as derivative upon the ownership of personal cognitive processes. Ownership of the former can be understood in terms of integration. But this project will work only if we have solved the problem of ownership for personal-level cognitive processes. The project we need to undertake is that of understanding the phenomenon of ownership at the personal level. And this I am going to understand as a constitutive rather than a criteriological project.

With respect to the constitutive project, a useful place to start is provided by the observation that, at the personal level, cognitive processes are, fundamentally, things we *do*: they are *activities*. Therefore, we might plausibly try to understand ownership of personal-level cognitive processes along the lines of ownership of activities in general. And, in general, we *own* our activities precisely because, and to the extent, that we *do* them. So, it seems we need to consider two questions:

1. If personal-level cognitive processes are activities, what sorts of activities are they?
2. In what sense do we perform these activities?

Of course, in one sense, to each different type of cognitive process there corresponds a different sort of activity: the activity of thinking is different from the activity of perceiving, which in turn is different from the activity of remembering, and so on. Nevertheless, this does not rule out the possibility that there is a more general activity-type that can subsume all personal-level cognitive processes.[8] I shall argue that there is. If this is correct, then understanding the sense in which we do or perform personal-level cognitive processes is a matter of understanding the sense in which we engage in this sort of activity. Both these questions are the subject of the rest of this book. Here, I simply want to provide a preparatory analysis of what it is to do or perform—and thereby to own—activities in general.

Suppose I am building a house, and am doing this on my own. In what sense, if any, might I be the *owner* of this activity? To the extent this question means anything, it is equivalent to the question: in what sense is it *me* and not anyone else who is *doing* the building? Ownership of an activity reduces to being the person who is engaged in it. I own an activity when I am the *author* of it.

However, this raises as many questions as it answers. To be the author of an activity—to be the person engaged in it—entails having authority over that activity. I have, intuitively, a certain sort of authority over my building activities, an authority that I do not have over, for example, my falling off the roof. I am the author of the former, but the victim of the latter. But what, precisely, does this intuitive sense of authority amount to?

It is common to suppose that my ownership of my activities can be explained in terms of my *intentions* (and associated intentional states—beliefs, desires, etc.). I am the author of the activity of building the house because I have the intention to build the house. And the various activities that go into this overall activity can similarly be explained in terms of my intentions to perform the necessary components of the overall activity of building the house. Conversely, I am the victim of my tumble from the roof because this was not the result of my intentions.

The appeal to intentions, however, will not help with the problem I have in mind: the appeal would only push that problem back a step. We need also to understand what constitutes ownership of intentions and other relevant intentional states. The problem of ownership in this regard can manifest itself in several different ways. Here is one that is particularly useful for our purposes: the problem of ownership manifests itself by way of a distinction between what we might call *practical* and *epistemic* authority. Each of these, I think, shades by degrees into the other; but the absence of a firm distinction is, of course, not the absence of a distinction. Since I am, *ex hypothesi*, the only person on-site, there is a clear sense in which I, and I alone, am doing the building. However, in building the house, I am using bricks and tiles made by someone else, wood supplied by someone else, tools manufactured by someone else, and so on. So, in what sense, and to what extent, is it I who am doing the building and not these people implicated in the overall process? The appeal to intentions will not help us with this question, for that appeal merely begs the question of how to distinguish those parts of the process with respect to which I do have intentions from those parts with respect to which I do not.

The sense in which I am doing the building, one might think, reduces to the sense in which I have *authority* over the process and the product. However, there are two different sorts of authority involved here. To see this, consider one part of the overall process: the laying of bricks. There are certain parts of this process over which I have *epistemic* authority. I am, of course, capable of identifying individual bricks—distinguishing one brick from another, and where necessary reidentifying individual bricks. I am, in short, acquainted with the bricks in all relevant and necessary ways. I can also, let us suppose, recognize the characteristics of good mortar work—I know the optimal amount of cement to put on each joint; I know, given the ambient air temperature, how much water should ideally be present in the cement; and so on. I know these things, and so a failure to satisfy them is a failure on my part—a failure of my *epistemic responsibility*.

Epistemic responsibility can be distinguished, at least in ideal cases, from *practical responsibility*. As a way of fleshing out what would be an ideal case, consider a situation where I can be reasonably be expected to have no knowledge of the internal constitution or properties of individual bricks. I am, let us suppose, in a foreign country, where I don't speak the language; there is only one manufacturer of bricks, and he is notoriously tight-lipped about the materials he uses in his bricks and the nature of the manufacturing process. In choosing to proceed with the bricks, I am *practically* responsible for them—I could have instead abandoned building, for example. However, in knowing essentially nothing about their internal constitution, I am not epistemically responsible for each brick. In such circumstances, we can (almost) neatly divide my authority over the brick-laying process into my *practical* authority over the bricks, and my *epistemic* authority over how each brick is laid. (I say "almost" because, of course, precisely the same issues that arose in connection with the bricks will also arise in connection with the cement I use to join them, etc.)

In reality, of course, matters will almost certainly be conceptually a lot messier. Epistemic responsibility shades by degrees into practical responsibility. In more realistic situations, there are certain other facets of the building process concerning which I may have my suspicions, but cannot really be sure. I may know nothing about the internal constitution of bricks. But I do know that factory A has a reputation for making good bricks, while factory B has a reputation for making cheaper but more questionable bricks. My decision to employ shoddy bricks from factory B then may be a partial failure of epistemic responsibility. But it may also be offset by other constraints—notably financial constraints, and/or the unavailability of bricks from factory A. However, crucially, what I am unable to do is identify the internal constitution of each brick in the way that I can identify the characteristics of good mortar work. So, although my employment of bricks of a certain sort may have epistemic aspects, it is largely a matter over which I have practical authority, but not epistemic authority.

So, subject to the vicissitudes of real-world messiness, we can distinguish practical authority and epistemic authority. Each of these senses of authority corresponds to, indeed coincides with, a sense of *responsibility*. My responsibility for the process and the product divides into my epistemic responsibility over certain parts of the construction, and my practical authority over the rest. But, one might argue, *pure* practical authority is little real authority at all. If the house fell down because of the inferior quality of the bricks, and if I were in a situation where I couldn't be expected to know this, then the house's demise, we would probably want to say, *was not really my fault*. If, on the other hand, it fell down because of shoddy pointing work on my part, then it would be my fault. I may be said to *own* certain parts of the building process, and certain parts of the result of the process, but not others. And this is equivalent to saying that I am responsible—*epistemically* responsible—for certain parts of the process and product, but not others.

For reasons that will become clear, I do not want to advance epistemic authority as a criterion of ownership of personal-level cognitive processes. What the concept of epistemic authority does provide us with, however, is a tolerably reliable way of distinguishing personal-level cognitive processes that we own from subpersonal processes that we also own (and whose ownership can be understood in terms of integration into the former). This is not, in general, enough for the purposes of this book, and in the final section of this chapter and in the chapters that follow, I shall attempt to push beyond the idea of epistemic authority to identify the deeper roots of ownership. However, even without this further excavation, the idea of epistemic authority does, I think, provide us with enough resources to successfully disarm the fourth standard objection to the amalgamated mind: the problem of cognitive bloat. It is to this that we now turn.

6   Authority and the Problem of Bloat

The concept of epistemic authority provides a useful way of thinking about the difference between personal and subpersonal ownership of cognitive processes. At the personal level, my epistemic authority over a process is a tolerably reliable indicator of my ownership of that process. The same is not true, of course, for subpersonal cognitive processes: these are characterized precisely by the *absence* of my authority. I am not author of, but hostage to, the processes that, for example, transform the raw primal sketch into the full primal sketch. Authority provides an epistemic criterion of ownership of cognitive processes. It clearly, then, is not the sort of criterion applicable to processes to which we lack epistemic access. Nevertheless, subpersonal processes can qualify as cognitive. And they qualify as cognitive because of the contribution they make to—the ways in which they are integrated into—personal-level cognitive processes to which the authority criterion is applicable. With this in mind, let us return to the problem of bloat.

We have no epistemic authority over the processes occurring inside the telescope, calculator, or computer. Therefore, they do not qualify as personal-level cognitive processes because, at that level, they would be processes owned by nobody. This is compatible, however, with their being subpersonal cognitive processes. They would qualify as such just in case they are appropriately integrated into the subject's (personal-level) psychological life. In this regard, they would occupy a role akin to subpersonal neural or computational processes: they can count as cognitive to the extent, and only to the extent, that they make the appropriate contribution to personal-level cognitive processes.

This, I think, renders anodyne the problem of bloat. First, the thesis of the extended mind is not committed to the idea that the processes occurring inside telescope, calculator, or computer are cognitive processes on a par with perceiving, remembering, reasoning, and thinking. None of these things occurs inside the telescope, calculator, or computer. Second, although the extended mind is committed to the claim that processes occurring inside these items can be subpersonally cognitive—on a par with, for example, the operations that transform the raw primal sketch into the full primal sketch—this is true only when the telescope, calculator, or computer is appropriately coupled with a cognitive subject: that is, a subject that satisfies conditions (1)–(3) of the criterion and is thus a subject of personal-level cognitive processes.

The problem of bloat is sometimes presented as if the thesis of the extended mind is committed to an uncontrollably expanding conception of the cognitive domain: as if my cognitive processes continue expanding ever outward into my notebooks, telephone directories, and Internet connections. This conception of the problem is unwarranted. According to the extended mind, the domain of the cognitive need extend no further than systems that are appropriately coupled to cognitive subjects—systems that, among other things, have epistemic authority over their activities. And even then, it is not every type of cognitive process that bleeds into the murky innards of artifacts: only subpersonal cognitive processes bleed in this way. And crucially, they do so only *when* the artifacts are appropriately coupled with cognitive agents.

Of course, according to the extended mind, personal-level cognition can also extend into the world in the form of my activities—my manipulation, exploitation, and transformation of information-bearing structures in the environment. However, with personal-level cognition also, this cognitive bleed is strictly limited: it extends no further than the activities over which I have epistemic authority. To the extent that epistemic authority is a matter of degree—merging gradually with mere practical authority—then the extension of my personal-level cognitive processes into the environment will also be a matter of degree. However, since the extent of the activities over which I have epistemic authority is strictly limited, so too will be the extension of my personal-level cognitive processes into the environment.

7 The Derivative Character of Epistemic Authority

It is important to realize what epistemic authority does and what it does not do. It allows us to distinguish, with a tolerable degree of accuracy, between personal-level cognitive processes that we own and subpersonal processes, whose ownership can be understood by way of integration into the former. Because it does this, it allows us to disarm the problem of bloat. Far from extending ever outward into notebooks, telephone directories, and Internet connections, cognitive processes extend no further than things appropriately coupled to cognitive subjects—and only *when* they are appropriately coupled to cognitive subjects. To the extent that cognitive processes bleed into the innards of computers and calculators, they do so only at the subpersonal level, and, again, only when these artifacts are

appropriately connected to cognitive subjects. The idea of epistemic authority can, I think, do this much for us. But what it cannot do is provide us
with a criterion of ownership for personal-level cognitive processes. Epistemic authority is best understood as a reasonably reliable accompaniment
of personal-level processes that we own. But it is not a criterion of ownership of these processes, because it is only a symptom of something more
basic. And the core of the idea of ownership is to be found at this more
basic level. In other words, the idea of epistemic authority is legitimate but
derivative. Roughly speaking, issues of epistemic authority arise only when
something goes *wrong* with our activities—or, at least, when they are not
proceeding as smoothly as they might. And we own these activities irrespective of whether or not they go awry. This fact is likely to be obscured
by the fact that personal-level processes themselves typically arise only
when our activities are not going as smoothly as they might.

This thought is, of course, a Heideggerian one. In his well-known but
often misunderstood analysis of the fundamental way in which we are *in
the world*, Heidegger (1927/1962) focuses on what he calls *equipment* (*Zeug*).
This he understands in a broad sense to incorporate whatever is useful:
tools, instruments, materials, modes of transport, clothing, dwellings, and
so on. In its essence, equipment is *something-in-order-to* (1927/1962, 97).
Equipment, in this sense, always refers to other equipment: for something
to function as equipment, in Heidegger's sense, there must be a network
of equipment.

Equipment—in accordance with its equipmentality—always is *in terms of* its belonging to other equipment: inkstand, pen, ink, paper, blotting pad, table, lamp, furniture, windows, doors, room. Taken strictly, there is no such thing as *an* equipment.
To the being of any equipment there always belongs an equipmental whole, in
which it can be this equipment that it is. (Ibid.)

The being of any equipment is determined by its place in this equipmental
whole. The fundamental way in which human beings are in the world is
as users or manipulators of these sorts of equipmental wholes. Being-in-
the-world in this sense consists in a certain sort of *understanding* we have
of that world, and this understanding, at least in its most basic form, consists in our using this equipment:

Where something is put to use, our concern subordinates itself to the "in-order-to"
which is constitutive for the equipment we are employing at the time; the less we
just stare at the hammer-thing, and the more we seize hold of it and use it, the more
primordial does our relationship to it become, and the more unveiledly it is encountered as that which it is—as equipment. (Ibid., 98)

Of course, we can know what a hammer is without necessarily having used one. But such understanding is what Heidegger would call "positive" rather than "primordial." The fundamental, or "primordial," way of understanding the hammer is to use it. This is true of all equipment.

When we use—and thus primordially understand—equipment, it has a tendency to *disappear* in the sense that it becomes *transparent* to us. Our consciousness passes through the equipment—all the way to the purpose or end for which we are using it.

The peculiarity of what is primarily available is that, in its availableness, it must, as it were, withdraw in order to be available quite authentically. That with which our everyday dealings primarily dwell is not the tools themselves. On the contrary, that with which we concern ourselves primarily is the task—that which is to be done at the time. (Ibid., 99)

When hammering a nail, "The hammering itself uncovers the specific 'manipulability' of the hammer" (ibid., 98) and is thus a form of *understanding* the hammer. However, I am not typically aware of the hammer or of any of its positive properties. All I am aware of is the task. My *concern* renders the hammer, and the equipmental whole in which it is situated— nails, wood, roof, house—transparent. My concern passes all the way through the equipment to the goal or end of the activity.

It is here, in these sorts of contexts, that we find our primary sense of agency. Many would deny that in these sorts of circumspective dealings with the world there is any sense of agency to be found at all. This is an indication of the grip in which a certain conception of agency holds us. The conception is that of agency as a conscious or otherwise intentional state of some sort. It is common to think of agency is terms of volitions or conscious *tryings*. A closely related view is that agency is to be identified with a sense or experience of effort, or is at least closely associated with such an experience. According to others, the sense of agency is thought of as the experiencing of an action as implementing an intention that I experience as my own. However, in normal contexts of activity, there is no sense of agency. This is not because we experience our actions as effortless. Rather, we do not experience them at all.

Typically, not only is the equipmental totality transparent; there is an important sense in which *I* am also transparent. While hammering the nail, I am absorbed in what I am doing, and so am not aware of myself as an entity distinct from the hammer or the nail. I have no awareness of myself as author of my actions. But this transparency of self is also transparency of my mental properties. I am not typically aware of the *effort* I am putting into the hammering. I am not aware of any mental states—and still less am I aware of them causing my hammering. I am not aware of my actions, of my intentions, or the contents of my intentions. And, therefore, I am hardly aware of my actions as implementing intentions that I experience as my own. Far from being explained in terms of our awareness of mental items—the self, intentions, volitions, and their contents—our fundamental (or as Heidegger would put it primordial) agential dealings with the world are characterized precisely by the *absence* of this sort of awareness. Our fundamental acquaintance with our own agency is constituted by this sort of transparent emptiness in which I am a pure directedness toward my goals.

Whether we want to describe this as a sense of agency, or reserve that expression for more familiar and overtly intentional contexts, is largely a matter of stipulation. What is important for our purposes is this idea: any account of agency formulated in terms of a subject's awareness of the contents of his or her own mind is in fact an account of agency that in some respect *misfired*. This sort of account is an account of agency that has, in one way or another, gone wrong. Mentalistic accounts of agency, in effect, describe senses of agency that occur when the equipmental nexus has broken down, and, as a result, the equipment, the subject, and his or her conscious states have become *opaque*.

Heidegger details three distinct kinds of equipmental breakdown, of progressively increasing order of seriousness: *conspicuousness*, *obstinacy*, and *obtrusiveness*. "Conspicuousness presents the available kind of equipment as in a certain unavailableness" (ibid., 102–103). The hammer becomes conspicuous because it is, say, too heavy. Equipmental breakdown due to conspicuousness is easily rectified: I simply lay down the hammer I have and pick up a lighter one, and normal circumspective dealings are quickly restored. Nonetheless, for a moment or two, the hammer becomes an object of my awareness: "Pure occurrentness announces itself in such equipment, but only to withdraw to the availableness of something with which one concerns oneself" (ibid., 103).

Obstinacy is a form of temporary breakdown of equipment, more serious than the simple unsuitability of a hammer that is too heavy. For example, perhaps the hammer is too heavy and there is no suitable alternative hammer available. Or perhaps the head has become detached from the handle, and needs to be reattached before my circumspective dealings can resume. In such circumstances, "the constitutive assignment of the 'in-order-to' to a 'towards-this' has been disturbed" (ibid., 105). Now I need to think about what I am doing: I need to engage in *deliberation*. How can

I reattach the hammer head to the handle? Do I have something that will allow me to do so? In such circumstances, I have to employ reflective planning of a certain sort. Sometimes this can extend significantly into the future: I don't have any means of reattaching the head to the handle, but the hardware store down the road does.

The most serious form of equipmental breakdown is *obtrusiveness*: a form of total equipmental breakdown. Perhaps the roof frame I have put on the house fails to stand up properly, owing to serious flaws in its design. Now, I must go "back to the drawing board." I must engage in theoretical deliberation concerning how to rectify those flaws. This is distinct from the deliberative but still essentially practical methods that I might have employed to reattach the hammer head to the handle (e.g., inserting a small wooden wedge into the gap where the handle inserts into the head). Now I am engaging in pure theory concerning how to proceed, and as Heidegger notes, such theory becomes necessary only when the possibility of ongoing circumspective activity is blocked:

> If knowing is to be possible as a way of determining the nature of the occurrent by observing it, then there must first be a *deficiency* in our having to do with the world concernfully. (Ibid., 88)

In other contexts, the distinction between conspicuousness, obstinacy, and obtrusiveness would be important. For our purposes, however, it is sufficient to note that they all share a common, and for our purposes crucial, feature: they are all ways in which intentions and other mental states that I formerly *lived through* are transformed into *objects* of my consciousness.

In my absorbed coping with the world, my consciousness has no explicit objects. This is true both of the equipment I employ and the mental life that allows me to employ them. My consciousness, we might say, is a *directedness* toward the world that passes through its objects toward my goals. When the equipmental whole breaks down, in one of the three ways specified by Heidegger, this is when I become aware of objects: of the hammer that is too heavy, of the head that has detached itself from the handle. But it is also here, when the circumspective going gets tough, that I experience my agency as emanating from my mental life. I experience the action as difficult or involving effort; I experience it as being caused by my beliefs and desires. I experience it as implementing intentions that I experience as my own. All these are ways in which I might experience my agency: they are all ways of characterizing, in particular contexts, the phenomenology of my agency. However, they are all phenomenological accounts of an agency that has been in some way blocked. They are all, therefore, phenomenological accounts of an agency that is secondary to, or derivative upon, a more fundamental form of agency.

8   The Continuum of Coping and Cognition

With regard to our activities in general, ownership is a matter of agency: we *own* them when we *do* them. But our doing them does not, in general, reduce to our having epistemic authority over them. At most, that is a symptom of our owning them that arises when our agency has in some way been stymied. However, if this Heideggerian analysis is correct, then at least some cognitive processes—thinking, reasoning, and so on—similarly arise only when our agency has been stymied. This is why it is natural to think of our ownership of our personal-level cognitive processes in terms of epistemic authority, and why there is a respectable internalist tradition in epistemology that does just that. The connection between (personal-level) cognition and epistemic authority—this reliable accompaniment of the former by the latter—is real but derivative. The connection between personal-level cognition and epistemic authority is a symptom of something deeper: a more, as Heidegger might put it, *primordial* sense of ownership that makes it tempting for us to think of personal-level ownership in terms of epistemic authority.

The remainder of the book is concerned with understanding the core primordial sense of ownership. I shall argue that the best way of thinking about the theses of the extended mind and embodied mind is in terms of the idea that personal-level cognitive processes are activities erected on a substructure of more basic ways of coping with the world. Not only do personal-level cognitive processes emerge from these more basic ways of coping, they are in an important sense *continuous* with these more basic ways of coping. It is not that when the equipmental totality breaks down that a radically new form of activity is introduced to the world: cognition. Rather, cognitive activity is continuous with these more basic ways of coping. In characterizing cognition as continuous with coping, I mean that cognitive activity and coping activity are, at least in one sense, fundamentally the same kind of activity: the same kind of activity that is implemented in different ways. If this is correct, there must be a more general characterization of these activities: a *sortal* concept under which coping and cognition can be subsumed. In the rest of the book, I shall argue that there is such a sortal concept: coping and cognition are both forms of *revealing* or *disclosing* activity. It is in the idea of revelation or disclosure that, I shall argue, we find the ultimate basis for our ownership of cognitive processes.

Finally—spoiler alert—I shall argue that once we have properly identified this basic sense of ownership, the amalgamated mind, in both its embodied and extended incarnations, emerges as a natural, indeed almost obvious, consequence. Like many coping activities, cognitive processes are a form of revealing or disclosing activity. And the revealing or disclosing activities that make up cognition are not restricted to the brain: they incorporate both bodily processes and things that we do in and to the world.

7 Intentionality as Revealing Activity

1 Introduction

In the remaining two chapters, I am going to defend the following claims:

1. Coping and cognition are both forms of *revealing* or *disclosing* activity. The idea of revelation or disclosure supplies the ultimate basis for our ownership of cognitive processes. There is no such thing as revelation or disclosure in itself. Disclosure is always disclosure *to* someone or something. Personal-level disclosure is disclosure to someone; subpersonal disclosure is disclosure to something. Cognitive processes are essentially owned because revealing activity is essentially owned.
2. Cognitive processes are extended because they are revealing activity. The revealing activity performed by an organism can, but often does not, stop at the organism's skin.
3. The reason that all cognitive processes are owned and many are extended is therefore, ultimately, the same: cognition is revealing activity.
4. Cognition is revealing activity because cognition is *intentional*. And, ultimately, intentional directedness toward the world is best understood as revealing activity.

This chapter develops further the idea of revealing activity. To this end, I want to look at states for which this idea can, at least initially, be most clearly developed. These are states that are both conscious and intentional. That is, my focus will be on *experiences*, in particular, *perceptual* experiences. The idea I shall defend is that perceptual experiences are intentional because they are a revealing or disclosing of the world. And they are conscious because they are a revealing or disclosing of the world to someone—their subjects. The final chapter will then extend these ideas to cognition and, on the basis of this, argue that we should expect much, but not necessarily all, cognition to be extended.

The arguments to be developed in this and the next chapter can therefore be regarded as having both a specific and a more general significance. The specific significance is that the arguments supply us with the means to account for the ownership of cognitive processes, thus completing the criterion of the cognitive, and so defusing the standard objections to the amalgamated mind. The more general significance is that the arguments collectively show something profoundly important about the thesis of the amalgamated mind. Far from being recherché doctrines, the ideas that cognitive processes should be embodied and extended are utterly quotidian—practically banal implications of a proper understanding of intentionality. In other words, the widespread perception that the theses of the embodied and extended mind are outlandish derives from a certain conceptualization of the intentionality of conscious experience. The implicated conceptualization of intentionality of conscious experience is widespread and tenacious. However, I shall argue that it is also incomplete. If we want to understand intentionality—directedness toward objects—then we must allow that there is an aspect of conscious experience that the tradition has, by and large, passed over in silence. This neglect is curious, for the alternative conception of conscious experience, and the intentionality that underlies it, is clearly present in some of the formative works of twentieth-century philosophy—both in the analytic and continental traditions.

This chapter comes in three parts. In the first, I shall identify, and delineate the influence of, the default view of conscious, perceptual experience. In the second part, I shall examine some of the aforementioned works of twentieth-century philosophy where the alternative conception of intentionality, and, as a result, of conscious experience, is clearly present. Although I do not take these to be the only representatives of the alternative conception, the three figures I shall focus on are particularly central to the way philosophy developed in the last century. These are Frege, Husserl, and Sartre. In the third part of this chapter, I shall develop and defend an argument that deepens and systematizes the somewhat disparate strands of this alternative conception of experience found in the work of these three thinkers. The argument, if successful, provides us with an understanding of the idea of intentionality as revealing activity that we can use to underwrite and justify the claims of the amalgamated mind.

2 Experiences as Empirical: The Pull of Objectivity

Most recent treatments of experience presuppose—sometimes implicitly but usually explicitly—that experiences are *objects* of some sort. By this, I do not mean, of course, that they think of experiences as objects as opposed to some other category of existent—events, states, processes, properties, facts, and so on. Rather, I mean that they conceive of experiences as items *of* which we are, or can be, aware. That is, in the terminology I am going to employ, they conceive of experiences as *empirical* items. I use this term in a recognizably Kantian sense. To say that an item is empirical is simply to claim that it is an actual or potential object of consciousness: it is the sort of thing of which I might become aware if my awareness is suitably engaged.

It is not only experiences but also their *properties* or *aspects* that can be empirical in this sense. I can attend both to my experience of a bright red apple and to, as Locke might put it, the forcefulness and vivacity of this experience. Moreover, among these properties is a particularly important—arguably definitive—one: *what it is like* to have or undergo the experience. This too is one of the things of which we can be aware in the having of the experience. What distinguishes me from my zombie twin, so the idea goes, is that when we have an experience of a given type, I am, but he is not, aware of what it is like to have the experience. It is my awareness of the *phenomenal character* of my experiences that distinguishes me from my zombie twin.

In an earlier work (Rowlands 2001), I argued that this empirical—or as I then preferred to call it, *objectualist*—model of experience is false. Here, I shall be somewhat less sanguine—but only because my former youthful level of sanguinity is not required for the arguments I am going to develop in the remainder of this book. Here, I shall argue that the empirical conception of consciousness is not so much false as *incomplete*. Experiences and their properties, I shall accept, may be items of which we are aware when our attending is suitably engaged. But they are also, necessarily, more than this. There is an aspect of any experience that cannot be an item of which we are aware in the having of that experience. It is here that we find the intentionality of the experience. I shall argue that understanding why this is so, and the sense in which it is so, is essential to a proper understanding of the thesis of the amalgamated mind.

The precise nature of the relation between a subject and her experiences required for her to be aware of these experiences and/or their properties is a matter of dispute. The following categories—not necessarily mutually incompatible ones—have proved influential:

1. Experiences and what it is like to have them are objects of *knowledge*.
2. Experiences and what it is like to have them are objects of *introspection*.

3. Experiences and what it is like to have them are items to which we have *access*.

Each of these claims can be subdivided further, depending on one's favored model of the implementation of each type of relation. It is here, for example, that the debate between first-order and higher-order models of consciousness becomes relevant. The discussion to be developed in this chapter, however, proceeds at this more abstract level represented by (1)–(3).

Frank Jackson's (1982, 1986) *knowledge argument* is explicitly predicated on claim (1). The knowledge argument is based on the assumption that what it is like to have an experience can be an object of knowledge—a peculiarly factive attitude, but nonetheless a form of awareness in the general sense invoked in this chapter. Mary, despite the impediment of being locked away in a monochromatic environment for her entire life, nevertheless becomes the world's leading authority on the neurology of color vision. In fact she knows everything there is to know about the neural processes involved in seeing colors. However, Jackson comments:

> It seems, however, that Mary does not know all there is to know. For when she is let out of the black-and-white room, she will learn what it is like to see something red, say. This is rightly described as learning—she will not say "ho, hum." Hence physicalism is false. (Jackson 1986, 292)

Before her release, she does not know what it is like to see red. After her release she does. This is what she learns upon her release. What it is like to see red, therefore, becomes an object of her knowledge. I am presupposing only a very minimal sense of "object of knowledge": if s knows that p, then p is an object of knowledge for s. This claim is distinct from, and does not entail, more specific claims concerning the nature of this knowledge or the object. For example, to claim that p is an object of knowledge for s does not entail that p is some sort of peculiar "mental object"—a particular with irreducible and intrinsic phenomenal qualities on which the mind can direct its knowledge-acquiring gaze. I doubt that there are any such objects, and I am using the term "knowledge" in such a way that it entails no such thing. The sense of the term is so broad that it is compatible with any proposal concerning what a subject knows when he or she knows what it is like to have an experience. If there is a presupposition here, it is a tautology.

Colin McGinn's (1989a,b, 1991, 2004) defense of his transcendental naturalist position explicitly requires claim (2). His arguments presuppose that what it is like to have an experience is an object of introspection—in the broad sense of "object" presupposed in this book. Thus:

Our acquaintance with consciousness could hardly be more direct; phenomenological description thus comes (relatively) easily. "Introspection" is the name of the faculty through which we catch consciousness in all its vivid nakedness. By virtue of possessing this cognitive faculty we ascribe concepts of consciousness to ourselves; we thus have "immediate access" to the properties of consciousness. (McGinn 1991, 8)

Through introspection, we become aware, introspectively, of what it is like to have a conscious experience, or, as McGinn puts it: it is through introspection that we catch consciousness in "all its vivid nakedness." What it is like is, thus, an object of our introspection: something given to us by a form of "immediate access." Again, given the broad conception of object presupposed in this book—one that is entirely neutral with regard to the nature of the object (and, indeed, the nature of introspection)—this is a tautology. If you can introspect what it is like to have or undergo an experience, then what it is like is an object of introspection.

I have been emphasizing the entirely unremarkable character of the idea that what it is like to have an experience is an object—in the sense required by this book—of awareness. If the claim that what it is like to have an experience is an object of awareness is tautological then it can hardly be false. Nonetheless, it is disingenuous because it is incomplete. The very ordinariness of the idea that consciousness is an object of awareness masks something deeply significant about consciousness. What this is begins to emerge if we turn our attention to (3). Here, Thomas Nagel's (1974) position is particularly instructive, because here we find an implicit commitment to (3), and this, in the work of the arch-champion of subjectivity, brings out just how widespread and tenacious—utterly unremarkable—is the empirical conception of experience. We also begin to see just what this conception hides.

In his seminal (1974) paper "What Is It Like to Be a Bat?" Nagel argued that (1) "Fundamentally, an organism has conscious mental states if and only if there is something that it is like to be that organism—something that it is like *for* the organism" (Nagel 1974, 166). However, (2) "If physicalism is to be defended, the phenomenological features of experience must themselves be given a physical account" (ibid., 167). But (3) "When we examine their subjective character it seems that such a result is impossible. The reason is that every subjective phenomenon is essentially connected with a single point of view, and it seems inevitable that an objective physical theory will abandon that point of view" (ibid., 167).

What is important for our purposes is not the success or otherwise of Nagel's argument, but a particular conception of subjectivity embodied in it. Nagel begins with a certain common understanding of objectivity. An "objective fact *par excellence*" is "the kind that can be observed and understood from many points of view" (ibid., 172). Objective facts are ones to which there exist many *routes of epistemic access*. It is the existence of such many and varied routes, capable of being adopted by many and varied individuals, that constitutes the objectivity of an item. In short, objective items are ones to which epistemic access is *generalized*. Taking this concept of objectivity as primary, Nagel then constructs a concept of subjectivity based on the guiding metaphor of a route of access. Subjective phenomena are ones to which our routes of access are reduced to one: they are items to which our access is *idiosyncratic*. To think of subjective phenomena in this way is to think of them as part of a region of reality that *in itself* is just like any other. This region of reality differs from other regions not in any of its intrinsic features: the only difference lies in our mode of access to it. Our port of epistemic entry to this region of reality is unusually small. Classically objective phenomena are like objects on a savannah, and can be approached from many different directions. Conscious phenomena are locked up in a remote canyon whose only route of access is a narrow tunnel.

This way of thinking about consciousness is, I think, part of the pull of the idea that all reality is intrinsically objective. Objectivity is taken as primary, and subjectivity is understood as a derivative and truncated form of objectivity. And the notion of a mode or route of access lies at the heart of both concepts. Thus, it is our having idiosyncratic (i.e., truncated) access to an item that constitutes the subjectivity of that item. If only our routes of access could somehow be *beefed up*; if only they could be suitably generalized, then the very same item would become objective. The idea that reality is intrinsically objective is the idea that this generalizing of routes of access could, in principle, take place without any change in the intrinsic nature of the object toward which this access is directed.

To see the significance of this way of understanding the subjective–objective distinction, consider Nagel's tendency to slide from claims such as:

Every subjective phenomenon is essentially *connected* with a single point of view. (Ibid., 167, emphasis mine)

to claims such as:

For if the facts of experience—facts about what it is like *for* the experiencing organism—are *accessible* only from one point of view, then it is a mystery how the true character of experiences could be revealed in the physical operation of that organism. (Ibid., 172)

The claim that a subjective phenomenon is one essentially *connected* with a single point of view mutates into the claim that a subjective phenomenon is one that is essentially *accessible* from only a single point of view. However, these two claims are not equivalent. To suppose that they are is a symptom of the grip exerted on us by the empirical conception of experience. To see why this is so, we must first look more closely at the alternative. This is to think of experience not as empirical but as *transcendental*. This term I am also employing in a recognizably Kantian sense that opposes the transcendental to the empirical. If empirical items are objects of consciousness, then transcendental items are what allow empirical items to be as such. Transcendental items are, as Kant put it, *conditions of possibility* of empirical items.

The idea that experiences have a transcendental as well as empirical element has the curious distinction of being both mundane and difficult (although not, of course, in the same respects). Here is the mundane part. According to the empirical conception, experiences and their properties are items of which we are, or can be, aware when we have those experiences with their properties. But experiences, of course, are not just objects of awareness but also *acts*. It is through inward engagement of my awareness that I make my experiences and what it is like to have them into objects of my awareness. My inward engagement is, in this case, an act of awareness. This claim is utterly unremarkable. If I am aware of a conscious state and/or its properties—I am aware of my pain or what it is like to have it—then my conscious experience at that time consists not just in that *of* which I am aware; it consists also in my awareness of it.

The idea that experiences are not merely empirical items but also transcendental ones is, in part, an expression of this rather commonplace observation. In general, experiences are not just items *of* which we are aware. They are also items *in virtue of* which we are aware, both of nonmental objects and their properties and also of other experiences. As acts of awareness, experiences are items that reveal objects to subjects. Thus, experiences are not simply empirical things: they are also *transcendental*. As transcendental, experiences are not objects of awareness but that in virtue of which objects—whether mundane physical objects or other experiences—are revealed to a subject precisely as objects of that subject's experience.

A more precise understanding of the idea of experiences as transcendental requires us to move from the mundane to the difficult. And, here, a good place to begin is one that might seem an unlikely one: Frege's ruminations on (and indeed tribulations with) the concept of *sense*.

3 Two Senses of Sense

The discussion to follow is perhaps best regarded as a constructive misreading of Frege's attempts to understand the idea of linguistic sense. It is a misreading because it attributes to Frege a concern with the psychological that he did not have, and so veers in the direction of a *psychologism* that he eschewed. It is constructive because the primary concern of this chapter is, of course, the psychological: specifically, conscious, intentional experience. The thesis I shall defend is that the advertised Fregean ruminations on sense translate almost exactly into contemporary discussions of consciousness. And this reveals an important way in which those discussions are incomplete.

As many commentators have noted, there is a pronounced tension in Frege's account of *sense* (*Sinn*). Frege wants to attribute two distinct types of feature or function to *senses* or *thoughts* (*Gedanken*). On the one hand, Frege claims that senses can be objects of mental acts in a way akin— although not identical—to that in which physical objects can be the objects of mental acts (Harnish 2000). Physical objects can be perceived; senses or thoughts (i.e., the senses of declarative sentences) can be *apprehended*. Moreover, when a thought is apprehended, Frege claims, "something in [the thinker's] consciousness must be *aimed at* the thought" (Frege 1918/1994: 34–35). In one of its guises, therefore, a sense is an intentional object of an act of apprehension.

However, according to Frege, senses also have the role of fixing reference. Although senses can be objects of reference, that is not their only, or even typical, role. In its second guise, the function of sense is to direct the speaker's or hearer's thinking not to the sense itself but to the object picked out by that sense. In this case, senses do not figure as intentional objects of mental acts, but as items in virtue of which a mental act can have an object. In their customary role, senses are *determinants* of reference: they are what fix reference rather than objects of reference.

It is clear that there is a tension between these two ways of understanding sense. It is not simply that these characterizations are distinct. More importantly, when sense is playing the role described in the first characterization, it cannot also play the role described in the second, and vice versa. This inability to play both roles simultaneously shows itself in a certain *noneliminability* that attaches to sense in its reference-determining role. In its first guise, a sense is an object of apprehension: an intentional object of a mental act. But the second characterization of sense tells us that whenever there is an intentional object of a mental act, there is also a sense that fixes reference to this object. If we combine these characterizations, therefore, it seems we must conclude that whenever sense exists as an intentional object of a mental act of apprehension, there must, in that act, be another sense that allows it to exist in this way. And if this latter sense were also to exist as an intentional object of a mental act, there would have to be yet another sense that allowed it to do so. Sense in its reference-determining guise, therefore, has a noneliminable status within any intentional act. In any intentional act, there is always a sense that is not, and in that act cannot be, an intentional object.[1]

It is the second way of thinking about sense, sense as determinant of reference, which underwrites the familiar idea that Fregean sense is *inexpressible*: as something that can be *shown* but not *said*. Dummett states the initial worry: "even when Frege is purporting to give the sense of a word or symbol, what he actually *states* is what its reference is" (Dummett 1973, 227). Some have tried to upgrade this worry to a charge of outright incoherence. Consider an analogy employed by Searle (1958). There is a collection of tubes through which marbles pass to drop into holes below; in some cases different tubes may lead to the same hole. We cannot succeed in getting a marble to lodge in a tube; it always passes through the tube to the hole beneath. Senses, it might be thought, are like this. And, if so, they are not the sorts of thing that can be grasped. Thus, sense in its reference-determining role undermines the possibility of its figuring as an object of apprehension.

This conclusion would, however, be premature. Searle's analogy invites us to think of sense as a *route* to a referent. This sits comfortably with Frege's idea that different senses can determine one and the same reference: there can, similarly, be many routes to one and the same location. However, the analogy introduces too much of a gap between sense and reference. One might imagine, for example, someone switching around the tubes so that they now pass into entirely different holes. A better way of thinking about reference is not as route to a referent, but as a *way or manner of presenting* a referent (Dummett 1981). If the sense of an expression is the manner in which we determine its referent, then should we want to convey the sense of an expression, all we can do is choose a means of stating the referent where this means displays the sense we wish to convey. Thus, we *say* what the referent of an expression is, and in choosing the particular means for saying this, we thereby *show* what the sense of the expression is (Dummett 1973, 227).[2]

Three ideas emerging from the foregoing discussion are particularly pertinent to the concerns of this chapter:

1. The notion of Fregean sense functions in two different ways: (a) as an intentional object of a mental act of apprehension, and (b) as that which determines reference.
2. As a determinant of reference, sense has a noneliminable role within any intentional act.
3. This combination of (1a) and (1b) is not incoherent as long as we are willing to accept that sense is simply a manner of determining a referent, and therefore is something that can be shown but not said.

I shall argue that clearly identifiable counterparts of these principles can be identified in recent attempts to understand consciousness: what it is like to have or undergo an experience. However, as we have seen, almost all recent discussions have been oriented around a conception of consciousness along the lines of Frege's first conception of sense: the idea of sense as an object of an act of apprehension. What it is like to have an experience is thought of as something of which we are aware in the having of that experience. What it is like to have an experience is an object of experiential *apprehension*. However, just as Fregean sense is more than an object of apprehension, what it is like to have an experience is more than an object of apprehension. Just as Fregean sense is that which determines reference, what it is like to have an experience is, in part, that which determines the objects of experiential acts. Its role in this regard is noneliminable in any such act.

In other words, Frege's distinction between the two roles of linguistic sense is structurally analogous to the distinction between empirical and transcendental conceptions of experience introduced earlier. As an empirical item, sense is an object of apprehension—something that I grasp when I understand the sense of a term or sentence. As empirical, sense is something toward which a thinker's act of apprehension is directed. As a transcendental item, sense is a determinant of reference: it is that in virtue of which a term or sentence can be about something outside it. As transcendental, rather than being an object of apprehension that is grasped, sense is that in virtue of which objects of apprehension are grasped.

In its transcendental role, sense occupies a noneliminable position in any intentional act. Any attempt to make sense into an object—and hence empirical—will require a further sense in virtue of which this transformation can be accomplished. Moreover, it is to sense in its noneliminable transcendental role that we must look if we want to understand the intentionality of thought—the directedness of thought toward its object.

Similarly, it is to experience in its transcendental role that we shall have to turn if we want to understand the intentionality of experience. The intentionality of experience is commonly understood as the directing of that experience toward its intentional objects. If this is correct, focusing on those intentional objects themselves is not going to enable us to understand intentional directedness toward them. To understand this, we need to understand what it is that permits these objects to appear to subjects as the intentional objects of their experiential acts. The distinction between empirical and transcendental concepts of experience mirrors the distinction between sense as object of thought and sense as determinant of the reference of thought.

This dialectic is not a peculiar eruption of Fregean thought. Although it has become oddly neglected in recent years, it played a pronounced role in early to mid-twentieth-century thought. Further important exemplars of this way of thinking about intentional directedness can be found in the work of Husserl and Sartre. Indeed, perhaps surprisingly for those not used to thinking of Frege in these terms, this way of thinking about intentional directedness strongly shaped the development of the phenomenological tradition. It is to an examination of this that we now turn.

4 Husserl on *Auffassungsinn, Noesis,* and *Noema*

As we have seen, the concept of sense, as employed by Frege, admits of both *empirical* and *transcendental* interpretations. Empirically, sense is the intentional object of an act of apprehension. Transcendentally, it is that in virtue of which any intentional act—an act of apprehension or an experiential or cognitive act more generally—can refer to, or be about, an object. Sense, as transcendental, occupies a noneliminable position in any intentional act: whenever there is a referent there is a sense that consists in the manner in which this referent is picked out. This true even when the referent of an act is also a sense: in such a case, there must be another sense—the sense in virtue of which the referent is presented in the manner in which it is presented. As a transcendental determinant of reference, sense is therefore a noneliminable component of any intentional act.

When a "thought"—the sense of a declarative sentence—is apprehended, Frege claims, "something in [the thinker's] consciousness must be *aimed*

at the thought" (Frege 1918/1994, 34–35). As something aimed at, therefore, the sense or thought remains an extrinsic object of an act of appre-
hending. Frege explains this in terms of an analogy concerning two
different ways in which something might be grasped or apprehended by
a hand:

The expression "apprehend" is as metaphorical as "content of consciousness" . . .
What I hold in my hand can certainly be regarded as the content of my hand but
is all the same the content of my hand in a quite different way from the bones and
muscle of which it is made and their tensions, and is much more extraneous to it
than they are. (Ibid., 35)

Senses or thoughts are grasped by the mind in a way (metaphorically) akin
to that in which a hand grasps an object. When grasped, they are therefore
"in" the mind in way that an object grasped by the hand is in the hand,
and not the way in which the bones and muscles that make up the hand
are in the hand. This, however, pertains only to senses as entities that are
grasped or apprehended. That is, it pertains only to senses as empirical.
Transcendentally, on the other hand, a sense is that in virtue of which an
object is picked out as falling under a given mode of presentation. Therefore, if senses are transcendental as well as empirical, indeed, if their
primary role is a transcendental one, then it seems that, as such, senses
must also be more akin to the bones and muscle of the hand than an object
grasped in it. The bones and muscle are precisely what allows the object
to be grasped in the hand: they are that in virtue of which the hand can
grasp things extrinsic to it. Similarly, as transcendental, senses are that in
virtue of which a mental act can have an intentional object.

   This, however, poses an immediate problem for Frege: it seems to
threaten his antipsychologism. If senses are the psychic equivalent of the
bones and muscles of the hand, then they seem to be mental entities of
some sort, and this undermines Frege's contention that senses are abstract
entities (belonging to, as he put it, realm three) rather than psychological
entities (belonging to, as he put it, realm one). This tension also insinuates
itself into the work of Husserl, where we find a dialectic that parallels, in
most important respects, the one we have found in Frege.

   In the *Logical Investigations*, Husserl assigned a central role to what he
called *Auffassungsinn* (McIntyre 1987). For Husserl, the *Auffassungsinn* is
the *content* of the mental act: it is not an object of the act, not something
apprehended or otherwise intended in the act, but something in the act
in virtue of which the act is a presentation of an object. In terms of Frege's
analogy, the act's *Auffassungsinn* is less like an object grasped in the hand

and more like the muscles and bone in virtue of which the hand can grasp that object. *Auffassungsinn* is sense understood *transcendentally*.

However, the existence of *Auffassungsinn* or the transcendental form of sense is a potential embarrassment for Husserl; and this is so for the same reason that the transcendental conception of sense is for Frege. The reason is that it potentially conflicts with Husserl's (and Frege's) *antipsychologism*. Both Frege and Husserl were insistent that senses should be understood as (i) objective, in the sense that they exist independently of the mental activity of any subject, and (ii) ideal in the sense that they are neither spatial nor temporal entities. However, this idea seems to work most naturally with the empirical conception of sense, assuming (which may not be the case) that we can understand the epistemic relation between mental acts and these objective, ideal entities: that is, assuming we can understand how a concrete, particular subject can grasp or apprehend an abstract, ideal entity (Harnish 2000). The problem with understanding the transcendental version of sense in this nonpsychologistic way is a subtly different one. As empirical, senses are extrinsic objects of mental acts—as the ball grasped by a hand is extrinsic to the hand. But as transcendental, they are not extrinsic in this sense at all. The worry, therefore, is that if senses are so intimately connected with mental acts—like the muscles and bones are connected to the hand—as to be determinants of their reference, then they must be the same sort of things as acts—subjective, spatial, temporal, dated, concrete particulars.

In the *Logical Investigations* Husserl's (1900/1973) proposed answer to this problem lies in his distinction between what he called the *real* and the *ideal* content of a mental act. Real content is specific to a particular mental act, whereas ideal content can be shared by different acts, whether in the same person or others. In other words, Husserl claimed that ideal content is a universal, instantiated by particular mental acts undergone by individuals, but independent of those acts and individuals. In his later (1913/1982) work, *Ideas Pertaining to a Pure Phenomenology and Phenomenological Philosophy*, volume I (henceforth, *Ideas I*), Husserl developed this general idea in terms of a distinction between *noesis* and *noema*.

There are, broadly speaking, two distinct ways of interpreting this distinction present in the literature. These have become known as the "East Coast" and "West Coast" interpretations. The former is associated with Robert Sokolowski (1987) and John Drummond (1990). The latter is associated with, among others, Dagfinn Føllesdal (1969) and Ronald McIntyre (1987). According to the East Coast interpretation, the distinction between *noesis* and *noema* is intended to track the distinction between

transcendental and empirical interpretations of sense. On this interpretation, *noesis* corresponds to sense understood transcendentally as
a determinant of reference; *noema* corresponds to sense understood
empirically, as an object of reference. In other words, when he introduces
the distinction between *noesis* and *noema* Husserl is recording the systematic ambiguity of the notion of sense, and effecting an appropriate
disambiguation. As such, the distinction has little to do with the worry
concerning psychologism canvassed above.

The West Coast interpretation, on the other hand, makes this worry
central to the *noema–noesis* distinction. The distinction is still importantly
connected to the distinction between empirical and transcendental conceptions of sense, but the connection is a more complex one. According
to the West Coast interpretation, the distinction between *noesis* and *noema*
is, in the first instance, connected to Husserl's distinction between real and
ideal content. Both *noesis* and *noema* are versions of the transcendental
interpretation of sense—sense as a determinant of reference rather than an
object of reference. However, the *noema* corresponds to the transcendental
conception of sense understood as belonging to an act individuated by
way of its ideal content. *Noesis* corresponds to the transcendental conception of sense understood as belonging to an act individuated by its
real content. That is, the distinction between *noesis* and *noema* tracks the
distinction between real and ideal content and is, in the first instance,
motivated by Husserl's desire to avoid psychologism.

However, even on this second interpretation, it is still true that the distinction between *noesis* and *noema* is ultimately motivated by the distinction between empirical and transcendental conceptions of sense. The
distinction between *noesis* and *noema* is, we might accept, the result of
Husserl's desire to safeguard the objectivity of sense. But it is the desire to
safeguard this objectivity *precisely* in the face of the problem posed by the
fact that sense has a transcendental as well as an empirical interpretation.
The possibility of a transcendental interpretation of sense entails that sense
is more closely connected to mental acts than merely being an extrinsic
object grasped by such acts. Husserl's suggestion is that the experiential
noema is, whereas the experiential *noesis* is not, an ideal reference-determining content (one that he now, in *Ideas I*, understands as an ideal particular, or trope, rather than, as in the *Logical Investigations*, as an ideal
universal). The *noesis*, on the other hand, is the real, concrete, psychic
counterpart to this ideal particular.

For our purposes, therefore, it is not important to endorse one of these
interpretations of the *noema–noesis* distinction over the other: both are, in

their different ways, predicated on the recognition that sense has a transcendental as well as empirical status. And what is important for our purposes is the existence of a clear, unequivocal conception of sense as a transcendental determinant of reference rather than an object of reference. In recognizing—in one way or the other—the distinction between transcendental and empirical conceptions of sense, Husserl's contribution decisively shaped the future development of phenomenology. Understood transcendentally, sense is what permits any given mental act to have or take an intentional object. As such, sense is not an object of *that* intentional act (although nothing has been said that precludes it from being the object of other intentional acts). Transcendentally, with respect to intentional act A, the sense of A is not an object of awareness for A's subject because this sense is what permits A to have an object. If the sense of A were to be made into an object, there would have to be another sense that allowed it to appear as such. This is not to say that there is a part of any experiential act that is *hidden* to the act's subject. This would follow only if we assumed that anything that is not an object of a subject's awareness is thereby hidden from that subject. The point is that the relation between a subject and the transcendental sense of her intentional acts is quite different from the relation between her and the empirical sense of her intentional acts. The latter is an object of her awareness. But the former is not like this at all. The connection between her and the transcendental sense of her intentional acts is a far more *intimate* one, and cannot be understood in dyadic subject–object terms. We shall, shortly, explore this point further in our discussion of Sartre.

The idea that a mental act contains a noneliminable component that is not available to the subject of that act in the form of an intentional object is one that indelibly marked the future development of phenomenology. Those who have been presented with a facile conception of phenomenology as quasi-introspectionist enterprise concerned largely with the description of experiences transparently presented to the scrutiny of a subject might find this claim surprising. But this is not what phenomenology is or could ever be. And the reason for this lies ultimately in Husserl's realization that even if sense is an object of apprehension, it must necessarily be more than this: it must also be what allows objects to be objects of apprehension. It was this realization that effectively determined the future direction of phenomenology. Thus, although he would hate the apparatus of intentional acts and senses in terms of which I have expressed the claim, the idea that phenomenology is the uncovering of what is proximally hidden in our dealings with the world, but can in principle be uncovered, is a central plank of Heidegger's conception of the discipline. We shall examine Heidegger's important contribution to our concerns in the next chapter. For now, let us look at how essentially the same dialectic as the one we have identified plays itself out in the work of Jean-Paul Sartre.

5 Sartre on Nothingness

Despite his repeated attempts to distance himself from Husserl, Sartre's *Being and Nothingness* (1943/1957) provides an important development of Husserl's ideas. Understood transcendentally, sense possesses two crucial features. First, it is noneliminable. Whenever an intentional act has an object, there must be a sense that permits this. If this sense is also an object of awareness, then there must be another sense that permits this. Always we are pushed back to a sense that is not an object of awareness. This entails the second crucial feature of sense understood transcendentally. Whenever a subject is aware of some object, there must be a sense that is not an object of that subject's awareness: this sense is not something of which the subject is aware in the having of her experience. This noneliminable aspect of consciousness that is not an object of the subject's awareness is what Sartre referred to as *nothingness*. Sartre's invocation of nothingness is simply a more colorful expression of Husserl's idea that the sense of an intentional act is, at least in part, irreducibly transcendental.

According to Sartre, to say that consciousness is nothingness is equivalent to saying that it has no *content*. Particularly significant here is Sartre's idea that this striking claim is a straightforward, almost banal, implication of the intentionality of consciousness. He writes:

All consciousness, as Husserl has shown, is consciousness *of* something. This means that there is no consciousness that is not a *positing* of a transcendent object, or if you prefer, that consciousness has no "content." (Sartre 1943/1957, 11)

What is important here is not the claim that consciousness has no content—although that is striking enough—but that Sartre thinks this claim is a straightforward implication of the idea that all consciousness is intentional. According to Sartre, objects of consciousness, of whatever sort, are *transcendent* in the sense that they are not proper parts of consciousness: they are outside consciousness, what consciousness is not. To be transcendent is, in this context, quite different from being *transcendental* in the sense introduced earlier in this chapter. To be transcendental is, in a rough sense that will be significantly clarified in the next chapter, to be what allows something to appear as an object of consciousness. A transcendental item is, again very roughly, a condition of possibility of an empirical item. But to say that an item is transcendent, in Sartre's sense, is simply a way of saying that it is outside of, or not a proper part of, consciousness.

The claim that all objects of consciousness are transcendent is one that Sartre takes to be a transparent entailment of the idea that consciousness is intentional. The question is: why? When applied to mundane worldly objects—tables, chairs, and the like—the claim that these are transcendent is simply part of a commonsense realism about the external world.[3] But Sartre wants to claim more than this: he is claiming that *all* objects of consciousness are transcendent.

Consider something that might be thought a prime candidate for inclusion among the contents of consciousness: a mental image. I close my eyes and picture the glass sitting on the table in front of me. To the extent that it is an object of consciousness, something of which I am aware, this image, Sartre claims, is a transcendent object: something irreducibly exterior to consciousness. His argument for this claim, in effect, presages a point more widely associated with Wittgenstein (1953). The image is, logically, just a *symbol*. In itself, it can mean anything at all, and therefore, in itself, means nothing at all. The image might signify the glass that sits on my table and from which I have recently been drinking. But it might signify glasses in general. Or it might signify glass objects in general; or things that have been on my table; and so on. In order to have meaning, it must be interpreted. For Sartre, unlike Wittgenstein, it is consciousness that interprets the image, and thus gives it meaning (or, more accurately, consciousness, in a given context, *is* the interpretation of the image—in the mode of not being it). Any intentionality possessed by the image is thus derivative on that supplied by the interpreting consciousness. Therefore, if all consciousness is consciousness of something, the mental image is not part of consciousness. The image has merely derived intentionality. The same holds true of all objects of consciousness. Nothing of which we are aware can be intentional in itself. Therefore, nothing of which we are aware can be part of consciousness. Thoughts, feelings, mental images, the ego: all these, for Sartre, are transcendent objects.

It would not be too much of an exaggeration to say that *Being and Nothingness* is nothing more than an attempt to work out the implications of this idea. Consider, to take just one example, Sartre's famous discussion of *anguish*, or consciousness of freedom. In one passage, Sartre discusses anguish in the face of the past:

[A]nguish in the face of the past . . . is that of the gambler who has freely and sincerely decided not to gamble any more and who, when he approaches the gaming table, suddenly sees all his resolutions melt away . . . what the gambler apprehends at this instant is again the permanent rupture in determinism; it is nothing which separates himself from himself. (Sartre 1943/1957, 69)

The "nothing" in question is consciousness conceived of simply as directedness toward objects that are outside it. Sartre continues:

After having patiently built up barriers and walls, after enclosing myself in the magic circle of a resolution, I perceive with anguish that *nothing* prevents me from gambling. The anguish is *me* since by the very fact of taking my position in existence as consciousness of being, I make myself *not to be* the past of good resolutions *which I am.* . . . In short, as soon as we abandon the hypothesis of the contents of consciousness, we must recognize that there is never a motive *in* consciousness; motives are only *for* consciousness. (Ibid., 70–71)

The gambler's resolution, as something *of* which the gambler is aware, is a transcendent object, and therefore has no meaning in itself. It is merely a symbol. For it to be about anything, and so possess an efficacy vis-à-vis the gambler's future behavior, it must be continually interpreted anew by the animating consciousness.

This animating consciousness is what we might think of as the noneliminable intentional core of experience. If we think of intentionality as directedness toward extrinsic—or as Sartre would put it, transcendent— objects, then we will look in vain to these objects if we want to understand intentionality. Intentionality cannot be found among transcendent things. Sartre's depiction of consciousness as nothingness is a reflection of the ideas that (i) consciousness is essentially intentional, and (ii) that intentionality is not to be found among transcendent things. But a list of the furniture of the world would be a list of all the things one can, in principle, encounter when one's consciousness is suitably directed. The world—being *en-soi* or in-itself—is a collection of transcendent things. Consciousness, as essentially intentional, is therefore not part of the furniture of the world. Consciousness is *nothingness*.

6 Systematizing the Strands: The Argument

Most recent treatments of experience presuppose, explicitly or implicitly, that experiences and their properties are *objects* of some sort. That is, they are items *of* which we are, or can be, aware. That is, in the terminology employed in this book, they conceive of experiences as *empirical* items. We have examined a clear historical strand of twentieth-century philosophy that suggests, strongly, that experiences must also have an aspect that is not like this at all. Whenever we are conscious of the world—that is, whenever the world appears to us as a collection of objects and properties—there must be an aspect of our experience of which we are not aware, and, when we are having that experience, cannot be aware. In Frege, this aspect appears in the form of sense playing one of its two possible roles. In Husserl, this aspect of experience is the *Auffassungsinn*, or, in his later work, the experiential *noesis* (East Coast interpretation) or *noema* (West Coast interpretation). In Sartre, the relevant aspect of experience is described as *nothingness*: consciousness as pure directedness toward the world. The underlying idea is, in each case, the same. When we have an experience, this is an aspect of the experience *with* which, or *in virtue of* which, the experience makes us aware of things. It is not something *of* which we are aware when we have that experience. If this historical line of argument is cogent, then consciousness does not consist simply in items of which we are aware—experiences and their various properties. Crucially, it also consists in that *of* which we are not aware: it consists in what allows us to be aware of whatever it is we are aware. Consciousness is not simply a collection of experiential objects. Consciousness is also (in a sense I shall try to make clear in the next chapter) the *condition of possibility* of experiential objects.

In the remainder of this chapter, historical analysis gives way to logical argument. I am going develop and defend an argument that systematizes the historical strands identified in the preceding sections—strands found in Frege, Husserl, and Sartre. However, although the argument I shall develop here legitimizes those strands, it is logically distinct from them, and stands or falls independently of whether the interpretations of Frege, Husserl, and Sartre proffered in the preceding sections are correct.

The argument I shall develop, in the first instance, is restricted to states that are both intentional and conscious: that is, it applies most obviously to experiences rather than sensations (and will apply to the latter only if the minority opinion that these are also intentional turns out to be true). I shall defend two claims:

1. Experiences contain a *noneliminable intentional core*; and in this core we find the essence of intentionality.
2. This essence of intentionality consists in a kind of *disclosing* or *revealing* activity.

In the next chapter, I shall argue that these claims have important implications for any non-Cartesian science of the mind. First, these claims allow us to make considerable headway in understanding the idea of ownership of embodied and extended cognitive processes. Second, and more important, the central claims of the amalgamated mind—embodiment and extendedness—emerge naturally and obviously from these two claims. If these two claims are correct, then the thesis of the amalgamated mind turns out to be obviously true. In the rest of this chapter, I am going to defend these two claims.

A. The Structure of Intentionality

It is not, of course, clear that all mental items are intentional. It is common to cite sensations—pain and associated genera—as examples of mental items that are not, although this claim is disputed by many. The argument I am going to develop, in the first instance, is one that pertains to the nature of intentionality, and so I shall be working only with states that are clearly both conscious and intentional—that is, experiences. In the next chapter, the focus will switch to cognitive states (and the consciousness condition will be relaxed). But, here, the argument will focus on, and be formulated in terms of, *perceptual experiences*—largely visual experiences.

More significantly, I shall be working with a model of intentionality that has become sufficiently widely accepted to be referred to as the *standard model*. According to this, intentionality has a tripartite structure, comprising: (i) act, (ii) object, and (iii) mode of presentation of that object. This can legitimately be referred to as the standard model, being widely accepted by writers in both the phenomenological and analytic traditions. Widespread acceptance is, of course, not universal acceptance. The claim that all forms of intentional directedness must conform to this model has come under attack in recent decades, largely owing to the work of Kripke (1980). The argument I shall develop in this chapter need not, and does not, dispute the possibility of forms of intentionality that do not conform to the traditional model. However, it assumes that at least some forms of intentional directedness do thus conform. It applies only to states that exhibit this form of intentional directedness. Happily, the claim that perceptual experiences exhibit this form of intentional directedness is commonplace.[4]

For example, it is common to hold that the content of perceptual experience is not *object-involving* (Martin 2002). Suppose you have a visual experience as of a bright red tomato. The claim that the content of your perceptual experience is not object-involving is the claim that it would be possible to replace the tomato with an exact duplicate without altering the content of your experience. In this, it is argued, the content of perceptual experience is different from that of demonstrative propositional attitudes, where substitution of the object would alter the content of the attitude. The nonobject-involving character of perceptual experience is easily accommodated by the standard or tripartite model of intentionality, since this ties the content to the mode of presentation of an object—a mode of presentation that could, in principle, remain the same given the substitution of an object with its exact duplicate. But it is more difficult to accommodate this claim on a Kripkean model.

Therefore, I shall assume that the standard model provides an accurate account of the intentional directedness of at least some conscious states—perceptual experiences in particular. In at least some cases, intentional directedness is a tripartite structure composed of act, object, and mode of presentation of that object. The key to the argument I am going to develop in this chapter lies in a proper understanding of the concept of a mode of presentation. I shall argue that this apparently univocal concept masks a systematic ambiguity (one that, in effect, parallels the dual nature of Fregean sense).

B. Modes of Presentation and the Noneliminable Intentional Core

According to the standard model, the mode of presentation is what connects intentional act to intentional object. Employing a terminology made famous by Kaplan (1980), we can say that the intentional act has a *character*, and the *content* of this act can be expressed in the form of a description. The intentional *object* of the act is the object that satisfies this description. The *mode of presentation* of the object, then, consists in the content expressed in the relevant description.

If an object satisfies the content-specifying description, however, this will be because the object possesses certain *aspects*: aspects that are picked out by the content-specifying description. Aspects are not to be identified with objective *properties* of objects. Aspects are objects of awareness in an intentional rather than an objective sense. Aspects are the ways in which objects are presented, the ways in which they appear, to subjects. And to the aspect there may or may not correspond an objective property of the object. An object may appear—be presented as—round, even if it, in fact, is not. A necessary condition of an object's having aspects is the intentional activity of a subject. Barring the sort of antirealism that sees all worldly properties as dependent on intentional activity, such activity is not a necessary condition of an object's having properties. Therefore, aspects are not identical with objective properties.

Since the *aspects* of the object are that in virtue of which it satisfies the content-specifying description, and since the mode of presentation of the object is the content expressed in that description, this invites the almost irresistible identification: we identify the *mode of presentation* of the object with that object's *aspects*. This identification, however, is problematic: it can be both true and false, depending on how we understand the concept of a mode of presentation. And this reveals that this concept is crucially ambiguous.

Aspects are intentional objects of awareness. I can attend not only to the tomato, but to its size, color, and luster. Indeed, typically I attend to the tomato in virtue of attending to these sorts of aspects. Thus, if we identify modes of presentation with aspects, and if we adhere to the standard model of intentionality as a relation whereby an object of awareness is determined only by way of a mode of presentation, it follows that whenever there is a mode of presentation—an aspect—there must be another mode of presentation to fix reference to it. Intentional directedness toward objects is mediated by way of a mode of presentation. Therefore, if aspects are intentional objects of experience, there must be a mode of presentation in virtue of which the intentional activity of a subject is directed toward these aspects.

In short, intentional objects require modes of presentation. If aspects of objects are themselves intentional objects, then there must be a mode of presentation that allows them to be as such. So if modes of presentation are aspects, then any experience that contains them as intentional objects must contain another mode of presentation—one that is not, in that experience, an intentional object. And if we were to make this second mode of presentation into an object of awareness—an *aspect* of our experience of which we are aware—there must be another mode of presentation that enables us to do this.

This is an issue of *noneliminability* rather than *regress*. It is not that any experience must contain an infinite number of modes of presentation. That regress is stopped as soon as we stop trying to make modes of presentation into objects of our awareness. For example, if we identify a mode of presentation of a tomato with an aspect of that tomato—its redness or shininess, for example—and so think of it as an intentional object of my experience, then it follows from the traditional model of intentionality that there must be another mode of presentation that allows it to be such. However, as long as I do not attempt to make this further mode of presentation into an intentional object, there is no need for an additional mode of presentation to fix reference to it. Therefore, in any given experience, there must be a mode of presentation that cannot, in that experience, be made into an intentional object. In the experience, this mode of presentation is not something *of* which we are aware (as we might, for example, be aware of aspects) but something *with* which or *in virtue of* which we are aware of the intentional object of our experience.

The concept of a mode of presentation, in other words, admits of both *empirical* and *transcendental* interpretations in the sense introduced earlier. An item is empirical if it is the sort of thing that can be an intentional object, an actual or potential object of consciousness: it is the sort of thing *of* which I might become aware if my awareness is suitably engaged. Aspects of objects are empirical in this sense. A transcendental item, on the other hand, is one that is not and cannot be an intentional object—at least not in its transcendental role—because it is that which permits objects to appear under aspects. That is, in its transcendental role, a mode of presentation is a *condition of possibility* of intentional objects. An empirical mode of presentation is an aspect of objects. A transcendental mode of presentation is what makes a given empirical mode of presentation *possible*. This, ultimately, is what justifies the rubric *transcendental*.

If we assume that the identification of modes of presentation with aspects is a legitimate way of understanding this concept—and it is certainly common to understand a mode of presentation in this way—then the standard model of intentionality has this clear entailment: any given experience must contain not only an empirical but also a transcendental mode of presentation. It is the transcendental mode of presentation that corresponds to Frege's first concept of sense—sense as determinant of reference rather than object of apprehension. It is in this transcendental mode of presentation that we find the *noneliminable intentional core* of the experience. If intentionality is understood as directedness toward objects, then it is in the transcendental mode of presentation that this directedness is to be found. Empirical modes of presentation—aspects—are simply objects consciousness is directed upon. They are not the sort of thing that could constitute the directedness of consciousness toward its objects. This is, in essence, the Sartrean point that underwrites his claim that consciousness is nothingness. Consciousness has no content, because consciousness is intrinsically intentional, and any content of consciousness (understood as something *of* which the subject is aware) would not be intrinsically intentional. The point is, ultimately, a straightforward one: any intentional object—mundane object, aspect, empirical mode of presentation—is something toward which consciousness or intentional activity is directed. Therefore, if we want to understand intentional directedness itself, we will have to look elsewhere. We will not find intentional directedness in the objects of that directedness.

The transcendental mode of presentation, on the other hand, is not an intentional object of the experience, and in its transcendental role cannot be an object of any experience. In its transcendental role, it is that which allows mundane worldly objects to be presented to subjects by way of aspects and, thus, that which allows the intentional states of subjects to be directed toward the world. If intentionality is understood as the *directedness* of consciousness toward its objects, it is in this noneliminable intentional core of experience that this directedness resides. This has one implication that is crucial for the purpose of defending the theses of embodied and extended cognition: intentional directedness toward the world consists in a form of *revealing* or *disclosing activity*.

C. Intentionality as Disclosing Activity

Suppose I have a visual experience as of a shiny, red tomato. The empirical mode of presentation of the tomato consists in the way it is presented to me—in this case, shiny and red. The transcendental mode of presentation of the experience, however, is that which allows the tomato to be presented to me as shiny and red. This characterization is intended to be neutral with regard to what it is that gets presented—and this neutrality is reflected in my use of the expression "as of." Historically, the candidates have been (i) the thing-in-itself conceived of as something lying behind the presentation, or (ii) a structured series of presentations. For our purposes, we need not adjudicate. I shall frame the discussion as if there is something lying behind the presentation—something that gets presented— but this discussion could just as easily be framed in terms of option (ii). If there is no tomato there, of course—if the experience is an illusion—then it is still true that some object in the world—that which is erroneously taken to be a tomato—is presented as shiny and red. In the case of a hallucination, there is no *object* that is taken to be red and shiny—erroneously or otherwise—but, nevertheless, there is a *region* of the world that is taken to be red and shiny. This localization to a region is what makes the hallucination a specifically *visual* hallucination.[5]

In each case, it is the transcendental mode of presentation of the experience that allows the world—object or region—to be presented in this way. The transcendental mode of presentation of my experience is that in virtue of which the tomato, or relevant part of the world, is *disclosed* or *revealed* to me as shiny and red. The noneliminable core of intentional experience, therefore, consists in a *disclosure* or *revelation* of the world. The fundamental sense in which intentional acts are directed toward objects, therefore, is that they reveal or disclose them as having certain *aspects* or *empirical modes of presentation.*

7 Summary

Any perceptual experience has a noneliminable intentional core, and it is in this core that we find the intentionality or directedness of experience. This core is the transcendental mode of presentation: that in virtue of which an experience presents an object as falling under a given aspect or empirical mode of presentation. In presenting an object in this way, the transcendental mode of presentation thus brings about, or effects, a certain disclosure or revelation of the object. The object is disclosed or revealed as falling under (i.e., possessing) a given aspect or empirical mode of presentation. The essence of perceptual intentionality is, accordingly, disclosure or disclosing activity.

In the rest of the book, I shall argue that the thesis of the amalgamated mind—understood as the conjunction of the theses of embodiment and extendedness—emerges as a natural, obvious, indeed almost banal implication of this understanding of intentionality. Intentionality is disclosing activity. But disclosing activity is, in general, indifferent to its location. Processes occurring in the brain can constitute (i.e., realize) disclosing activity. But this is also true of processes occurring in the body. And it is also true of things we do—activities we perform—in the world. Intentionality is revealing activity. Our revealing activity typically—not always, not necessarily, but typically—extends out from the brain through the body and out into the things we do in the world. This, I shall argue, is the ultimate justification for the thesis of the amalgamated mind, and so provides the ultimate basis for the new science itself.

8   The Mind Amalgamated

1   From Perception to Cognition

The previous chapter defended the following claims:

1. Any experience—any conscious state intentionally directed toward an object—must possess a noneliminable intentional core. It is in this core that the intentional directedness of the experience is to be found.

2. This core is identical with the transcendental mode of presentation of the experience. A transcendental mode of presentation is not something *of* which the subject of the experience is aware when he or she has the experience: if it were, then the experience would have to contain another transcendental mode of presentation in virtue of which the subject could be aware of the first transcendental mode of presentation. As determinants of empirical modes of presentation, transcendental modes of presentation occupy a noneliminable role within any experience.

3. The transcendental mode of presentation is that aspect of the experience *in virtue of which* the experience's object is presented as falling under, or possessing, a given aspect or empirical mode of presentation.

4. The noneliminable, transcendental core of the experience, therefore, consists in a form of *revealing* or *disclosing activity*.

5. The essence of intentionality—of intentional-directedness toward the world—is, therefore, disclosing or revealing activity.

In this final chapter, I shall argue that the ultimate basis and justification of the thesis of the amalgamated mind lies in this conception of intentionality. If this conception of intentionality is accepted, then the amalgamated mind emerges as an obvious, almost mundane, consequence. If the arguments of the previous chapter are correct, then this conception of intentionality should be accepted for the case of experiences—understood as states that are both conscious and intentional. However, the amalgamated mind—the conjunction of the embodied mind and the extended mind—is a claim concerning primarily the nature of cognition rather than experience. The first stage in the argument of this chapter, therefore, is to extend the account of intentionality already developed from experience to cognition.

The general contours of this extension are already fairly clear. Suppose I am *thinking* about an object—say, a tomato—and I am thinking about the fact that it is unusually red and shiny. The aspects of the tomato—redness and shininess—are objects of my thought. I am thinking about the tomato by thinking about its redness and shininess. Thus, in the terminology introduced in the previous chapter, redness and shininess are empirical modes of presentation of the tomato. The standard model of intentionality, however, has a straightforward implication. Intentional directedness toward an object is mediated by a mode of presentation. An empirical mode of presentation is an object of an intentional state—in this case, of my thought. Therefore, the standard model entails that my thought must contain another, distinct mode of presentation: that which permits the tomato to be thought of as falling under empirical modes of presentation (redness and shininess). This is the transcendental mode of presentation of my thought about the tomato. Just as the transcendental mode of presentation of my perceptual experience is that aspect of the experience in virtue of which the tomato is visually presented to me as falling under the empirical mode of presentation of being red (or being shiny), so too the transcendental mode of presentation of my thought is that in virtue of which the tomato is presented to me, in thought, as being red (or shiny). That my thought should possess this noneliminable transcendental mode of presentation is, similarly, a straightforward implication of the standard model of intentionality according to which intentional directedness toward an object is brought about via a mode of presentation of that object. If a mode of presentation is an object of my thought, then the standard model entails that there must be another mode of presentation that allows it to be such. This noneliminable, transcendental core of my thought is that in virtue of which the thought discloses or reveals, to me, the object as falling under, or possessing, a given aspect or empirical mode of presentation. The transcendental core consists, therefore, in a form of revealing or disclosing activity. It is in this core of revealing activity that we find the intentionality of thought. The various empirical modes of presentation of the tomato are objects of intentional directedness. So we will look in vain at these if we want to identify intentional directedness itself. Intentional directedness itself consists in the revealing or disclosing activity that allows an object of intentional directedness (e.g., a tomato) to be presented as falling under another object of intentional directedness (e.g., the empirical mode of presentation of redness).

In short, cognition no less than perception reveals objects as falling under empirical modes of presentation. Both the objects and the empirical mode of presentation are objects of intentional directedness. The intentionality of both perception and cognition is precisely that in virtue of which one type of intentional object (an object *simpliciter*) is disclosed as possessing or falling under another type of intentional object (an aspect or empirical mode of presentation). The intentional directedness of both perception and cognition is the noneliminable revealing activity in virtue of which this sort of disclosure takes place.

Therefore, the idea of revealing or disclosing activity lies at the heart of the intentionality of both perception and cognition. This is why it is plausible to suppose that the sort of model developed in the previous chapter for perception can also be applied to cognition. This extension is the first stage in the argument of this chapter. The next stage is to disambiguate the concept of disclosing or revealing activity.

2   Causal versus Constitutive Disclosure

The idea of disclosure is not unambiguous, and it is important to distinguish two forms. In essence, the distinction I am going to develop is a vehicle–content distinction. Acts of both perception and cognition have content (though not, perhaps, of the same sort). The content of a perceptual or cognitive act reveals an object as falling under an empirical mode of presentation. That is, content can effect one type of disclosure of an object. However, whenever there is content, there is also a vehicle of that content. And this vehicle can also effect a type of disclosure of the object. However, crucially, the way in which a given content discloses an object is different from the way in which a vehicle of that content discloses that object. A content discloses an object by providing a *logically sufficient* condition for the object to fall under a given empirical mode of presentation. A vehicle of content discloses an object by providing only a *causally sufficient* condition for that object to fall under a given empirical mode of presentation.

These claims are not as unfamiliar as they might sound. To begin with I shall focus on experience. Here, the vehicle–content distinction is more typically rendered as a distinction between an experience and its material realizations. The claims, therefore, amount to this: there is an important difference between the way in which an experience discloses its object and the way in which the material realization of the experience discloses that object. As we shall see, this does not presuppose any form of dualism about experience. Rather, it is an expression in an unfamiliar language of a, by now, very familiar point: there is an *explanatory gap* between conscious experience and its material bases.

Suppose, again, that I have a visual experience as of a shiny, red tomato. The tomato is disclosed to me as red and shiny because, roughly, there is *something that it is like* to see the tomato. At the level of the content of an experience that is essentially characterized by there being something that it is like to have it, this "what it is like" is the transcendental mode of presentation of that experience. Thus, the transcendental mode of presentation of the tomato given to me in my experience of it consists in what it is like to see the tomato: what it is like to see the tomato is that in virtue of which the tomato is revealed to the subject as red and shiny.[1] The expression "in virtue of" should be understood as expressing a *logically sufficient* condition: what it is like to see the tomato, in its concrete phenomenal particularity, is, in this case, a logically sufficient condition for the tomato to be revealed to the subject as red and shiny. If a subject has an experience with the requisite what-it-is-like-ness, then there is no logically possible way in which the tomato (or region, etc.) cannot be revealed to him as red and shiny. If the experience is an illusion, then some other—that is, nontomato—object will be revealed as red and shiny. But it is still true that the content of the experience provides a logically sufficient condition for that object to be revealed as red and shiny. If the experience is a (visual) hallucination, then it is still true that some region of the world is revealed as red and shiny—the region that appears to be a red, shiny tomato. And the content of the hallucination provides a logically sufficient condition of the region's being revealed in this way.

Transcendentally, what it is like to have or undergo an experience is not something of which we are aware in the having of that experience—although we may, in suitable contexts, become aware of its empirical counterpart (but see note 1). Rather, it is that in virtue of which the world is revealed to us as being a certain way: that is, as falling under a given aspect or empirical mode of presentation. It reveals the world in this way by providing a logically sufficient condition for the world to be presented in this way. Whether it also provides a logically necessary condition is an interesting question, but not one that needs to be addressed here.[2]

Let us switch focus, now, from the visual experience as of a shiny red tomato to the material realization—the vehicle—of this experience. By "material realization," I simply mean a *supervenience* or *realizing* base of the experience, where the idea of supervenience is understood in the usual way: as a one-way relation of determination with modal status. The material realizations of experience also reveal or disclose the world, but they do so in a quite different way: the revealing activity performed by the material realization of an experience has a quite different status from that of the experience itself. This, ultimately, is why there is an explanatory gap between conscious experience and its material realizations.

Consider, for example, the mechanisms whereby, it is thought, my retinal image of a red tomato is progressively transformed into a visual representation of a tomato. Let us, for now, work with our favorite paradigmatically internalist model of this process: Marr's (1982) account. The retinal image is transformed into a 3D object representation by way of its progressive transformation through raw primal sketch, full primal sketch, and 2½D sketch. To identify the mechanisms responsible for these transformations, if Marr's account is correct, would be to identify the mechanisms that are *causally* responsible for my visual experience of the tomato and its specific aspects.

The successive transformations that collectively produce the visual experience of the red tomato are a form of disclosing activity. However, this is quite different from the form of disclosure exhibited by transcendental modes of presentation, at least when these are understood at the level of content. In no part of the Marrian story—or in any story like it—do we find *logically* sufficient conditions for the disclosure of the world as being, for example, shiny and red. This disclosure undoubtedly has physically sufficient conditions in certain psychophysical events, occurring, perhaps, both inside and outside the body. But these *physically* sufficient conditions do not add up to *logically* sufficient conditions. There is no logical contradiction involved in supposing that there are two subjects in whom exactly the same Marrian processing operations are being performed on exactly the same retinal image, but where, as a result of these processes, one of the these subjects experiences a tomato as shiny and red where the other experiences it as dull and green (or experiences nothing at all).[3] This may be physically impossible, but the absence of logical contradiction shows that it is not logically impossible. Indeed, this is one way—a simple translation into the language of disclosure—of understanding the force of the various explanatory gap intuitions.

The shift from *physically* to *logically* sufficient conditions is, in effect, a move from what *produces* a given item to what a given item *consists in*. At the level of the content of experience, a transcendental item is that in which the appearance of an item as empirical consists. Thus, understood transcendentally, the phenomenal character of my visual experience—what it is like to see a shiny red tomato—does not (causally) *produce* the revealing of the tomato as red. Rather, it is what the revealing of the tomato as red consists in. We can use the ambiguous expression "in virtue of" to express this idea—the phenomenal character of my experience is that in virtue of which the object of the experience is revealed in the way that it is—but only if we are clear that this is a *constitutive* rather than *causal* sense of that expression.

It is useful, for the purposes of extending this idea to cognition in general, to formulate it explicitly in terms of the distinction between vehicle and content. Visual experiences possess phenomenal content. The phenomenal content of an experience discloses the intentional object of that experience by providing a logically sufficient condition for the object to fall under a given empirical mode of presentation. The vehicles of that content provide only a causally sufficient condition for the object to fall under this mode of presentation.

Cognitive states—thoughts, beliefs, memories, and so on—also possess content. Their content is semantic. Much work has recently been done with a view to delineating the relation between semantic and phenomenal content. Does phenomenal content reduce to semantic content? Or is the former *sui generis*? We need not get involved with these questions. For our purposes, it is enough to point out that semantic content, whatever its relation to phenomenal content, discloses objects in a different way than does the vehicle of that content. Semantic content provides a logically sufficient condition for an object to be disclosed as falling under a given empirical mode of presentation. The vehicles of that content provide only a causally sufficient condition. Thus, if am entertaining a thought with the content "That tomato sure looks shiny and red," then this is a logically sufficient condition for the tomato to be revealed to me, *in my thought,* as shiny and red. There is no logically possible way that the tomato could not be revealed in thought in this way given that my thought has the content it does. However, whatever causal mechanisms we identify in the brain—whether these mechanisms are neurologically specified or identified in terms of a more abstract functional role—these provide only a causally sufficient condition for the tomato to be revealed to me, in thought, in this way. As a matter of natural necessity, given that these neurological or functional mechanisms are activated in the right way, I must be thinking of the tomato as shiny and red. But this natural necessity does not translate into logical necessity. There is no contradiction in supposing that, even given the appropriate activation of the mechanisms, I am thinking of the tomato in some other way, or not thinking of the tomato at all. The semantic content of my thought constitutively discloses the tomato as shiny and red. The neurological or functional mechanisms causally disclose the tomato as shiny and red.

Therefore, we should be alive to the distinction between causal and constitutive disclosure: to the distinction between disclosure by means of causally sufficient conditions and disclosure by means of logically sufficient conditions. The distinction is not insignificant, and in other contexts it might be crucial. It is unclear, for example, where the constitutive disclosure of the world takes place. Indeed, I have argued elsewhere (Rowlands 2001, 2002, 2003) that it takes place nowhere at all. If this is correct, then we would have to allow that there is an aspect of consciousness that is real but nowhere at all; that the bounds of the real do not coincide with those of the spatial. Even I am willing to accept that this is a controversial claim. Happily, for the purposes of this book, we do not need it.

As we have seen, the thesis of the amalgamated mind—the conjunction of the theses of the embodied mind and the extended mind—is a thesis about the *vehicles* of cognition, not the *content* of cognition. It claims that the vehicles of cognition include processes of exploiting bodily structures and/or processes of manipulating environmental structures. If we are going to use the apparatus of disclosure to understand this thesis, then the relevant sort of disclosure will be that belonging to the vehicles of cognition rather than the content of cognitive states. That is, the relevant sort of disclosure will be causal rather than constitutive, and from now on my focus will be exclusively on causal disclosure.

Causal disclosure is a part of the world in the normal way. On Marr's account, for example, causal disclosure takes place in the various mechanisms and processes that make up the progressive transformation of the retinal image into the 3D object representation. If we could successfully transform this algorithmic description into an implementational one, then we will have thereby identified where this particular causal disclosure of the world takes place.

In the rest of this chapter, *pace* Marr, I am going to argue that there are reasons for supposing that, in general, causal disclosure of the world does not take place purely inside the head of a subject. The essence of intentionality is disclosing activity. The sort of disclosing activity occasioned by the vehicles of intentional states and processes—the sorts of vehicles pertinent to the theses of embodied and extended cognition—is causal disclosure. Causal disclosure can be effected or brought about by states and processes occurring in the brains of subjects of intentional states. But, in general, it is not restricted to neural states and processes. There are many ways of causally disclosing the world—many vehicles through which the world may be causally disclosed to subjects—and brain-based ways are only a subset of these. In general, the vehicles of causal disclosure do not stop at the boundaries of the brain, but extend out into the activity we perform in the world, activity that is both bodily and incorporates wider environmental performances. In the following sections I shall elaborate and defend these claims.

3   Intentionality as a "Traveling Through"

I have argued that the noneliminable core of intentionality consists in a *disclosure* or *revelation* of the world. The fundamental sense in which intentional acts are directed toward the objects, therefore, is that they reveal or disclose them as having certain *aspects* or *empirical modes of presentation*. Two forms of revelation or disclosure can be distinguished: causal and constitutive. The concerns of this book require only the former. But, whichever sense of disclosure we focus on, the idea that intentional directedness is to be understood in terms of disclosure has a crucial, but largely overlooked, implication: as directedness toward objects, intentional acts are also, necessarily, a *traveling-through* of their material realizations.

This idea can perhaps best be clarified, in the first instance, by way of a well-known example; indeed, by now, possibly a hackneyed example: Merleau-Ponty's (1962, 143ff.) famous discussion of the perceptual role played by a blind person's cane (cf. Polanyi 1962, 71). As Merleau-Ponty notes, it is possible to tell two quite different stories about this role. The first story treats the cane as an empirical object: in this case, an object of theoretical scrutiny and explanation. The resulting empirical story is a familiar one. Tactile and kinesthetic sensors in the blind person's hands send messages to the brain. Various events then occur in the person's sensory cortex, and these are interpreted as the result of ambient objects standing in certain relations to the person's location. When suitably filled out, there is nothing wrong with this story. However, it only describes the blind person's consciousness from the outside, as an empirical phenomenon. The story from the inside—the transcendental story in the sense introduced earlier—is quite different. The cane—in conjunction, of course, with the requisite neural and other biological machinery—*discloses* or *reveals* objects as possessing or falling under certain *aspects* or *empirical modes of presentation*. Thus, an object may be disclosed to the blind person as being "in front" of him or her, as "near," "farther away," "to the left," "to the right," and so on.

Merleau-Ponty is at pains to emphasize—quite correctly—the phenomenology of the resulting perception of the world. The blind person does not experience aspects of the objects he encounters as occurring in the cane, even though this is (part of) the material basis of his perception of these aspects. Still less does he experience them as occurring in the fingers that grip the cane; and less again in the sensory cortex that systematizes the experiential input. The cane can be both an *object* of awareness and a *vehicle* of awareness. But when the blind person uses the cane, it functions as a vehicle, not an object, of awareness. The cane is not something of which the blind person is aware; it is something *with* which he is aware. Phenomenologically, the consciousness of the blind person passes all the way through the cane to the world.

Essentially the same sort of point was also made by Sartre. In his famous discussion of the body in *Being and Nothingness*, part 3, Sartre notes:

I do not apprehend my hand in the act of writing but only the pen which is writing; this means that I use my pen in order to form letters but not my hand in order to hold the pen. I am not in relation to my hand in the same utilizing attitude as I am in relation to the pen: I *am* my hand. (Sartre 1943/1957, 426)

Similarly:

Thus in a duel with swords or quarter-staffs, it is the quarter-staff which I watch with my eyes and which I handle. In the act of writing it is the point of the pen which I look at in synthetic combination with the line or the square marked on the sheet of paper. But my hand has vanished; it is lost in the complex system of instrumentality in order that this system may exist. It is simply the meaning and orientation of the system. (Ibid.)

One may legitimately contest whether Sartre has described the phenomenology correctly in these cases. It seems that Sartre has, for example, little experience of dueling with quarter-staffs (in particular, if, as he appears to suggest, the quarter-staff at which you are looking is the same as the one you are handling, then, one might suspect, you are going to have a painful afternoon). Nevertheless, the general phenomenological point is a legitimate one: when I am doing things with my hand, then phenomenologically my consciousness passes through my hand to the instruments it employs (and often, of course, it needn't stop there—as Merleau-Ponty's blind person shows).

As points concerning the phenomenology of absorbed coping experience, Merleau-Ponty's and Sartre's claims can, I think, scarcely be contested.

However, here I want to distinguish these claims concerning the phenomenology of experience from quite distinct ones concerning the underlying structure of intentional directedness. My primary concern is with the latter claim. And this latter claim is also, I suspect, more basic: the claims concerning phenomenology are grounded in the claims concerning the structure of intentional directedness in the sense that the truth of the former derives from the truth of the latter.

Intentional directedness, I have argued, consists in a form of disclosure or revelation. Intentional acts are directed toward the world in the sense, and to the extent, that they are disclosing or revealing activity. But where does the blind person's revealing activity occur? When the person discloses an object as being in front of him, for example, where does this disclosing activity occur? It occurs, in part, in the brain. But it also occurs in the body, and also, crucially, in the cane and the cane's interaction with the world. Revealing activity, by its nature, *does not stop short of the world*: it *travels through* its material realizations out to the world itself.

The role of the cane, when used in this way, is not one of *object* of disclosure but *vehicle* of disclosure. The blind person does not, it is commonly observed, experience the object as "on the end of the cane," nor does he experience it as a blocking or resistance to the cane. But a question seldom asked is: why should the phenomenology of his experience be like this? Why wouldn't he experience aspects of the objects he encounters as occurring in the cane? Why wouldn't he experience them as occurring in his fingers that grip the cane? These facts about the phenomenology of his experience are grounded in the underlying nature of intentional directedness. Phenomenologically, the blind person's experience does not stop short of the world because (1) this experience is intentionally directed toward the world, (2) intentional directedness is revealing or disclosing activity, and (3) disclosing activity does not stop short of the world. Thus, it is *in virtue of* the object's being on the end of the cane, and *in virtue of* the resistance it provides to the cane, that the blind person experiences the object as spatially located in the world. In employing the cane, the blind person ceases to experience the cane. As revealing activity, his experience travels all the way through the cane to the object itself. That is why his experience can be a disclosing of the aspects of those objects.

The concept of *traveling through* should be distinguished from the superficially similar idea of *living through*. It is quite common to talk of consciousness as, for example, living through the brain. Claims of this sort typically advert to a one-way relation of dependence that can be characterized in terms of the concept of supervenience or realization. In this sense, consciousness lives through the brain to the extent that the brain is *respon-sible* for consciousness—that without the requisite neural activity there would be no consciousness. It is true to say, in this sense, that the blind person's perceptual consciousness lives through his cane. The cane is part of the realization of his perception of the world. Nevertheless, although it is true that the blind person's perceptual consciousness lives through his cane, this is not what I mean by describing his experience as a traveling through the cane.

Suppose you are utterly engrossed in a novel. Your consciousness passes through the words on the page—these are not explicit objects of your awareness—through to the characters and plot-lines these words commu-nicate. When I talk of consciousness traveling through its material realiza-tions, I intend this to be something akin to the way in which consciousness passes through the words of a book to the characters that these words describe. This example, however, might suggest that the idea of traveling through is fundamentally a phenomenological one. Phenomenologically, from the point of view of what it is like to have or undergo the relevant experiences, the blind person experiences the objects around him as objects in the world rather than modifications of the cane. Phenomenologically, we might say, his consciousness does not stop short of the world. Similarly, in reading the novel, my consciousness stops not at the words on the page but passes all the way through to the characters those words describe.

However, the concept of traveling through is one that pertains, funda-mentally, not to the phenomenology of experience, but to the underlying nature of intentional directedness as disclosure, something in which the phenomenology is grounded. In this respect, a useful template for thinking about revealing activity is provided by processes such as *exploration*—a paradigmatic example of revealing activity. I am, let us suppose, exploring an unfamiliar terrain. I walk across the clearing, toward the large tree that obstructs my view, and in so doing reveal the lie of the land behind the tree. This is a form of revealing activity. It takes place partly in the brain: if my brain were made of sawdust, no disclosure of the terrain would occur. But it also takes place in my body—the body that propels me across the clearing toward the tree. And it also takes place in the things I do in and to the world. Barring more remote forms of exploration (telescope, satellite imagery, etc.), exploration of a new and unfamiliar terrain requires that I situate myself in that terrain: my exploration of the terrain does not stop short of the terrain itself. This is not to say, of course, that this activity is to be identified with intentionality. All intentionality is revealing activ-ity, but not all revealing activity is intentionality. The point here is that revealing activity, in general, is something that is done in the head, in the body, and also in the world. By its very nature, revelation or disclosure of a given region of the world does not stop short of that world: if it did, it would by definition be unsuccessful (or even fail to be a case of revealing activity at all). Revealing activity is, in this sense, essentially *worldly*.

4   Heidegger and De-severance

This rather difficult idea of might become clearer if we compare it to the position defended by Heidegger (1927/1962). Some might, not entirely unreasonably, be skeptical of the idea that comparison with Heidegger is even the *sort* of thing that can help in a process of clarification. But even if we overlook this kind of skepticism, such comparison is not without its difficulties, since Heidegger would eschew the conceptual apparatus in terms of which I have developed the argument: the apparatus of consciousness, experience, intentionality, mode of presentation, and the like. For Heidegger, these are "positive" rather than "primordial" phenomena. That is, they are phenomena that are essentially derivative on more basic ways of relating to the world. Nevertheless, while he would hate the terms in which this argument is expressed, there remains an idea in the work of Heidegger that closely engages with the argument developed here. The idea is that of human beings (*Dasein*) as essentially *de-severant* or *de-distancing*:

"De-severing" [*Entfernen*] amounts to making the farness vanish—that is, making the remoteness of something disappear, bringing it close. Dasein is essentially de-severant: it lets any entity be encountered close by as the entity which it is. (Heidegger 1927/1962, 139)

And again:

Proximally, and for the most part, de-severing is a circumspective bringing-close—bringing something close by, in the sense of procuring it, putting it in readiness, having it to hand. But certain ways in which entities are discovered in a purely cognitive manner also have the character of bringing them close. *In Dasein there lies an essential tendency towards closeness*. (Ibid., 140)

For example, in connection with walking along the street toward someone one has seen, Heidegger writes:

One feels the touch of it at every step as one walks; it is seemingly the closest and Realest of all that is ready-to-hand, and it slides itself, as it were, along certain portions of one's body—the soles of one's feet. And yet it is farther remote than the acquaintance whom one encounters "on the street" at a "remoteness" of twenty paces when one is taking such a walk. Circumspective concern decides as to the closeness and farness of what is proximally ready-to-hand environmentally. (Ibid., 142)

As with Merleau-Ponty's discussion of the blind person, we can take these remarks in two ways: as a point about the phenomenology of our experience, or as a point about the structure of consciousness (or, as Heidegger would prefer it, *Dasein*). It is clear which way Heidegger wants to think of it: he regards de-severance as a constitutive feature of *Dasein*. Indeed, this is a consequence of his regarding the phenomenology of experience as positive rather than primordial. To claim that phenomenological content is positive is to claim that it is derivative upon something more basic. And, for Heidegger, this more basic element was the form of self-interpreting world disclosure that he called *Dasein*. Heidegger regarded de-severance as a fundamental constitutive feature of *Dasein*—a primordial rather than positive phenomenon. So, it is reasonably clear that he is not contenting himself with making a relatively mundane claim about the nature of visual phenomenology.

I have, in effect, argued for an analogous position with regard to the relation between the phenomenological idea of traveling through and the structural version of traveling through: the former is grounded in the latter. The objects in the environment of Merleau-Ponty's blind man are located at the end of his cane. But he does not experience them as such: his consciousness passes all the way through the cane to the objects itself. Understood as a point about the phenomenology of what it is like to experience the world in the way that the blind man does, these claims are not really contestable. But nor, on the other hand, are they particularly profound. The claim is, I think, far more significant when they are understood as a claim about the nature or structure of intentional directedness. Intentionality is revealing activity, and this activity takes place, in part, in the cane (and in the brain and in the body, etc.). The cane can with as much justification be regarded as the (partial) locus of the blind man's revealing activity as his brain. The nature of the blind person's revealing activity is that it travels through his brain, through his body, through his cane, out into the world itself.

There is another way of putting this general idea: *there is no intentionality at a distance*. In classroom discussions of the concept of intentionality we might find chalk arrows arcing out across the void that lies between a person's mental representation and the external item that the representation is about. But intentional directedness, I have argued, is not like this at all. Intentional directedness is revealing activity, and revealing activity does not take place in a void. Activity is always done by something and with something. So, to employ Heidegger's example, when I see my acquaintance on the street at a distance of twenty paces, I do so by revealing, visually, what is on the street as (presumably among other things) a person with whom I am acquainted. But what, in this case, are the analogues of the blind man's cane? What is the intentional ether in which my revealing activities can be grounded or given form? What, in other words, are the vehicles of disclosure—vehicles through which my consciousness travels all the way through to my acquaintance herself?

5   The Vehicles of Perceptual Disclosure

Consider the disclosing activities of a visually unimpaired subject. It is tempting, indeed it is typical, to think of these activities as restricted to processes occurring in the eyes themselves and subsequent neural processing operations. Such processes are, of course, vehicles of disclosure, not objects of disclosure. I am not aware *of* these processes: they are processes *with* or *in virtue of* which I am aware of other things. Relative to those things *of* which I am aware—the *empirical* objects of my awareness—the status of these processes is *transcendental*. These processes form part of my causal disclosure of the world.

  However, my causal disclosure of the world is not restricted to these inner processes. In addition to the various neural processes occurring in my eyes and brain we can also identify various activities that I perform in the world; and these activities also form part of my causal disclosure of the world. It is useful to break down these activities into three different, but partially overlapping, kinds: (i) saccadic eye movements, (ii) probing and exploratory activities involved in the identification of sensorimotor contingencies, and (iii) the manipulation and exploitation of the optic array. These categories do not exhaust the kinds of extraneural disclosing or revealing activities appropriate to visual perception. But they are, I think, absolutely central.

Saccadic eye movements   When I perform visual tasks, my eyes engage in various movements—*saccades*. Yarbus (1967) has demonstrated that (i) different tasks result in quite different scan paths, and (ii) the pattern of saccadic eye movement is systematically related to the nature of the visual task. In a famous series of experiments, Yarbus (1967) asked subjects, prior to their viewing of a painting, to perform certain tasks. The painting showed six women and the arrival of a male visitor. Subjects were asked to either:

1. View the picture at will.
2. Judge the age of the people in the painting.
3. Guess what the people had been doing prior to the arrival of the visitor.
4. Remember the clothing worn.
5. Remember the position of objects in the room.
6. Estimate how long it had been since the visitor was seen by the people in the painting.

Yarbus demonstrated that the required task had an impact on the visual scan path that the subject took: different tasks resulted in quite different visual scan paths. Subjects asked questions concerning the appearance of people in the painting—for example, questions about their ages—focused on the area around the face. Subjects asked questions concerning the theme of the painting focused on various points throughout the picture. And different themes also resulted in different scan paths. For example, subjects asked what the people doing before the visitor arrived employed a different scan path from those asked to estimate how long it had been since the visitor was last seen by the family. In general, Yarbus showed, the scan varies systematically with the nature of the task.

Saccadic eye movements, and the more general patterns of search in which such movements are situated, are part of the vehicles of perceptual disclosure. Being a person I saw only last week is an empirical mode of presentation of an object. So too is being a person I haven't seen for years. My saccadic scan paths, in the sort of context described here, are part of the means with or in virtue of which the world is disclosed as falling under one or another empirical mode of presentation—for example, as containing a collection of people who have not seen the visitor for many years rather than a collection of people who saw him last week.

Saccadic scan paths are, of course, not objects of awareness—typically, we have little or no idea what our eyes are doing when we extract information from a visual scene. Phenomenologically, we are typically not aware of the eye movements, but of what these movements help us reveal: an object falling under an empirical mode of presentation. And this phenomenological point concerning what we are and what we are not aware of is grounded in the deeper point concerning the nature of intentional directedness: as revealing or disclosing activity, intentional directedness passes all the way out to the objects revealed. In this case, it travels through the saccadic eye movements out to the world itself.

Sensorimotor activity Recall the *enactive* or *sensorimotor* account of visual experience outlined in chapters 2 and 3. Such an account accords a central role to a certain sort of activity: the probing or exploratory activity required to identify the sensorimotor contingencies pertinent to a given visual scene. Earlier, I cast doubt on whether enactive accounts could properly be regarded as versions of the extended mind. Here I simply want to focus on the role of exploratory visual activity. Whether or not enactive accounts are of a piece with extended accounts, it is still true that the sorts of exploratory activities invoked by enactive accounts are among the vehicles of perceptual disclosure. And this latter claim is all we need for present purposes.

Suppose, to use an example of Dennett (1991), you are looking at a wall of photographs of Marilyn Monroe, à la Andy Warhol. Your foveal vision subtends no more than three or four of these photographs, and your parafoveal vision is insufficiently precise to discriminate Marilyns from squiggly shapes. Nevertheless, it seems to you as if you are confronted with a wall of Marilyns, and not three or four Marilyns surrounded by a sea of squiggly shapes. The wall of Marilyns, in its entirety, is phenomenologically present to you.

The explanation supplied by the enactive account of this sense of phenomenological presence is simple and elegant. First, the impression we have of seeing everything—the wall of Marilyns in its entirety—derives from the fact that the slightest flick of the eye allows any part of the wall to be processed at will. This gives us the impression that the whole wall is immediately available (O'Regan and Noë 2001, 946). Is this impression erroneous? It would be erroneous only if seeing consisted in the production of an internal representation isomorphic with the part of the world seen. If, on the other hand, we accept that seeing consists in combining the results of environmental probing with knowledge of laws of sensorimotor contingency, we are indeed seeing the whole scene, for probing the world, and knowledge of these laws, is precisely what we do and have as we cast our attention from one aspect to the next.

Second, in addition to our ability to direct our attention, at will, to the visual world, the visual system is particularly sensitive to *visual transients*. When a visual transient occurs, a low-level "attention-grabbing" mechanism appears to automatically direct processing to the location of the transient. This means that should anything happen in the environment, we will generally consciously see it, since processing will be directed toward it. This gives us the impression of having tabs on everything that might change, and so of consciously seeing everything. And if seeing consists in exploratory activity combined with knowledge of sensorimotor contingencies accompanying such exploration, then this impression is not erroneous. We do, indeed, see everything. The suspicion that we do not derives from a residual attachment to the idea that seeing consists in the production of an internal representation that maps onto the outside world.

Casting one's attention at will to any part of the visual scene, or having one's attention drawn by a visual transient to a part of the scene: these are both examples of probing or exploratory activity.[4] Like saccadic scan paths, these sorts of activities are vehicles of perceptual disclosure: they are that with which or in virtue of which, in part, the visual world is disclosed in the way that it is. That is, the activity is that in virtue of which a given part of the world is revealed as falling under one or another empirical mode of presentation—for example, a falling under the empirical mode of presentation "wall of Marilyns" rather than the mode of presentation "wall of indeterminate shapes." These probing, exploratory activities are not, typically, things *of* which we are aware when we visually experience the world: they are things *with* which we visually experience the world. That is, they are activities with which the world is disclosed to us as falling under one or another empirical mode of presentation. That is, these activities are among the vehicles of causal disclosure of the world; part of the means by which, in the case of vision, our intentional directedness toward the world is achieved or effected. As such, our visual consciousness both lives through and travels through these activities no less than it does through processes occurring in our eyes and brain.

Manipulation of the optic array   Consider, now, Gibson's (1966) account of visual perception outlined earlier. A key component of Gibson's account is the idea that by acting on the optic array, and thus transforming it, the perceiving organism makes available to itself information that was, prior to the action, present but not available. When an observer moves, the optic array is transformed, and such transformations contain information about the layout, shapes, and orientations of objects in the world. More specifically, by effecting transformations in the ambient optic array—by transforming one array into another systematically related array—perceiving organisms can identify and appropriate what Gibson calls the *invariant* information contained in the optic array. This is information contained not in any one static optic array as such, but in the transformation of one optic array into another. The proper function of the transformation of one optic array into another is to transform the status of this invariant information from the merely present to the available.

The manipulation of the optic array, manipulation that is carried out by movement on the part of the perceiving organism, is another vehicle of perceptual disclosure. The perceiving organism need not be, and typically is not, aware of its manipulative activities: these activities are vehicles of disclosure, not objects of disclosure. That is, the activities are ones *with* or in virtue of which the perceiving organism becomes aware of certain features of its environment; they are not, typically, activities *of* which the organism is perceptually aware. Phenomenologically, the perceptual awareness of the organism passes through the activities to the world that those activities, in part, disclose to it. Crucially, where does the organism's perceptual disclosure of the environment take place? It takes place, in part, wherever the activities take place. And these activities do not stop short of the external optic array. One cannot manipulate an external structure unless one's manipulation reaches out to that structure.

Like saccadic scan paths and sensorimotor probing, manipulation of the optic array is one of the vehicles of causal disclosure of the world. That is, in the case of visual perception, manipulation of the array is one of the means by which our intentional directedness toward the world is brought about; it is one of the means by way of which a part of the world is revealed as falling under some or other empirical mode of presentation. Our visual consciousness both lives and travels through these manipulative activities no less than it occurs in processes occurring in the eye and brain.

6   The Return of Otto

The story so far looks like this. Intentionality—intentional directedness toward the world—should be understood as revealing or disclosing activity. This is the activity in virtue of which the world is presented to the subject as falling under one or more aspects or empirical modes of presentation. If intentional directedness consists in disclosing activity, it takes place wherever this disclosing activity takes place. Such activity exists in many places. Processes occurring in the eyes and the brain can be part of this disclosing activity: they are certainly part of the activity in virtue of which the world can be disclosed to a subject as being a certain way—that is, as falling under a given empirical mode of presentation. However, there is little reason for thinking that the disclosing activity constitutive of intentionality is restricted to processes occurring inside the brain. Certain things we do in and to the world can, no less than neural processes, be part of the activity that discloses the world to a subject as falling under a given empirical mode of presentation. When Merleau-Ponty's blind man uses a cane to disclose the world as containing objects in a particular orientation to him, this is part of the activity through which he discloses the world. When a visually unimpaired subject employs a certain saccadic scan path in order to identify salient information in a visually presented scene, this is part of the disclosing activity of that subject. When he probes and explores the world in a manner that reveals its sensorimotor contingencies, this probing and exploration forms parts of his disclosing activities. When he manipulates the optic array in order to make available information that was, prior to this, present but unavailable, this too is part of his disclosing or revealing activities. If intentionality consists in disclosing activity, then this intentionality is not restricted to processes occurring inside the brain.

The discussion, so far, has supplied two things. First, there is the general model of intentionality as revealing activity. Second, there is the application of this general model to perception—in particular, visual perception. However, the amalgamated mind—the conjunction of the embodied mind and extended mind—is a thesis about cognition in general, not merely perception. Therefore, the next stage is to switch focus and apply the model of intentionality as revealing activity to cognitive processes more generally. With this goal in mind, let us return to Clark and Chalmers's case of Otto.

Wanting to see the exhibition he has just read about in the newspaper, Otto consults his notebook, and sees that the Museum of Modern Art is on 53rd Street. On Clark and Chalmers's version of the extended mind (at least as this is usually understood), the entry in Otto's notebook is identical with one of his beliefs. For reasons outlined earlier, I do not endorse this claim. The sentence-tokens in Otto's book are the *wrong* sorts of tokens to be identical with belief-tokens. Therefore, we should not identify the sentences in Otto's book with token cognitive states. According to my version of the extended mind, on the other hand, Otto's manipulation of his notebook counts as part of his process of remembering the location of the Museum. If the account of intentional directedness defended here is correct, then it is clear why this should be so. The manipulation of the book forms part of the vehicles of causal disclosure of the world. That is, the activity of manipulating the book is part of the means whereby, in the case of memory, Otto's intentional directedness toward the world is brought about. The manipulation of the notebook is, in part, that in virtue of which the world is disclosed to Otto, in memory, as falling under a specific empirical mode of presentation. That is, in virtue of Otto's activity, the museum is disclosed as falling under the empirical mode of presentation of being located on 53rd Street. The intentional directedness of Otto toward the world both lives and travels through his manipulation of the notebook. For this manipulation is nothing more than what, in part, reveals the world to him, in memory, as being as certain way.

This is why it is legitimate to regard Otto's manipulation of his book as part of his process of remembering. The manipulation is part of the vehicle of his intentional directedness toward the world—intentional directedness that, in this case, takes the form of remembering. There is, as I argued earlier, no intentional directedness in the void. Intentional directedness always takes place through some or other vehicles—intentional ether, if you like. In the case of Otto, the vehicles are, in part, brain processes: the processes, for example, that allow him to detect the sentence that is written on the page and form beliefs about the content of this sentence. The processes are also bodily: for example, ones that allow his arms, hands, and fingers to move in such a way that they can manipulate the book. But they are also, finally, environmental processes—processes of manipulating the book in such a way that information that was hitherto unavailable to Otto now becomes available. In the case of Otto, all of these processes—neural, bodily, and environmental—form proper parts of the overall process of disclosing the world, in memory, as falling under a given empirical mode of presentation. But to talk of disclosing the world, in memory, as falling under a given empirical mode of presentation is simply to talk of remembering the world as falling under a given empirical mode of presentation. To remember is simply to disclose the world in memory. Therefore, in the case of Otto at least, all of these processes—neural, bodily, and environmental—can properly be regarded as forming part of the overall process of remembering.

This way of understanding the case of Otto has another advantage: it allows us to defuse what many take to be an important objection to the extended mind. One objection to regarding Otto's consultation of his book as part of the process of remembering is that Otto's access to his book is fundamentally different from Inga's access to her memories. Otto's access to his book is perceptual; Inga's access to her memories or beliefs is not. In considering this objection, Clark and Chalmers accept the premise of the objection: Otto's access to his notebook entries is indeed perceptual and Inga's access to her beliefs is not. But they deny that this disqualifies the notebook entries from counting as among Otto's beliefs. The difference in mode of access is not sufficiently significant to result in this disqualification. Consider, they say, a cyborg of the Arnold Schwarzenegger *Terminator* genre. The terminator's access to its stored information—both about the world and its internal states—takes the form of a quasi-perceptual display on a virtual visual display unit (VDU). This does not seem to preclude ascribing to the terminator, when the appropriate virtual display is activated, the belief that, for example, the fleeing suspect is indeed John Connor. Whether or not an item counts as a belief is not something essentially determined by one's mode of access to it. Rather, as we have seen, for Clark and Chalmers, it is the item's functional role that is decisive.

In an earlier chapter, I provided some reasons for doubting that the moral of the case of Otto is that the entries in his notebook qualified as a subset of his beliefs. I argued that it was more plausible to frame the conclusion in terms of processes rather than states: Otto's manipulation of his notebook could, in the appropriate circumstances, be regarded as part of the process of remembering. The point I want to develop in this section, however, is indifferent to whether we want to understand the case of Otto in terms of states or processes. My discussion to follow, therefore, will follow Clark and Chalmers's version of the extended mind more than I think, in other contexts, would be advisable.

The problem with Clark and Chalmers's response is perhaps clear from the earlier discussion of the role played by liberal functionalism in the extended mind. On most accounts of functional role, of course, the mode of access one has to one's beliefs would be counted as part of the functional role of those beliefs. This is because the functional role of an item is defined in terms of its typical causes and typical effects. But the effects typical of a virtual VDU would be different from those of a belief traditionally understood. For example, among the causal effects of the virtual VDU would be the belief that I am having a visual experience of a particular sort. This would not be true of belief in its traditional form. Therefore, the causal roles are in fact distinct. Therefore, if we are relying on a functionalist account of belief to justify our claims concerning Otto, we would have to deny that the entries in his notebook qualify as his beliefs. The only way around this is to regard the sorts of functional difference in question as shallow ones—not significant enough to make a difference in the way we type psychological states or processes. But this will only work if we think there is a more abstract level of description of function that preserves the important aspects of functional role while whittling away these unimportant ones. This more abstract functional description would, in other words, allow us to justify the claim that there are certain aspects of functional role that are sufficiently unimportant to be safely ignored. But this, as we might have guessed, leads us straight back to the dispute between liberal and chauvinistic forms of functionalism—and, therefore (i) to the possibility of stalemate, and, more seriously, (ii) to a standoff between the extended and embodied strands of the amalgamated mind.

The account of intentional directedness I have developed allows us to sidestep the issue of the appropriate level of functional description for psychological kinds. From the point of view of the account of intentional directedness developed in this book, the claim that Otto's access to his notebook entries is perceptual while Inga's access to her beliefs is not is, of course, true; but it is also misleading and irrelevant. Consider, first, why it is misleading. When Otto looks in his book and reads "The Museum of Modern Art is on 53rd Street," what is the phenomenology of this visual experience? Is he aware of the words and letters? Is this a correct way of thinking about the visual phenomenology of reading in general? In one sense of "aware," then, of course, when one reads, one is aware of the words that one is reading, and the letters that make up these words. We shall look more closely at what this sense of awareness amounts to in due course. For now, let's simply assume that Otto is aware of the words and sentences written in his book. Without awareness in this sense, Otto can scarcely be thought of as reading.

However, to suppose that this is *all* Otto is aware of would be a mistake that disguises the true nature of the phenomenology of reading. When reading, if things are going well, one is aware not primarily of the words on the page but of what those words describe—what they are about. To be aware only, or even primarily, of the words or letters on the page is a sure sign of intentionality that has been stymied or otherwise thwarted. Earlier, we looked at Heidegger's discussion of the sorts of environmental break-down that could thwart one's intentional directedness in this way. Applied to Otto, perhaps his writing is not particularly legible, and he must stare intently at the sentence to work out whether the indistinct scrawl at part of the sentence is a "5" or a "3." In such circumstances, Otto might well be aware primarily of the words on the page, and not what those words are about. But such circumstances are abnormal. Following Heidegger we might imagine various levels of environmental breakdown—conspicuous-ness, obstinacy, and obduracy—of varying degrees of severity. Perhaps Otto must don his spectacles in order to read some of the sentences—but after he does so he can resume his normal circumspective dealings with the book (conspicuousness). Perhaps even with his spectacles on, some of the sentences are not particularly legible, and he must stare intently at them in order to try and decipher what they are saying (obstinacy). Or perhaps his book is nowhere to be found, and Otto must try and work out how he is possibly going to cope without it (obdurateness).

However, these are all circumstances where something has gone wrong. In normal circumstances matters are not like this at all. The relevant sense of "normal," here, is a normative rather than statistical sense: perhaps, for Otto, things go wrong more often than not. In normal circumstances, where things are going as they should, Otto's consciousness passes through the words of his notebook to what those words are about. He is not primarily aware of the sentence "The Museum of Modern Art is on 53rd Street." He is aware of the *fact* that the Museum of Modern Art is on 53rd Street. Similarly, Inga is not aware of her neural states. Her consciousness passes through those states to what they are about: the fact that the Museum of Modern Art is located on 53rd Street. In both cases, when it is not stymied by unfortunate environmental circumstances, the intentional directedness of both Otto and Inga passes through their material realizations out to the world itself.

This is why the appeal to visual phenomenology is also, ultimately, irrelevant. To see why, consider the sense in which Otto is aware of the sentence "The Museum of Modern Art is on 53rd Street." The pronounced temptation to suppose that he is aware of the sentence results from the conflation identified and examined in earlier chapters: the confusion of awareness *of* and awareness *with*. Fundamentally, when things are going as they should, Otto is not aware of the sentence—this is not the intentional object of act. Rather, the sentence in his book is something *with* which, or *in virtue of* which, he is aware of other things—notably the *fact* of the location of the museum. The sentence is, in part, what discloses to Otto the empirical mode of apprehension under which the museum falls— being located on 53rd Street. Otto's manipulation of his notebook is, no more and no less than Inga's consultation of her memory, a way of revealing the world, in memory, as falling under a given empirical mode of presentation—that is, as containing the Museum of Modern Art that is located on 53rd Street. As such, Otto's manipulation of his notebook is a way of revealing or disclosing the world, and his consciousness, typically, passes all the way through the words on the page to what those words are about.

The neural states of Inga, and the notebook entries of Otto, are both vehicles of disclosure. They are both items with which Inga and Otto are aware of objects in the world. And they are both items of this sort because they are both, in part, the vehicles by which the world is disclosed as containing objects that fall under one or more empirical mode of presentation. They are, in this sense, both vehicles of Inga's and Otto's revealing or disclosing activity. They are vehicles in virtue of which, in part, the world is disclosed as being a certain way: as containing as the Museum of Modern Art that is located on 53rd Street. This, I think, is the justification for regarding Otto's manipulation of his notebook as part of his process of remembering. Otto's manipulation of his notebook forms part of the vehicle of his cognitive disclosure of the world. The museum is disclosed, in memory, as falling under the empirical mode of apprehension "located on 53rd Street." Otto's manipulation of his notebook forms part of the vehicle of this disclosure. And that is why the manipulation should be regarded as part—a cognitive part—of a cognitive process.

7   Disclosure and Cognitive Disclosure

I can already envisage attempts to parody this position. I walk around the corner, thereby disclosing things that would have otherwise remainder undisclosed. Therefore, walking around the corner is a cognitive process. But this, of course, is nothing more than a parody. Walking around the corner is a means of disclosure. But not all disclosure is cognitive disclosure. Therefore, not all disclosure forms part of a cognitive process. What is the difference between cognitive and noncognitive disclosure? That's easy: cognitive disclosure is disclosing activity that satisfies the criterion of the cognitive. Cognitive disclosure is disclosure that takes the form of (1) the manipulation and transformation of information-bearing structures, where this (2) has the proper function of making available, either to the subject or to subsequent processing operations, information that was hitherto unavailable, where (3) this making available is achieved by way of the production, in the subject of the process, of a representational state, and (4) the process belongs to a cognitive subject, understood as an organism that satisfies conditions (1)–(3).[5]

Walking around the corner does not consist in the manipulation or transformation of information-bearing structures. Therefore, it does not satisfy condition (1). Walking around the corner is something that can be done for many reasons, and so does not have the proper function of making information available, either to a subject or to subsequent processing operations. Of course, it may, as a matter of fact, make information available to the subject or to its processing operations. But if it does so this will not be a matter of fulfilling its proper function—for it has no such function. It has no proper function—other than, perhaps, the generic one of "getting around the corner"—because it can be done for a variety of purposes and with a variety of effects. Therefore, it fails to satisfy condition (2). And since it has no proper function, it can hardly satisfy this function by way of the production in the subject of a representational state. As a result of walking around the corner, a new representational state may well be produced in the subject. But this production can hardly be the result of fulfilling the proper function of walking around the corner. Therefore, walking around the corner fails to satisfy condition (3).

Walking around the corner may be a vehicle of disclosure—part of the means whereby an object is disclosed as falling under an empirical mode of presentation. But it is not, at least not typically, a vehicle of cognitive disclosure. Therefore, there is no reason to regard walking around a corner as part of a cognitive process.[6] A further advantage of this account is that it emphasizes the significant commonalities between cognition and action in a useful way, but without collapsing the one into the other. Cognition is a means by which an object in the world is disclosed as falling under an empirical mode of presentation, where this means satisfies the criterion of the cognitive. Some forms of action can also be means by which an object is disclosed in this way—means that also satisfy the criterion. So some action is cognitive, but not all action is.

8 Cognition Embodied and Extended: Back Together Again

The amalgamated mind is the conjunction of the theses of the embodied and extended mind. The central goal of this book has been to provide a conceptual framework within which the claims of the amalgamated mind could be advanced and most fruitfully understood. A serious problem with this project was seen to lie in the differing attitudes of the embodied mind and the extended mind to functionalism. The extended mind is predicated on a liberal form of functionalism. The embodied mind is characterized by a general antipathy toward functionalism: at most it could countenance chauvinistic forms of functional specification but not their more liberal counterparts. Therefore, one of the most important tasks in developing a conceptual underpinning for the amalgamated mind was to find a way of reconciling embodied and extended accounts.

This book has attempted, insofar as this is possible, to take functionalism out of the equation. This is not to say that functionalism has been rejected, simply that it has largely been ignored. The role of functionalism in motivating the extended mind has been replaced with the idea of intentional directedness as revealing or disclosing activity—activity that reveals objects as falling under empirical modes of presentation—and the resulting idea of intentionality as traveling through its material realizations. Crucial to the reconciliation of the mind embodied and the mind extended is the idea that revealing activity subsumes, for the same reasons and in equal measure, both bodily and environmental components of this activity.

Suppose the world is disclosed in a given way: an object is disclosed, either in perception or in thought, as falling under a certain aspect or empirical mode of presentation. From the perspective of the model of intentional directedness developed in this book, the key question is: what are the vehicles of (causal) disclosure? That is, what are the vehicles causally responsible for the disclosure of the world as being this way? As we have seen, the vehicles can be of several sorts. Neural processes are, obviously, in all cases among the vehicles of disclosure. This is why any sane version of both the embodied and the extended mind thesis will recognize that there is a noneliminable neural component involved in every cognitive process. However, often—not always, not necessarily, but often— neural processes do not exhaust these vehicles of disclosure. Sometimes, disclosure is implemented by bodily processes. These processes are among the vehicles of causal disclosure. Sometimes, disclosure is implemented by way of wider environmental processes—things that the subject does to and with things in its environment. An item counts as part of a cognitive process if it forms part of the means whereby that process, in a manner specified by the criterion of the cognitive, discloses the world as falling under a given empirical mode of presentation.

In the case of any given process, it is an open empirical question as to what constitutes the vehicles whereby that process discloses the world as falling under a given empirical mode of presentation. Different processes will employ different vehicles; some of them will be purely neural, but some will not. However, the general model of intentional directedness defended here is indifferent to whether the vehicles of disclosure of the world are neural, bodily, or environmental. The vehicles—whether neural, bodily, or environmental—all contribute to the same thing: the disclosure of the world as falling under some empirical mode of presentation. The model of intentional directedness defended here, therefore, provides the general theoretical picture that unites the theses of the mind embodied and the mind extended.

9   The Problem of Ownership

In the first half of this book, I argued that all of the major objections to the thesis of the extended mind could be traced back to the *mark of the cognitive* objection. I provided a mark of the cognitive—a list of conditions that were collectively sufficient for an item to count as cognitive. Of these, the most problematic condition was the ownership condition: anything that was to count as a cognitive process must be owned by a cognitive subject (understood as a subject that satisfied the first three conditions of the criterion). Earlier attempts to understand ownership were faltering. I restricted my attention to personal-level cognitive processes and argued that the ownership of subpersonal cognitive processes was derivative upon these. Then I explored the idea that personal-level ownership has something to do with authority, and something to do with agency. But these arguments were far from conclusive. In particular, the phenomena of authority and agency seemed to be derivative.

The model of intentional directedness defended here allows us to cut through these problems. A cognitive process belongs to me if it discloses the world to *me*. It can do this in two ways. It can disclose the world to me directly, in the form of my personal level processes—thoughts, perceptions, experiences, and the like. These processes are essentially characterized by the fact that they are items in virtue of which something in the world is disclosed to me—in perception, in memory, in thought, and so on—as falling under an empirical mode of presentation. Or it can, in the form of an informational state, disclose the world to my subpersonal cognitive processes. These processes count as mine, ultimately, because of the role they play in underwriting personal-level processes that disclose the world to me directly.

To add a little flesh to the bones of this account, recall the distinction between *causal* and *constitutive disclosure*. The former applies at the level of the vehicles or material realizations of thoughts, perceptions, memories, experiences, and the like. The latter applies at the level of the content of thoughts, perceptions, memories, and experiences. Consider, for example, the content of experience. What it is like to have or undergo an experience is, I argued, identical with the transcendental mode of presentation of the experience. But whenever there is an experience for which there is something that it is like to have or undergo it, the *mineness* of the experience is built into it as part of what it is like to have it. That is, part of what it involved in having an experience characterized by there being something that it is like to have it is to recognize that the experience is *mine*. Thus, the question of to whom the experience belongs does not arise. *Here is an experience; to whom does it belong*? That is not the sort of question that, except in the most atypically pathological of circumstances, makes sense. The *mineness* of an experience is part of its phenomenological character— part of its *what-it-is-like-ness*.

This phenomenological fact follows from the nature of intentional directedness as disclosure or revelation. There is no such thing as disclosure in itself. Disclosure is a relational concept: disclosure is always disclosure to *someone* (or, if it takes place at the subpersonal level, to something). Thus, what it is like to have or undergo an experience consists in the way the world is disclosed when a subject has an experience that is essentially characterized by this what-it-is-like-ness. The mineness of the experience—part of its what-it-is-like-ness—therefore consists in the fact that in the having of the experience the world is not only disclosed as falling under a given empirical mode of presentation; it is disclosed in this way *for me*.

We can provide the same sort of account for the content of thoughts, memories, and other cognitive states. "Here is a thought; to whom does it belong?" is a question that, in normal circumstances, makes no sense. This phenomenological point about thoughts derives from their nature as revealers or disclosers of the world. The content of a thought or memory consists in the revealing or disclosing of an item in the world as falling under a given empirical mode of presentation. The content of a thought or memory is a logically sufficient condition of a certain sort of disclosure. The vehicle of that content is a causally sufficient condition of this disclosure. But there is no disclosure in itself; disclosure is relational: it is always disclosure to something.

The vehicles of cognition—the proper subject matter of the new science—are causal rather than constitutive disclosers of the world. They provide a causally, rather than logically, sufficient condition for the world to be disclosed to a subject as falling under a given empirical mode of presentation. Nevertheless, we can give a parallel account of what makes these processes mine. Cognitive processes—whether neural, embodied, or extended—belong to me when they disclose the world to me. They can do this directly—as the causal means whereby a part of the world is disclosed as falling under an empirical mode of presentation. Or they can do it indirectly—by making information available to my subpersonal processes that then contribute to the personal-level processes defined by their world-disclosing function. At the personal level, a cognitive process is mine when it causally discloses the world to me. And structures and processes—whether neural, embodied, or extended—belong to this process when they form part of the means, part of the vehicles, of this causal disclosure. Thus, a perceptual process is mine when it, causally rather than constitutively, discloses the tomato to me as being shiny and red. The saccadic eye movements I employ, the exploratory processes I perform, the manipulation of the optic array in which I engage: these are all parts of the perceptual process if they are part of the (causal) means, or vehicle, by which the world is disclosed to me in this way. A belief is mine when it causally discloses the world to me as containing the Museum of Modern Art on 53rd Street. The notebook forms part of this process of causal disclosure when it forms part of the means by which, or in virtue of which, the world is disclosed to me in this way.

With this general account in mind, let us revisit the problem of bloat. Recall, now, the case of the telescope. The intratelescopic processes—reflections of light—satisfy conditions (1)–(3) of the mark of the cognitive defended earlier. Do they satisfy condition (4)? Yes, but only when I am appropriately engaged with the telescope. In such circumstances, they form part of the vehicles of my causal disclosure of the world as containing an object, say, the planet Saturn, which falls under the empirical mode of presentation of having rings. This, however, only yields the anodyne form of bloat. First, as I have argued earlier, the intratelescopic processes at most qualify as cognitive in a subpersonal sense. We are now in a position to add an important qualification to this. If the telescope were left pointing at Saturn after I had finished looking through it, then exactly the same intratelescopic processes would be occurring. But now they would not be cognitive, not even subpersonally. In order to qualify as cognitive, a process must belong to a subject. And it belongs to a subject only when it plays a role in disclosing, to that subject, the world as falling under a given empirical mode of presentation. The problem of bloat is, therefore, undercut by the fact that all cognition must ultimately relate back to the revealing activity of a subject. To be cognitive, a process must play a role in causally disclosing the world to a subject. If there is no subject to which the world is disclosed, there is no cognition. But more importantly, if there is no world disclosure of a particular form occurring at any given time, then neither is there cognition. If the telescope is, at a given time, not being used—neither by me nor by anyone else—as a vehicle of disclosing that, for example, Saturn falls under the empirical mode of presentation of having rings, then there is no part of any cognitive process that is occurring inside the telescope. There is no problem of bloat on the view defended here: the bounds of cognition are limned by the activities of world disclosure.[7]

10   A Weird New Science?

The extended mind is generally thought of as a "weird" thesis. Even its defenders accept this. The embodied mind is, I gather, regarded as slightly less outlandish—perhaps because it doesn't relocate the mental so far from its traditional home—but still distinctly peculiar. If either thesis were to turn out to be demonstrably true—this would strike many—almost certainly the vast majority—as a surprising result. The new, non-Cartesian science, therefore, would be born with the taint of the strange, peculiar, or otherwise bizarre.

This taint, I have argued, is the result of a tacit commitment to a particular conception of intentionality. There is a pervasive tendency to misunderstand the nature of intentional directedness: to think of it as an essentially inner process. What I mean when I mean something by a word is an entirely inner state or process. What I mean by a word or expression is something I can identify by turning my attention inward. Intentional directedness, it is assumed, is something we encounter when we turn our attention inward; an object of our inner, introspective engagement. If we think that this is what intentionality is, and if we take intentional states to be paradigm cases of the mental, then the amalgamated mind will indeed seem outlandish.

But I have argued that we will not find intentional directedness if we turn attention inward; all we can find are objects of this directedness. Intentional directedness is best understood in terms of the idea of world disclosure. Intentional directedness is the process of revealing or disclosing an item within the world as falling under one or more aspects or empirical modes of presentation. Depending on the level at which we cast our analysis—depending, that is, on whether our concern is with contents or vehicles of content—with experiences or their material realizations—this world disclosure can take one of two forms: constitutive or causal.

The theses of embodied and extended cognition emerge as a straightforward, almost banal, implication of the idea that the vehicles of cognition are causal disclosers of the world. World disclosure, in general, is entirely neutral over the nature and location of its vehicles. Sometimes they are neural operations, but sometimes they are processes taking place in the body, or even processes that extend into the world in the form of manipulation, exploitation, and transformation of environmental structures.

Once we accept this, the theses of embodied and extended cognition are not weird at all. They are stunningly obvious. Therefore, so too is the thesis of the amalgamated mind: the conjunction of the mind embodied and the mind extended. Suppose there were a new science of the mind to be built on the foundation of the amalgamated mind. Any stigma of the strange or deviant that attaches to this new science would, therefore, simply be the result of our implicit, and illicit, commitment to an untenable model of intentional directedness.

Notes

1 Expanding the Mind

1. For its growing presence in popular culture see, e.g., Fred Hapgood's "When Robots Live Among Us" In the June 2008 edition of *Discover* magazine, and David Brooks, "The Outsourced Brain" in the *New York Times*, October 26, 2007.

2. Interestingly enough, recognizable forerunners of neural network models actually predated the "cognitive revolution" of the 1960s. The well-known *pandemonium* model developed by Oliver Selfridge (1959) was a clear forerunner of today's connectionist networks. Moreover, Selfridge was building on earlier work of this general *oeuvre* developed by Warren McCulloch and Walter Pitts (McCulloch and Pitts 1943, 1947).

3. For this debate, see Fodor and Pylyshyn 1988 and Smolensky 1987, 1988.

4. In fact, I believe the conversation in question took place over lunch in Cardiff, at a situated cognition workshop organized by Alessandra Tanesini and Richard Gray. That was when Shaun coined the expression 4e. It subsequently formed the title of a conference he organized at the University of Central Florida in October 2007: 4e: The Mind Embodied, Embedded, Enacted, Extended.

5. *Spoiler alert*: I am, in fact, going to argue for a 2e non-Cartesian conception of the mind.

6. By "new" I mean whatever is left of the 4e conception once the process of identification, clarification, clarification, and rendering consistent has been carried out.

7. At least one of Rupert's (2004) criticisms of my position rests on failing to appreciate this distinction (or on attributing to me a failure to appreciate this distinction). I should, therefore, emphasize that I think the mind is embodied, embedded, enacted, or extended only if, and to the extent that, it is made up of, or constituted by, mental states and processes. If the mind is conceived of as something that is distinct from and underlies these states and processes—as something to which these

states and processes attach—then there is no reason for thinking that the mind is outside the head.

8. My thanks to Mike Wheeler for this.

9. This interpretation of Descartes, or rather of what Descartes needs to make sense of his account, is due to Keith Campbell (1970).

10. An alternative interpretation denies that Descartes attributed spatial location to minds, and is based on distinguishing between (i) where, for Descartes, the mind is located and (ii) where mind–brain interaction takes place. According to this interpretation, the mind may be nowhere while the interaction between mind and body might take place at a specified location—the pineal gland. I am grateful to Mike Wheeler for this suggestion. However, though this interpretation is part of a more general, and somewhat fashionable, process of rehabilitating Descartes, I think there are serious conceptual obstacles in its way. Most obviously: how can something that exists nowhere do something (i.e., act on the brain) somewhere? I shall, therefore, adhere to the more traditional interpretation of Descartes advanced in the main body of this section. If you don't buy into this interpretation of Descartes, just think of it as a way Descartes has commonly been interpreted, and then think of the label "Cartesian" as picking out the view commonly attributed to, rather than view actually held by, Descartes.

11. See Brooks, "The Outsourced Brain."

12. Or, in the case of my GPS, often the junction just behind me—she's not too quick off the mark. Or maybe it's me.

13. Andy Clark's (1989) "007 principle"—know only what you need to know—predates the barking dog principle and makes essentially the same point.

14. This objection has been championed, in slightly different ways, by Robert Rupert (2004) and Fred Adams and Ken Aizawa (2001; 2010). I think they have done a great service to anti-Cartesians by forcing them to considerably sharpen their statements of the non-Cartesian alternative. I shall discuss their objections in much more detail later on.

2   Non-Cartesian Cognitive Science

1. Burge (1986) demurs, presenting Marr's theory of vision as an example of externalist, or non-Cartesian, theorizing. However, his case turns on the role of "assumptions" about the nature of the environment that Marr builds in to his account of vision. Put in terms of the discussion of the previous chapter, these assumptions—or rather the environmental circumstances—provide a useful framework or scaffolding within which the processes that make up vision are embedded. But there is nothing in Marr's account that suggests that these environmental circumstances form part of the processes that make up vision itself. Therefore, I shall,

I think legitimately, employ Marr's account as an example of Cartesian cognitive science. If this is correct, it, once again, illustrates that environmental embedding of cognitive processes is by no means anathema to Cartesian cognitive science. For more on this see chapter 3.

2. I have Tony Chemero to thank for this.

3. Thanks to Mike Wheeler for drawing my attention to this.

3   The Mind Embodied, Embedded, Enacted, and Extended

1. I say Hume "might have held a view similar to it" but I actually don't think he did. See Craig 1982, chapter 3, for reasons for thinking that he did not, in fact, hold this view. Nevertheless, this view of the mind is attributed to him with sufficient regularity for it to be called the *Humean* view of the self.

2. In Rowlands 1999, I distinguish between ontic and epistemic versions of the extended mind thesis (or, as I preferred to call it in those days, "environmentalism"). That is, I distinguished the extended mind thesis as an ontic claim about what mental processes are from an epistemic claim about the best way to understand mental processes. I argued that the latter was an important corollary of the former, but that the former—the ontic claim—was the most interesting and important way of understanding the extended mind. The discussion of this section is, in part, an application of this distinction to the thesis of the embodied mind. However, here I am going to distinguish two different versions of the ontic thesis.

3. This point, in the context of the extended mind rather than the embodied mind, has been made forcefully (and in my view correctly) by both Adams and Aizawa (2001, 2010), and Rupert (2004).

4. In Rowlands 1999, I argued that the extended mind (aka environmentalism) was best understood as an ontic claim of constitution (rather than dependence). But I did not explicitly distinguish between dependence and constitution versions of the ontic claim. I do so now thanks, in part, to the work of Adams and Aizawa (2001, 2010) and Rupert (2004).

5. This line of thought can be discerned in Rupert 2004.

6. There are other possible ways of understanding the thesis of the extended mind, but this was the status of the thesis I developed and defended in Rowlands 1999.

7. This is because this epistemic claim is also a corollary of a weaker claim to be discussed shortly: the thesis of the *embedded mind*.

8. It is truly surprising how often one finds it necessary to repeat this obvious point.

9. Someone, with an enthusiasm bordering on the rabid, might even find him- or herself tempted to claim: some mental processes are *necessarily* constituted by processes of environmental manipulation. This *de re* version of the necessity claim would be even more plausible than the modalized *de dicto* claim.

10. See, especially, work by the "Edinburgh functionalists," Clark 2008a,b and Wheeler 2008, for the connection between the extended mind and functionalism.

11. Adams and Aizawa (2001, 2010) and Rupert (2004) both use the distinction between dependence and constitution as a way of attacking the extended mind on the grounds that the arguments used to support only establish the dependence of cognitive process on, rather than the constitution of cognitive processes by, environmental processes. Their argument will be discussed in more detail in the next chapter.

12. Of course, I have not argued for this claim yet. That is, I have not yet argued that a manipulative process that transforms the information contained in an external structure from the merely present to the available is thereby a properly cognitive part of a larger cognitive process. The argument for this claim will be developed in subsequent chapters.

13. Mackay's example is cited by O'Regan and Noë (2001).

14. Thanks to Tony Chemero for planting the seeds of doubt in my mind on this point.

15. This is the principal moral of the *change blindness* results discussed extensively by O'Regan and Noë (2001). The fact that subjects can, under appropriate masking conditions, fail to notice even significant changes in a visual scene suggests strongly, O'Regan and Noë argue, that they have formed no detailed or complex internal representation of this scene.

16. See Heidegger 1927/1962; Dreyfus 1992; Wheeler 2005.

17. I am not, here, rehearsing Stanley and Williamson's (2001) claim that there is no distinction between knowing how and knowing that. On the contrary, I think Stanley and Williamson are clearly mistaken. There is a legitimate distinction, but Noë fails to draw it. In particular, on his account, the expectations constitutive of sensorimotor knowledge are expectations *that*.

18. Not all of them, of course. My ability to mentally picture and count the number of windows in my house when I am sitting miles away in my office is an ability that is not composed of wider bodily structures and processes. The possession of this ability seems to depend purely on what is going on in my brain.

19. This, of course, is not necessarily a weakness of the enactivist view. Failure to entail an extended account might be regarded by many as a strength rather than a

weakness. My concern here is only to properly distinguish enactive and extended accounts.

20. This charge has been leveled by Siewert (2006).

21. It is true that he puts this in interrogative form. But it is clear from the context that this is a claim he wishes to endorse.

22. I would like to thank Andy Clark for drawing my attention to this.

23. This point originally goes back to Davidson (1987). For something to be sunburn, it must stand in a certain relation to solar radiation. But it does not follow that the sunburn must "extend" into the solar radiation. The planet example is due to Macdonald (1990).

24. A similar claim is endorsed by Clark (forthcoming).

25. Indeed, it is not even clear that the claim of environmental embedding is justifiable. As the example of the planet makes clear, one can be an internalist about experience and accept with equanimity the claim that the possession of a given property by an experience depends on a "characteristic extended dynamic." This seems to stretch the idea of embedding beyond the bounds of the acceptable.

4   Objections to the Mind Amalgamated

1. Understood deductively, the argument would, of course, be fallacious.

2. I think Richard Menary was the first to clearly see this—certainly he got there a long time before I did. See, especially, Menary 2006, 2007. He had been making this point at conferences long before the publication of these papers.

3. The significance of the contribution of the enactivist account in this context is, of course, moderated by the arguments of the previous chapter. If those arguments are correct, enactivism, at least in the form defended by Noë, does not yield an extended account of perceptual processing.

4. Susan Hurley (1998) also provides a powerful defense of this idea.

5. This point is made by Martin Godwyn (unpublished ms), "Who's Afraid of Cognitive Bloat?"

6. I am grateful to a conversation with Richard Samuels for the example.

7. The scales fell from my eyes on this particular point thanks to Mike Wheeler, who, as far as I am aware, was the first to make it in a paper he gave at the Extended Mind II conference, "Phenomenology, Activism, and the Extended Mind." Subsequently, he has made this point in print in "Minds, Things, and Materiality" (2008) and "In Defense of Extended Functionalism" (2010).

5   The Mark of the Cognitive

1. This criterion can, I think, be regarded as an explicit version of the criterion with which I was working—or at least should have been working—in *The Body in Mind* (Rowlands 1999). There are, however, two differences. First, the arguments of *The Body in Mind* do not employ the idea of ownership. In this regard, the criterion I adopted there was incomplete. Second, in *The Body in Mind* I defined the idea of a cognitive process in terms of the idea of a cognitive task, where the latter was defined by ostension. I have Aaron Wilson to thank for convincing me that this move was unnecessary. In this respect, the criterion I employed in *The Body in Mind* was a little flabby.

2. I take no stand on whether it is, in fact, possible for a process to make information available both to a subject and to subsequent processing operations. Some—for example, McDowell (1994b)—might want to deny this on the grounds that there is no common content that could be transmitted to both. My claims are simply that (i) subpersonal processes make information available only to other subpersonal processes and not to the subjects of those processes, and (ii) personal-level processes make information available *at least* to subjects. This is all I need for the arguments to follow. I thank Mike Wheeler for allowing me to clarify this.

3. More accurately, it is to allow us to understand what, in principle, might be only an important subset of cognitive processes—those currently dealt with in cognitive-scientific practice. The restriction is required because the proposed criterion provides only a sufficient condition for something to count as cognitive, and not a necessary condition.

4. Thanks again to Michael Wheeler for allowing/forcing me to clarify this.

5. Of course, there is nothing in the idea of the amalgamated mind that would require us to deny that external structures can possess nonderived *information*. Whether the external information-bearing structure possesses nonderived information would presumably, vary from case to case. Thus, in the examples discussed above, the information carried by the *kvinus* is derived, but that carried by the optic array is not. Whether nonderived information adds up to nonderived content depends, of course, on whether content can be explained exclusively in terms of information. For a variety of familiar reasons, I suspect that it cannot.

6. Though, again, see Rowlands 2006 for an alternative.

7. After writing this, I discovered that Wilson and Clark (2008) make essentially the same point. Also, to my chagrin, I discover that they have made it in a far more colorful and entertaining way. Just to demonstrate what a willful curmudgeon I can sometimes be, I am going to stick with my boring version.

6   The Problem of Ownership

1. Thanks to Mike Wheeler for encouraging me to clarify this point.

2. Thanks to Fred Adams, who raised this objection in correspondence.

3. Wilson (2001) seems to display an appreciation of the importance of the issue of ownership in the context of the extended mind. However, his discussion is vitiated by a fairly obvious conflation of the issue of (i) what an entity must be like in order to have mental properties attributed to it, with (ii) an account of what it is for such an entity to own such properties—because he fails to even address the second question. This second question is the focus of the present chapter.

4. Richard Samuels suggested this example to me in conversation.

5. Adams and Aizawa (2001) also use the example of digestion but with a somewhat different purpose. They use it as an example of a process that can be externalized—for example, a fly digesting its food. They claim that cognition, too, could be externalized but, in fact, is not. I am not using the example of digestion, here, to support to the idea of external cognition. With respect to the process of digestion, my concern is simply with the issue of *ownership*—and not with the issue of *location*.

6. I know I said earlier that I proposed to take functionalism out of the equation, at least insofar as this is possible. However, the advertised riddance of functionalist principles takes place in the argument I am going to develop for the amalgamated mind—and this will be developed in the following two chapters. Here I am talking about the ownership of cognitive processes. And in supplying an account of ownership of subpersonal cognitive processes I simply don't think it is possible to possible to take functionalism out of the equation (hence the qualification "insofar as this is possible"). As we shall see in the following chapters, matters are significantly different when we turn our attention to personal-level cognitive processes. Thanks to Mike Wheeler for urging this point of clarification.

7. See, e.g., Hurley 1998, chapter 3. Note that we would have to assume that these are psychological duplicates except in the case of indexical thoughts about themselves (and demonstrative thoughts about their environments).

8. And also one that can subsume sensory detections and motor responses performed by an organism. This goes back to the need to account not only for cognitive processes but also the fixed frame of reference. We cannot assume, at the outset, that ownership of sensory detections and motor responses is unproblematic.

7   Intentionality as Revealing Activity

1. Indeed, this is one way—a translation into the language of sense—to understand the commonplace idea that intentionality consists in *directedness-toward* objects. If

intentionality is indeed directedness-toward objects, and if this directedness-toward objects is distinct from the objects thus directed-toward, then we will look in vain at those intentional objects if we want to understand intentionality itself. The problem is, of course, that there is nothing else for us to look at.

2. This commits me to aligning myself with Evans and McDowell in attacking Frege's claim that empty proper names—proper names that have no bearer—should be regarded as having sense but no reference. Evans and McDowell insist that empty proper names should be regarded as devoid of sense. I am happy to side with Evans and McDowell on this.

3. Sartre was not, in fact, a commonsense realist about the world. But he was a phenomenological realist. The reality and objectivity of objects is to be understood in terms of their being constituted by a potentially infinite series of appearances, appearances that subsume and incorporate what we might regard as the "hidden" aspects of objects (e.g., their chemical structure). Appearances are, for Sartre, transcendent items rather than being parts of, or constructions out of, consciousness. The independence of things from consciousness and their ontological priority over consciousness is essential to Sartre's view, forming the basis of what he calls his "ontological proof," and his characterization of his view as a "radical reversal" of idealism.

4. This, of course, is not the place to become embroiled in the dispute between description and causal theories of reference—that would be another book entirely. The recent resurgence in description-theoretic approaches, of course, does me no harm. But even if we assume a causal (or informational, etc.) account of the reference of some terms, the idea that we can account for the mode of presentation of an experience in causal terms alone was always a distinctly minority view. That is all I assume here.

5. Remember that my focus here is on perceptual (indeed, largely visual) intentionality and related modes of illusion and hallucination. In effect, I am making a case for perceptual intentionality to be understood as a form of disclosing activity. The extension of this model to cognition more generally will be attempted in the next chapter.

8   The Mind Amalgamated

1. Here I am utilizing a point I have defended at much greater length (Rowlands 2001, 2002, 2003, 2008). It is consistent with the point I am defending in the present book that one can also regard what it is like to have an experience as an empirical mode of presentation—something of which we are aware in the having of an experience—something that I would have denied in at least some of these other places. All I need here is that the claim that what it is like to have an experience is, among other things, that in virtue of which the object of the experience is presented in a

given way to a subject. That is, I assume it is legitimate to think of what it is like to have an experience as a transcendental mode of presentation. If you do not like this assumption, nothing much turns on it. We can reformulate the above arguments in terms of the idea of a transcendental mode of presentation rather than what it is like to have an experience. I use the latter here because of its greater familiarity to most readers.

2. I vacillate on this—a lot—but at the time of writing of the final typescript, I suspect not.

3. The two possibilities, of course, correspond (roughly) to the well-known possibilities of inverted qualia and absent qualia.

4. This claim is, of course, compatible with my earlier questioning of whether the enactive approach entails a form of extended mind. The key question, to reiterate, is this: does the enactive approach require *exercise* of the ability to explore the world or does it merely require the *ability* to do this? If it requires the former, then the enactive model qualifies as a version of the extended mind. If not, then it does not so qualify. My concern in the present section, of course, is with the process of exploration itself—i.e., the exercise of the ability.

5. The criterion of the cognitive has been advanced as a sufficient but not a necessary condition for a process to qualify as cognitive. Therefore, the criterion is compatible with cognitive disclosure taking some other form than the one outlined here. However, for our purposes, the important point is that the position defended in this book is not, by any stretch of the imagination, committed to the idea that walking around the corner is a form of cognition.

6. Of course, this is not to deny that there might be conceivable circumstances in which walking around a corner might be part of a cognitive process. The qualification "at least typically" is intended to allow for such a possibility. I can't, off the top of my head, imagine what those circumstances might be. But the important point, of course, is that, for the most part, walking around a corner is *not* a cognitive operation.

7. Remember, of course, that even when it is being employed, the processes occurring within the telescope never amount to anything more than subpersonal cognitive processes. The subject has no epistemic authority over these processes, and that precludes their counting as personal-level cognitive processes. Therefore, to the extent that we have to be willing to face up to a problem of bloat, this is only with respect to subpersonal cognitive processes. This is what I identified earlier as the anodyne form of the problem.

References

Adams, F., and K. Aizawa. 2001. The bounds of cognition. *Philosophical Psychology* 14:43–64.

Adams, F., and K. Aizawa. 2010. Why the mind is still in the head. In *The Extended Mind*, ed. R. Menary. Cambridge, Mass.: MIT Press.

Baumeister, R., E. Bratslavsky, M. Muraven, and D. Tice. 1998. Ego depletion: Is the active self a limited resource? *Journal of Personality and Social Psychology* 74: 1252–1265.

Bechtel, W., and A. Abrahamson. 1991. *Connectionism and the Mind: An Introduction to Parallel Processing in Networks*. Oxford: Blackwell.

Beer, R. 1995. Computational and dynamical languages for autonomous agents. In *Mind as Motion: Explorations in the Dynamics of Cognition*, ed. R. Port and T. van Gelder, 121–148. Cambridge, Mass.: MIT Press.

Bergson, H. [1908] 1991. *Matter and Memory*. Trans. N. M. Paul and W. S. Palmer. New York: Zone Books.

Blackmore, S., G. Brelstaff, K. Nelson, and T. Troscianko. 1995. Is the richness of our visual world an illusion? Transsaccadic memory for complex scenes. *Perception* 24:1075–1081.

Brewer, William. 1996. What is recollective memory? In *Remembering Our Past*, ed. D. C. Rubin, 19–66. Cambridge: Cambridge University Press.

Brooks, D. 2007. The outsourced brain. *New York Times*, October 26.

Brooks, R. 1991. Intelligence without representation. *Artificial Intelligence* 47: 139–159.

Brooks, R. 1994. Coherent behaviour from many adaptive processes. In *From Animals to Animats 3*, ed. D. Cliff, P. Husbands, J.-A. Meyer, and S. W. Wilson. Cambridge, Mass.: MIT Press.

Burge, T. 1986. Individualism and psychology. *Philosophical Review* 45:3–45.

Campbell, J. 1994. *Past, Space, and Self*. Cambridge, Mass.: MIT Press.

Campbell, J. 1997. The structure of time in autobiographical memory. *European Journal of Philosophy* 5:105–118.

Campbell, K. 1970. *Body and Mind*. Notre Dame: Notre Dame University Press.

Chalmers, D. 1996. *The Conscious Mind: In Search of a Fundamental Theory*. Oxford: Oxford University Press.

Clark, A. 1989. *Microcognition: Philosophy, Cognitive Science, and Parallel Distributed Processing*. Cambridge, Mass.: MIT Press.

Clark, A. 1997. *Being There: Putting Brain, Body and World Back Together Again*. Cambridge, Mass.: MIT Press.

Clark, A. 2008a. Pressing the flesh: A tension on the study of the embodied, embedded mind. *Philosophy and Phenomenological Research* 76:37–59.

Clark, A. 2008b. *Supersizing the Mind: Embodiment, Action, and Cognitive Extension*. Oxford: Oxford University Press.

Clark, A. Forthcoming. Spreading the joy: Why the machinery of consciousness is (probably) still in the head. *Mind*.

Clark, A., and D. Chalmers. 1998. The extended mind. *Analysis* 58:7–19. Reprinted in Menary 2010.

Clark, A., and J. Toribio. 1994. Doing without representing? *Synthese* 101:401–431.

Craig, E. 1982. *The Mind of God and the Works of Man*. Cambridge: Cambridge University Press.

Damasio, A. 1994. *Descartes' Error*. New York: Grosset Putnam.

Damasio, A. 2004. *Looking for Spinoza: Joy, Sorrow, and the Feeling Brain*. New York: Mariner Books.

Davidson, D. 1970. Mental events. In *Experience and Theory*, ed. L. Foster and J. Swanson. London: Duckworth.

Davidson, D. 1984. *Inquiries into Truth and Interpretation*. Oxford: Oxford University Press.

Davidson, D. 1987. Knowing one's own mind. *Proceedings of the American Philosophical Association* 60:441–458.

Dennett, D. 1987. *The Intentional Stance*. Cambridge, Mass.: MIT Press.

Dennett, D. 1991. *Consciousness Explained*. Boston: Little, Brown.

Donald, M. 1991. *Origins of the Modern Mind*. Cambridge, Mass.: Harvard University Press.

Dretske, F. 1981. *Knowledge and the Flow of Information*. Oxford: Blackwell.

Dretske, F. 1986. Misrepresentation. In *Belief*, ed. R. Bogdan. Oxford: Oxford University Press.

Dreyfus, H. 1992. *Being-in-the-World*. Cambridge, Mass.: MIT Press.

Drummond, J. 1990. *Husserlian Intentionality and Non-Foundational Realism*. Dordrecht: Kluwer.

Dummett, M. 1973. *Frege's Philosophy of Language*. London: Duckworth.

Dummett, M. 1981. *The Interpretation of Frege's Philosophy*. London: Duckworth.

Fodor, J. 1986. *Psychosemantics*. Cambridge, Mass.: MIT Press.

Fodor, J. 1990. *A Theory of Content and Other Essays*. Cambridge, Mass.: MIT Press.

Fodor, J. 2009. Where is my mind? *London Review of Books* 31(3):13–15.

Fodor, J., and Z. Pylyshyn. 1988. Connectionism and cognitive architecture: A critical analysis. *Cognition* 28:3–71.

Føllesdal, D. 1969. Husserl's notion of noema. *Journal of Philosophy* 66:680–687.

Frege, G. [1892] 1960. On sense and reference. In *Translations from the Philosophical Writings of Gottlob Frege*. Ed. P. Geach and M. Black. Oxford: Blackwell.

Frege, G. [1918] 1994. The thought: A logical inquiry. In *Basic Topics in the Philosophy of Language*, ed. R. Harnish. Englewood Cliffs, N.J.: Prentice Hall.

Gallistel, C. 1993. *The Organization of Learning*. Cambridge, Mass.: MIT Press.

Gibson, J. 1966. *The Senses Considered as Perceptual Systems*. Boston: Houghton-Mifflin.

Gibson, J. 1979. *The Ecological Approach to Visual Perception*. Boston: Houghton-Mifflin.

Godwyn, M. (unpublished ms). Who's afraid of cognitive bloat?

Gould, D. 1967. Pattern recognition and eye movement parameters. *Perception and Psychophysics* 2:399–407.

Hapgood, Fred. 2008. When robots live among us. *Discover* (June).

Harnish, R. 2000. Grasping modes of presentation: Frege vs. Fodor and Schweizer. *Acta Analytica* 15:19–46.

Haugeland, J. 1995. The mind embodied and embedded. In *Having Thought: Essays in the Metaphysics of Mind*. Cambridge, Mass.: Harvard University Press.

Heidegger, M. [1927] 1962. *Being and Time*. Trans. J. Macquarie. Oxford: Blackwell.

Hume, D. [1739] 1975. *A Treatise of Human Nature*. Ed. L. Selby-Bigge. Oxford: Oxford University Press.

Hurley, S. 1998. *Consciousness in Action*. Cambridge, Mass.: Harvard University Press.

Hurley, S. 2010. Varieties of externalism. In *The Extended Mind*, ed. R. Menary. Cambridge, Mass.: MIT Press.

Husserl, E. [1900] 1973. *Logical Investigations*. Trans. J. Findlay. London: Routledge.

Husserl, E. [1913] 1982. *Ideas Pertaining to a Pure Phenomenology and Phenomenological Philosophy*. Trans. F. Kersten. The Hague: Martinus Nijhoff.

Hutchins, E. 1995. *Cognition in the Wild*. Cambridge, Mass.: MIT Press.

Jackson, F. 1982. Epiphenomenal qualia. *Philosophical Quarterly* 32:127–132.

Jackson, F. 1986. What Mary didn't know. *Journal of Philosophy* 83:291–295.

Kaplan, D. 1980. *Demonstratives*. The John Locke Lectures. Oxford: Oxford University Press.

Keijzer, F. 1998. Doing without representations which specify what to do. *Philosophical Psychology* 9:323–346.

Kirsh, D., and P. Maglio. 1994. On distinguishing epistemic from pragmatic action. *Cognitive Science* 18:513–549.

Kripke, S. 1980. *Naming and Necessity*. Cambridge, Mass.: Harvard University Press.

Lloyd, D. 1989. *Simple Minds*. Cambridge, Mass.: MIT Press.

Locke, J. [1690] 1975. *An Essay Concerning Human Understanding*. Ed. P. Nidditch. Oxford: Oxford University Press.

Loftus, G. 1972. Eye fixations and recognition memory for pictures. *Cognitive Psychology* 3:525–551.

Luria, A., and L. Vygotsky. [1930] 1992. *Ape, Primitive Man, and Child: Studies on the History of Behavior*. Cambridge, Mass.: MIT Press.

Macdonald, C. 1990. Weak externalism and mind–body identity. *Mind* 99: 387–405.

Mack, A., and I. Rock. 1998. *Inattentional Blindness*. Cambridge, Mass.: MIT Press.

Mackay, D. 1967. Ways of looking at perception. In *Models for the Perception of Speech and Visual Form*, ed. W. Watthen-Dunn. Cambridge, Mass.: MIT Press.

Marr, D. 1982. *Vision*. San Francisco: W. H. Freeman.

Martin, M. 2002. The transparency of experience. *Mind and Language* 17:376–425.

Maturana, H., and F. Varela. 1980. *Autopoiesis and Cognition*. Dordrecht: Reidel.

McCulloch, W., and W. Pitts. 1943. A logical calculus of ideas immanent in nervous activity. *Bulletin of Mathematical Biophysics* 5:115–133.

McCulloch, W., and W. Pitts. 1947. How we know universals: The perception of auditory and visual forms. *Bulletin of Mathematical Biophysics* 9:127–147.

McDowell, J. 1986. Singular thought and the extent of inner space. In *Subject, Thought, and Context*, ed. P. Pettit and J. McDowell, 136–169. Oxford: Oxford University Press.

McDowell, J. 1994a. *Mind and World*. Cambridge, Mass.: Harvard University Press.

McDowell, J. 1994b. The content of perceptual experience. *Philosophical Quarterly* 44:190–205.

McDowell, J. 1992. Meaning and intentionality in Wittgenstein's later philosophy. *Midwest Studies in Philosophy* 17:30–42. Reprinted in his *Mind, Value, and Reality* (Cambridge, Mass.: Harvard University Press, 1998).

McGinn, C. 1982. The structure of content. In *Thought and Object*, ed. A. Woodfield, 207–258. Oxford: Oxford University Press.

McGinn, C. 1989a. Can we solve the mind–body problem? *Mind* 98:349–366.

McGinn, C. 1989b. *Mental Content*. Oxford: Blackwell.

McGinn, C. 1991. *The Problem of Consciousness*. Oxford: Blackwell.

McGinn, C. 2004. *Consciousness and Its Objects*. New York: Oxford University Press.

McIntyre, R. 1987. Husserl on sense. *Journal of Philosophy* 84:528–535.

Menary, R. 2006. Attacking the bounds of cognition. *Philosophical Psychology* 19:329–344.

Menary, R. 2007. *Cognitive Integration: Attacking the Bounds of Cognition*. Basingstoke: Palgrave-Macmillan.

Menary, R., ed. 2010. *The Extended Mind*. Cambridge, Mass.: MIT Press.

Merleau-Ponty, M. 1962. *The Phenomenology of Perception*. London: Routledge.

Millikan, R. 1984. *Language, Thought, and Other Biological Categories*. Cambridge, Mass.: MIT Press.

Millikan, R. 1993. *White Queen Psychology and Other Essays for Alice*. Cambridge, Mass.: MIT Press.

Milner, A., and M. Goodale. 1995. *The Visual Brain in Action*. Oxford: Oxford University Press.

Nagel, T. 1974. What is it like to be a bat? *Philosophical Review* 83:435–450. Reprinted in his Mortal Questions (New York: Cambridge University Press, 1979). All page references are to the latter.

Neisser, U. 1979. The control of information pickup in selective looking. In *Perception and Its Development*, ed. A. Pick. Hillfield, N.J.: Erlbaum.

Noë, A., ed. 2002. *Is the Visual World a Grand Illusion?* Special edition of *Journal of Consciousness Studies* 9.

Noë, A. 2004. *Action in Perception*. Cambridge, Mass.: MIT Press.

O'Regan, K. 1992. Solving the "real" mysteries of visual perception: The world as an outside memory. *Canadian Journal of Psychology* 46:461–488.

O'Regan, K., H. Deubel, J. Clark, and R. Rensink. 2000. Picture changes during blinks: Looking without seeing and seeing without looking. *Visual Cognition* 7:191–212.

O'Regan, K., and A. Noë. 2001. A sensorimotor account of vision and visual consciousness. *Behavioral and Brain Sciences* 23:939–973.

O'Regan, K., and A. Noë. 2002. What it is like to see: A sensorimotor theory of perceptual experience. *Synthese* 79:79–103.

O'Regan, K., R. Rensink, and J. Clark. 1996. "Mud splashes" render picture changes invisible. *Investigative Ophthalmology and Visual Science* 37:S213.

Polanyi, M. 1962. *Personal Knowledge*. London: Routledge.

Putnam, Hilary. 1960. Minds and machines. In *Dimensions of Mind*, ed. S. Hook, 148–180. New York: New York University Press.

Rensink, R. O'Regan, K., and Clark, J. 1997. To see or not to see: The need for attention to perceive changes in scenes. *Psychological Science* 8:368–373.

Rowlands, M. 1995. Against methodological solipsism: The ecological approach. *Philosophical Psychology* 8:5–24.

Rowlands, M. 1997. Teleological semantics. *Mind* 106:279–303.

Rowlands, M. 1999. *The Body in Mind: Understanding Cognitive Processes*. Cambridge: Cambridge University Press.

Rowlands, M. 2001. *The Nature of Consciousness*. Cambridge: Cambridge University Press.

Rowlands, M. 2002. Two dogmas of consciousness. in *Is the Visual World a Grand Illusion?* Special edition of *Journal of Consciousness Studies* 9, ed. A. Noe, 158–180.

Rowlands, M. 2003. *Externalism: Putting Mind and World Back Together Again*. London: Acumen.

Rowlands, M. 2006. *Body Language: Representation in Action*. Cambridge, Mass.: MIT Press.

Rowlands, M. 2007. Understanding the "active" in "enactive." *Phenomenology and the Cognitive Sciences* 6:427–443.

Rowlands, M. 2008. From the inside: Consciousness and the first-person perspective. *International Journal of Philosophical Studies* 16:281–297.

Rowlands, M. 2009a. Extended cognition and the mark of the cognitive. *Philosophical Psychology* 22:1–20.

Rowlands, M. 2009b. Enactivism and the extended mind. *Topoi* 28:53–62.

Rowlands, M. 2009c. The extended mind. *Zygon* 44:628–641.

Rumelhart, D., McClelland, J., and the PDP Research Group. 1986. *Parallel Distributed Processing*, 3 vols. Cambridge, Mass.: MIT Press.

Rupert, R. 2004. Challenges to the hypothesis of extended cognition. *Journal of Philosophy* 101:389–428.

Russell, B. 1921. *The Analysis of Mind*. London: Allen & Unwin.

Ryle, G. 1949. *The Concept of Mind*. Oxford: Blackwell.

Sartre, J.-P. [1943] 1957. *Being and Nothingness*. Trans. H. Barnes. London: Methuen.

Searle, J. 1958. Proper names. *Mind* 67:166–173.

Sedgwick, H. 1973. The visible horizon: A potential source of information for the perception of size and distance. Ph.D. dissertation, Cornell University.

Selfridge, O. 1959. Pandemonium: A paradigm for learning. In *Proceedings of the Symposium on Mechanisation of Thought Processes*, ed. D. Blake and A. Uttley, 511–529. London: HMSO.

Shannon, C. 1948. A mathematical theory of communication. *Bell System Technical Journal* 27:379–423, 623–656.

Shapiro, L. 2004. *The Mind Incarnate*. Cambridge, Mass.: MIT Press.

Siewert, C. 2006. Is the appearance of shape protean? *Psyche* 12(3).

Simons, D. 2000. Attentional capture and inattentional blindness. *Trends in Cognitive Sciences* 4:147–155.

Simons, D., and C. Chabris. 1999. Gorillas in our midst: Sustained inattentional blindness for dynamic events. *Perception* 28:1059–1074.

Simons, D., and D. Levin. 1997. Change blindness. *Trends in Cognitive Sciences* 1:261–267.

Smart, J. 1959. Sensations and brain processes. *Philosophical Review* 68:141–156.

Smolensky, P. 1987. The constituent structure of connectionist mental states: A reply to Fodor and Pylyshyn. *Southern Journal of Philosophy* 26 (supplement):137–163.

Smolensky, P. 1988. On the proper treatment of connectionism. *Behavioral and Brain Sciences* 11:1–23.

Sokolowski, R. 1987. Husserl and Frege. *Journal of Philosophy* 84:521–528.

Stanley, J., and T. Williamson. 2001. Knowing how. *Journal of Philosophy* 98:411–444.

Sutton, J. 2010. Exograms and interdisciplinarity: History, the extended mind, and the civilizing process. In *The Extended Mind*, ed. R. Menary. Cambridge, Mass.: MIT Press.

Thelen, E., and L. Smith. 1994. *A Dynamic Systems Approach to the Development of Cognition and Action*. Cambridge, Mass.: MIT Press.

Thompson, E. 2007. *Mind in Life*. Cambridge, Mass.: Harvard University Press.

Tulving, E. 1983. *Elements of Episodic Memory*. Oxford: Oxford University Press.

Tulving, E. 1993. What is episodic memory? *Current Directions in Psychological Science* 2:67–70.

Tulving, E. 1999. Episodic vs. semantic memory. In *The MIT Encyclopedia of the Cognitive Sciences*, ed. F. Keil and R. Wilson, 278–280. Cambridge, Mass.: MIT Press.

van Gelder, T. 1995. What might cognition be, if not computation? *Journal of Philosophy* 92:345–381.

Webb, B. 1994. Robotic experiments in cricket phonotaxis. In *From Animals to Animats 3*, eds. D. Cliff, P. Husbands, J. Meyer, and S. Wilson. Cambridge, Mass.: MIT Press.

Wheeler, M. 1994. From activation to activity. *Artificial Intelligence and the Simulation of Behaviour (AISB) Quarterly* 87:36–42.

Wheeler, M. 2005. *Reconstructing the Cognitive World: The Next Step*. Cambridge, Mass.: MIT Press.

Wheeler, M. 2008. Minds, things, and materiality. In *The Cognitive Life of Things*, ed. C. Renfrew and L. Malafouris. Cambridge University Press.

Wheeler, M. 2010. In defense of extended functionalism. In *The Extended Mind*, ed. R. Menary. Cambridge, Mass.: MIT Press.

Whitehead, A. 1911. *An Introduction to Mathematics*. New York: Holt.

Wilson, R. 2001. Two views of realization. *Philosophical Studies* 104:1–31.

Wilson, R. 2004. *Boundaries of the Mind: The Individual in the Fragile Sciences*. New York: Cambridge University Press.

Wilson, R., and C. Clark. 2008. How to situate cognition: Letting nature take its course. In *The Cambridge Handbook of Situated Cognition*, ed. P. Robbins and M. Aydede, 55–77. New York: Cambridge University Press.

Wittgenstein, L. 1953. *Philosophical Investigations*. Ed. E. Anscombe, R. Rhees, and G. von Wright. Trans. E. Anscombe. Oxford: Blackwell.

Yantis, S. 1996. Attentional capture in vision. In *Converging Operations in the Study of Selective Visual Attention*, ed. A. Kramer, M. Coles, and G. Logan, 45–76. Washington, D.C.: American Psychological Association.

Yarbus, A. 1967. *Eye Movements and Vision*. New York: Plenum Press.

Index

Abilities
  embeddedness of, 79
  embodiment of, 78
  exercise of, 77 82
  extendedness of, 77–82
  in perception, 53, 72, 74, 77–82
Access, to experience, 167–169
Action, cognition and, 213
Active externalism, 58
Activity. *See* Agency
Adams, F., 86, 91, 116, 117, 128–133, 225n5
Adequacy conditions, 115
Agency, 151–155
  basic account of, 152–153
  consciousness of, in breakdown of worldly relations, 158–161
  ownership of, 152–153, 161
Aizawa, K., 86, 91, 116, 117, 128–133, 225n5
Algorithms, 14
Alien thought-transitions, 143, 145
Amalgamated mind
  challenges to, 85, 126–133
  derivation of concept of, 83–84
  functionalism and, 104–105
  future development of, 104–106
  internal and external processes in, 85–93, 127, 129
  obviousness of, 140, 162, 182, 187, 189, 218
Anguish, 179–180

Antipsychologism, 174, 175
Architecture. *See* Subsumption architectures
Artificial intelligence, 1
Aspects, 183–185
Auffassungsinn (content of the mental act), 174–175
Authority
  and cognitive bloat, 155–156
  derivative character of epistemic, 156–161
  ownership and, 152–153, 157
  and personal cognitive processes, 155–157, 161
  responsibility and, 153–154
Availability, of information, 16–18, 36, 58, 63, 112–113, 125, 138–139
Awareness
  of an activity one is performing, 158–160, 210–211
  of beliefs, 62
  of experience, 165–167, 169
  intentionality and, 183–185
  mind not an object of, 9
  in reading, 210
  Sartre on, 178–180
  the transcendental not available to, 177–178, 181, 185, 189

Barking dog principle, 16, 19
Behaviorism, 2
Being-in-the-world, 75–76, 157

experience and, 215
fixed frame of reference needed for, 148–150
functionalism and, 141–142, 225n6
importance of, 94–95, 105–106
input-output model for determining, 149
integration and, 140–144, 148–150
intentionality and, 152, 215–217
personal vs. subpersonal, 139–140
primordial sense of, 161
problematic nature of, 134–162, 214–217
"subject" defined for, 135–136

Pandemonium model, 219n2
Parity, in extended mind, 86–90
Pattern association, 42
Pattern completion, 42
Pattern mapping, 42, 43
Pattern recognition, 42
Pattern transformation, 42
PDP Research Group, 44
Perception. *See also* Visual perception
abilities as factor in, 53, 72, 74, 77–82
cognitive science and, 16
common sense view of, 26
embodied mind thesis and, 53–54
enactive approach to, 71–72
expectations as factor in, 72, 74–75
extending, 122–124
intentionality of, 182–187
learning distinguished from, 80–81
Perceptual psychology, 1
Peripheral nervous system, 8
Person, concept of, 145, 146
Personal cognitive processes
as activities, 151–155
authority over, 155–157, 161
defined, 113, 138–139
emergence of, from basic coping behaviors, 161

fundamental nature of, 146–147, 151
and integration, 144–147
ownership and, 138–140
representation in, 118
subpersonal vs., 117
target of, 143–144
Phenomenal content, 194
Phenomenological presence, 71–73
Phenomenology, 177–178
Pineal gland, 8
Pitts, Walter, 219n2
Point particles, 11
Positive phenomena, 158, 200–201
Practical authority/responsibility, 152–154
Presentness
of information, 16–18, 58, 63
phenomenological, 71–73
Primal sketch, 27, 29
Primordial phenomena, 158, 200–201
Procedural memory, 40
Process, cognition as primarily, 63, 66–67, 135
Process externalism, 67
Programs, mental processes as, 2
Proper function, 112
Psychology, 1, 2

Rational consistency and coherence, 145–146, 148
Rawls, John, 110
Raw primal sketch, 27, 117, 120
Realization, in computer context, 4
Reasoning
cognitive science and, 16
human competence and incompetence in, 43–44
neural networks and, 43–45
Recollective memory, 40
Reference, sense and, 170–173
Remembering. *See also* Memory
cognitive science and, 16
extended account of, 125–126

as subordinate to personal cognitive
processes, 146–147, 151
target of, 143–144
Substance
defined, 10
mind as, 10–11
Subsumption architectures, 46–48
Sufficient conditions, 108

Telescopes, 94, 137, 217
Thinking. *See* Cognition
Thompson, E., 71
3D object representations, 28–29, 121
Threshold of activation, 42
Token identity theory, 4–5
Tokens, 64–67
Transcendental, the
experience and, 169, 180–181,
192–194
intentionality and, 173, 185–187, 190,
192, 202
sense and, 172–178
transcendence vs., 178–179
Transformation
and cognition, 67, 124, 126, 132
as contentless, 131
as disclosing activity, 193
as element of amalgamated mind, 84
and environmental interaction, 59
extended mind and, 58–60, 67, 73
information processing and, 111–112
in visual perception process, 120–123,
205
Transformational rules, 27–30
Transparency, of equipment, 158–159
Traveling through, 196–201
Truth conditions, 115
2½D sketch, 28–29, 120–121
Type identity theory, 4

Vehicle externalism, 58
Vehicles. *See also* Material realizations
of cognition, 195, 216

content vs., 191, 194
of disclosure, 191, 194–196
of intentionality, 208, 214
objects vs., 197–198
of perceptual disclosure, 202–206
Vertical microworlds, 45–46
Vertical sandwich model, 37–39
Visual perception, 7
Cartesian theory of, 26–30, 33, 37–38,
68, 113, 117, 120–121, 131–132, 193,
195, 220n1
change blindness phenomenon,
30–32
ecological theory of, 33–37, 122–123
epistemological claim concerning, 123
metaphysical claim concerning, 123
stages in, 120–121
vehicles of disclosure in, 202–206
Visual transients, 145, 204–205
Vygotsky, Lev, 15, 37–39, 41, 124

Wheeler, M., 75–76
Whitehead, Alfred North, 19
Williamson, T., 222n18
Wilson, R., 225n3
Wittgenstein, Ludwig, 179
Written language, 15

Yarbus, A., 202–203